EVERYDAY SPANISH

This book is designed to help those who already know a little Spanish—having perhaps learnt it at school or worked through an elementary Spanish course such as *Teach Yourself Spanish*—and want to advance further. Each of the twenty lessons is divided into four parts: Grammar, with explanations and exercises; Conversation, showing how modern Spanish is spoken; Commercial, providing an introduction to business language; and Spanish Literature, giving an outline from the Middle Ages to the present day.

TEACH YOURSELF BOOKS

Without doubt this manual is the best value for money which has been offered to the Spanish student for years. It is comprehensive, modern, lively and progressive.

Scottish Educational Journal

EVERYDAY SPANISH

L. D. Collier

M.A.

TEACH YOURSELF BOOKS
Hodder and Stoughton

First printed 1957
Eighteenth impression 1987

This volume is available in the U.S.A. from David McKay Company Inc., 750 Third Avenue, New York, N.Y. 10017

ISBN 0 340 27223 6

Printed in Grest Britain
for Hodder and Stoughton Educational,
a division of Hodder and Stoughton Ltd,
Mill Road, Dunton Green, Sevenoaks, Kent,
by Richard Clay Ltd, Bungay, Suffolk

FOREWORD

THIS book is designed to help you if you already know a little Spanish, perhaps learned a good while ago at school or in evening classes, and since then largely forgotten, or if you have recently worked through an elementary Spanish course (such as *Teach Yourself Spanish* in this series) and now want to advance further. While it is intended primarily for older people who have left school, and who either in evening classes or at home want to improve their Spanish, the book will be also found useful for Sixth Form pupils who are studying for the various levels of the General Certificate of Education, who need a thorough revision of grammatical details, and who will enjoy the wide acquaintance with literature introduced in the last section of each lesson.

Whatever your reason for reviving or extending your Spanish, the book will help you. Each of the twenty lessons is in four parts: grammar, conversation, commercial Spanish, and extracts from Spanish literature. The grammar section, while not pretending to be entirely complete, provides extremely careful explanations and practice exercises to help you to overcome all the chief difficulties. The conversations show you how modern Spanish is spoken, and careful study of these will give you an invaluable store of phrases and expressions that you will find useful in conversation at any time—special care has been taken *not* to include any of those slangy expressions (common to all languages) which a native can use effectively but which sound objectionable when used by a foreigner. In addition, these conversations, which are between four friends, two English travellers and two Spaniards, follow the course of a holiday journey through Spain from San Sebastián to Seville, and they contain many unobtrusive hints about what to do and to expect in Spain. Two famous Spanish legends are included in the later lessons in the conversation sections. The third section of each lesson gives you an introduction to the special forms of expression used in business language. In this section there are included some things not normally found in Spanish courses, such as a careful explanation of Spanish surnames and the method used for putting through a trunk call by telephone. The last section of each lesson provides you with a brief sketch of Spanish literary history from the Middle Ages to the present day, with specimens of the works of some of the most interesting writers. In arranging the literary extracts chronologically *backwards* the plan employed in *Everyday French* in this series has been followed as, although contrary to the usual way of presenting literature, this method has the advantage of introducing you to modern, not to medieval, literature in the first chapter.

It may be of interest to readers to know that some of the grammatical material and exercises, with a few other features incorporated in this book, were devised by the author during the late war in Japanese prisoner-of-war camps in Java, for the benefit of pupils of all ranks who worked with him there, many of whom made remarkably good progress.

L. D. C.

ACKNOWLEDGMENTS

I wish to acknowledge my great indebtedness to my friend don Fermín Soriano Saury, of Granada, for a great deal of kind help with several parts of this work. For permission to quote from their works I am grateful to don Salvador de Madariaga and to Dr J. E. Varey, and I wish to express my thanks to Mr Brian Park and to Mr Harry Eccles, of Exeter College, Oxford, who have energetically performed helpful research on my behalf. Thanks are also offered to Mr Charles Thomas, the Oxford University Press, the Oxford Local Examinations Board in respect of copyright quotations which they have permitted to be used in this book.

L. D. C.

HOW TO USE THIS BOOK

TRY the following plan :

First, go over the Grammar section at the beginning of Lesson I, and note especially the points that seem to you to be in any way difficult. It is most helpful to memorize short sentences which contain examples of the correct use of these harder points of grammar. Then tackle the translation exercise that follows the Grammar section—you will find that every sentence contains at least one example of the grammar rules that you have just seen stated. Of course there are other points of Spanish grammar in these sentences also, points which will be fully reviewed in Grammar sections later in the book, and if in working through the exercise you find you are undecided whether or not, for instance, to use the subjunctive, either turn up the rules in the elementary Spanish Course which you have used already or turn up the lessons in this book which deal with the subjunctive and see what they say (the table of contents will tell you that the subjunctive is dealt with in Lessons XIII, XIV, and XV). For this translation you are most likely to need your English–Spanish and Spanish–English dictionary. When you have worked out all the sentences in the exercise, turn to the Key at the end of the book, and see how far your effort agrees with the version given there (but think hard first, don't turn to the Key too soon, and don't *necessarily* be discouraged if your version contains something different, there is often more than one correct way of expressing a statement).

Then pass on to the Conversation section. Read through the Spanish carefully, and note any expressions that seem to you specially useful—copy them into a special notebook, and memorize them later on. When you have read it over once or twice in Spanish, turn to the English version given in the Key, and try to turn it back into Spanish, seeing how near you can get to the original.

The Commercial section will obviously be of more interest

to people who are improving their Spanish for business purposes than to those with more general interests, but much of the matter in these sections of each lesson has been designed to convey information useful to anyone travelling in Spain, or who has dealings with Spaniards. You are likely to need a little practice in the writing of formal letters, sooner or later, and it will possibly be more interesting than you expect.

When you reach the Literary section, try the idea of reading it aloud to yourself first—Spanish is a magnificent language to read aloud. Then when you have a reasonably clear idea of the sense, and have made notes of difficult words that you have had to look up in your dictionary, translate the passages into English. The Key, which is there to help you when you have finished, will tell you whether you have misunderstood anything—but again, do not expect your own translation to be word for word exactly like the Key. Your version may still be perfectly correct.

It is a good plan to try to cover a definite amount of work each week, say a lesson, or at most, two; neither working too fast nor too slowly. Your brain has its own pace at which it can do its best work, and if you do too much in a single burst of energy you are as likely to forget what you have studied as if you leave too long a gap between one phase of work and the next. " Little and often " is the best way for language study.

Now go ahead with the work, and good luck to it !

L. D. C.

CONTENTS

PART 1

INDEX OF GRAMMATICAL POINTS

PART 1

LESSON I

THE ARTICLES

ENGLISH people learning Spanish are often uncertain about when to use the articles *un, una* ; *el, la, los, las* and when to leave them out. A safe guide is to put the articles in Spanish where a corresponding English sentence would express them, and leave them out where the English leaves them out, *unless there is a grammatical reason for doing the opposite.*

These examples illustrate the rules for the cases in which the Spanish usage is different from the English :

1. " Soap is cheap." (" Soap " in a general sense, not a restricted quantity.) *El jabón es barato.*

But : " Bring me soap and water." (" Some " is understood before the noun.) *Tráigame jabón y agua.*

2. Proper nouns, if accompanied by adjectives, require the article, but not if used alone.

> *Vivía en España para poder estudiar allí la España moderna.* He was living in Spain so as to be able to study modern Spain there.
>
> *El viejo Jorge no nos vio, porque era ciego.* Old George did not see us, because he was blind.

Similarly if a name is accompanied by a title, the article is needed :

> *El Señor García me hablaba.* Mr. García was talking to me.

BUT, if the person is being spoken *to*, omit the article :

> *¿Cómo está Vd, Señor García?* How are you, Mr. García ?

3. With names of languages put the article except after *hablar* or *en*.

> *El francés es más difícil que el alemán.* French is more difficult than German.

BUT :

> *¿ Quiere Vd decírmelo en inglés ?* Will you say it to me in English?
> *Hablaremos español mañana.* We will talk Spanish tomorrow.

AND with the word *castellano* use the article, even with *hablar*.

> *Aprendemos a hablar el castellano.*

4. Never put the indefinite article *un, una* before *otro, cierto, ciento, mil*, and *tal*.

> *Otra señora vino a verme el otro día.* Another lady came to see me the other day.
> *¿ Cuántos libros tiene Vd ? Tengo mil, y pienso comprar otros ciento.* How many books have you? I have a thousand, and I intend to buy a hundred others.
> *Tal hombre no dice nunca la verdad.* Such a man never tells the truth.

5. Omit *un, una* after the verb " to be " in Spanish before *unmodified* nouns denoting occupation or nationality.

> *Mi hermano es médico.* BUT *Es **un** médico importante.*
> *Este señor es norteamericano.* BUT *Su padre era **un** italiano muy pobre.*

6. The infinitive used as a noun is masculine :

> *El comer demasiado le ha puesto enfermo.* Eating too much has made him ill.

7. With names of countries, follow rule 2 (e.g., *Francia, Portugal*, but *La Gran Bretaña, el Asia Menor, los Estados Unidos*), but note that there are a few—mostly names of countries that are a long way from Spain—that always require the article. These are best verified from a diction-

ary, but amongst the most important are *La China, el Japón, el Perú, el Brasil.*

8. The neuter article *lo* is placed before an adjective used as a noun :

> *Se ruborizó hasta lo blanco de sus ojos.* He blushed to the whites of his eyes.
>
> *No sabe lo mucho que le agradezco su favor.* He does not know how grateful I am to him for his help.

1 (*a*)

Now practise these sentences :

1. The man who has just arrived is a Russian, but he is now living in the United States.

2. Give me another pair of grey socks, please, Mrs. Martínez.

3. He stopped before a certain old house at the end of the street.

4. Their lodger is a very coarse Portuguese, he is a sailor and he is often drunk and has no money.

5. King George VI died on the sixth of February 1952 ; a hundred years earlier Queen Victoria was on the throne.

6. Doctors say that drinking iced water when you are too hot is bad for you.

7. I have never heard of such a thing ! Don't tell me any more about it.

8. French is easy enough to learn if you live a year or so in France, Belgium, or Switzerland.

9. Here are two newspapers, one is dated yesterday, and the other is a week old. The former is in German, the latter is in Dutch.

10. Faith, hope, and charity are the three Christian virtues. Let us always have a little more charity.

1 (*b*) Conversation

(*De sobremesa en casa de* MARTÍN *e* ISABEL, *en Londres. Sus amigos españoles* ANTONIO *y* MARÍA *están cenando con ellos.*)

ANTONIO : Conque piensan Vds ir de vacaciones este año a España. ¿ Qué parte van a visitar ?

MARTÍN : Primero iremos en avión hasta París, para evitar lo incómodo de la travesía del Canal de la Mancha. Preferimos no correr el riesgo de que Isabel se maree.

ISABEL : Sí, de veras, ¡ cualquier cosa para evitar eso !

ANTONIO : Bien, ¿y luego? ¿Por qué no van Vds directamente hasta Madrid? Hay servicios buenos, ingleses y españoles, que tienen vuelos directos desde Londres, y no tardan más de dos o tres horas en hacer este trayecto.

ISABEL : Pues de las cinco semanas de vacaciones que tenemos este año, deseamos pasar algunos días en el norte de España, en San Sebastián y en Pamplona, y hemos pensado que por esto nos sería mejor atravesar Francia desde París por ferrocarril, y luego estaríamos precisamente donde queremos estar.

ANTONIO : Sí, claro. Los trenes franceses son muy rápidos y bastante cómodos también, sobretodo si Vds hacen reservar los asientos de antemano.

MARTÍN : Sí, como empezaremos el viaje a mediados de julio, esto será imprescindible, pues con las fiestas francesas del día 14 los trenes estarán muy llenos.

ISABEL : Pero María, ¿ no han dicho que van Vds también a España este verano?

MARÍA : Sí. Ya sabe Vd que Antonio siempre tiene que tomar sus vacaciones por agosto, por esto iremos a Córdoba a pasar un par de semanas con mi cuñada, que tiene cerca de allí una casa de campo. ¿Le parece posible que nos veamos allí? Martín, que es arquitecto, debería bajar hasta Andalucía para ver por lo menos la mezquita de Córdoba, y tal vez Sevilla y Granada.

MARTÍN : Sí, quiero ir por allí, pues hace muchísimos años que no he estado en Andalucía. Sólo estuve allí una vez cuando era estudiante, antes de la guerra civil.

ANTONIO : Entonces, si pasan por Córdoba mientras estemos nosotros allí, irán a vernos. A mi hermana le gusta tener muchos amigos en casa, y fácilmente se les puede acomodar.

ISABEL : Gracias, Antonio. Claro es que mucho depende de lo que nos cueste el viaje y la estancia en el Norte y en Madrid, donde queremos pasar por lo menos unos pocos días. Pero yo creo que podremos ir a verles,

y tengo muchas ganas de visitar a Andalucía, donde no
he estado nunca.

MARÍA : Me alegro mucho. Por la primera o segunda
semana de agosto les esperaremos en Córdoba, entonces.
Y para que avisen cuando vayan a llegar, aquí le doy las
señas de mi cuñada. (*Se las da, escritas en una tarjeta.*)

COMMERCIAL SPANISH, 1
Spanish Names

Commercial Spanish does not present many difficulties
to English people who have learned the elements of Spanish
grammar and acquired a fair working vocabulary. The
special words and expressions used in commercial correspondence will, of course, to some extent differ in different
types of business, but there is a broad common basis of
customary language which is used in all Spanish business
letters, and it is this that will be dealt with in this part of
each lesson.

An important thing which non-Spaniards find puzzling
in tackling Spanish correspondence—and other associations
with Spanish people, too—is the Spanish use of family names.

If a Spaniard calls on you and presents a visiting-card
bearing the name *Francisco López García*, you refer to him
in conversation as *Señor López*, or if you get to know him
much better, as *Don Francisco*, or *Don Francisco López*
(*Don*, feminine *Doña*, is used only before a *Christian* name).
García, which in conversation you omit, is his mother's
surname, but it is part of his legal signature. Sometimes
the conjunction *y* appears between the two surnames,
your acquaintance may be *Don Fernando Linares y Ordóñez*,
in which case in conversation *y Ordóñez* is dropped. When
writing to him, however, always put *Señor Don Francisco
Linares y Ordóñez* at the head of the letter and on the
envelope.

There are a few exceptional family surnames which consist
of more than one word, and these are at first slightly con-
fusing. Thus *Don Ramón **Bernaldo de Quirós** y Martínez*
should be referred to as *Señor Bernaldo de Quirós*, or *Don
Ramón Bernaldo de Quirós*—the last three words forming
the family name inherited from his father.

Women follow the same principle until their marriage, when they usually drop their mother's maiden surname, and put their husband's surname after their father's, as follows : *Julia Sánchez Sevillano*, after marriage to *Antonio Gómez Ruiz*, writes her name *Julia Sánchez Gómez*—and is referred to in conversation as *Señora Gómez* or more familiarly *Doña Julia*. And since it is common for both men and women to insert *de* before the surname, this lady could be referred to as *Doña Julia de Gómez*, or *Señora de Gómez*. It is always wrong, however, to refer to Spaniards (when the title *Señor* is dropped) as *de Gómez* or *de Martínez*. The famous musical composer, *Manuel de Falla*, should therefore be referred to, not as is sometimes wrongly done, as *de Falla*, but simply as *Falla*.

These facts need to be borne in mind when addressing Spanish firms, in order to avoid mistakes which may possibly offend correspondents' susceptibilities. When in doubt, it is generally fairly safe to call a Spaniard by the *last but one* of his legal names.

The equivalent of the English " & Co." in the title of a firm is *y Cía* (for *Compañía*), and if a Limited Company the letters *S.A.* (for *Sociedad Anónima*) are put last, after the rest of the title.

If you are writing to a firm, known, say, as *Vespasiano Cuesta y Cía*, do not put any *Señor Don* before the firm's title, simply write the firm's name directly without any courtesy decorations. Similarly, omit the *Señor Don* if the letters *S.A.* appear in the style of the firm.

As to addresses, Spanish street names are put first, then the number of the building in the street, then, often, the number of the floor in the building in which the office or apartment is situated. The abbreviations *dcha* or *izq* may follow, to indicate whether the office or flat is to the right or left of the staircase, going up.

1 (c)

Try these examples :

1. A Spaniard's father's surname is *Ramírez* and his mother's is *Valdés*. His Christian name is *Ramón*. How

would you address him : (a) on an envelope; (b) if he paid
a business call at your office; (c) if you got to know him
fairly well socially ?

2. The same man marries a lady named *Isabel*. Her
father's surname is *Avellaneda* and her mother's is *Narváez*.
What are : (a) her legal names before her marriage;
(b) her legal names after her marriage ? And (c) how would
you address her in polite conversation if you did not know
her well ?

3. A firm is a Limited Company and bears the name of its
founder, *Manuel Morales*. Its office is in Barcelona at
no. 17, *Calle de San Ignacio*, third floor on the right.
Give the correct title and address of the Company.

SPANISH LITERATURE, 1
Modern Novelists

The year 1898, when Spain lost the last of her American
colonies in the Spanish–American War, is often taken as
the beginning of a new period in Spanish literary and
intellectual history. The loss of the war was the cause
of much disillusionment in Spain, but it acted as a spur to
novelists, poets, and essayists, who strove, in the years that
followed, to depict truth, often stark and sometimes cruel,
though sometimes supremely lovely. These writers have
come to be known as the " Generation of 1898 ", and a list
of them should include world-famous writers such as the
philosopher Miguel de Unamuno (whose *Sentimiento
Trágico de la Vida* appeared in 1913), and José Ortega y
Gasset (one of whose most interesting works, *La Rebelión
de las Masas*, came out just before the fall of the monarchy
in 1930).

It is impossible to mention more than a very few novels
in a book of this length, but the work of three novelists,
most of whose work has appeared since about 1900, will
well repay a student's more detailed study.

Vicente Blasco Ibáñez (1867–1928), whose international
fame rests perhaps chiefly on *Sangre y Arena* and on *Los
Cuatro Jinetes del Apocalipsis*, also wrote several very fine
novels dealing with life in the east coastal region of Spain,
near Valencia. *Entre Naranjos* and *La Barraca* are two

of these, while *Cuentos Valencianos* is an excellent collection of short stories with a similar background. Most of his works depict well the way in which various human failings can react on the lives and characters of families and other social groups.

Ramón Pérez de Ayala (1880–1962) is a thoughtful writer from Asturias, whose novels show much of the struggle between the old and the new which has so much occupied Spain in the present century. *Tigre Juan, Luna de Miel, Luna de Hiel,* and *La Pata de al Raposa* are amongst his best.

Pío Baroja (1872–1957), a Basque, has produced a very large number of novels, often depicting disillusionment among middle-class characters, but almost always with a very finely described and rapidly changing background. *Zalacain el Aventurero,* from which the following extract is taken, deals with adventures during the Second Carlist War in the eighteen-seventies.

1 (d)

Estaba Fernando de aprendiz en la zapatería del difunto Ichtaber, el *Chato de Tolosa,* y no sé si vosotros sabréis, pero Ichtaber era un zapatero viejo y muy rico. Tenía Fernando de novia una chica muy guapa; pero Ichtaber, el *Chato,* al verla, la empezó a cortejar y a decir si se quería casar con él, y, como era rico, ella aceptó. Solían verse la muchacha y el viejo en la zapatería, y el granuja de Ichtaber, para estar más libre, mandaba a Fernando con cualquier pretexto, a la trastienda. El hacía como que no se incomodaba, pero se vengó. Fue a ver a su novia y habló con ella.

—Sí—la dijo—. Ichtaber es buena persona y hombre de fortuna, es verdad; pero como es zapatero y chato y ha andado toda la vida con pieles, huele muy mal.

—¡ Mentiroso !—dijo ella.

—No, no, fíjate. Ya verás.

Fernando fue a la zapatería, cogió un fuelle grande y lo rellenó de esa casca que queda después de curtidos los pellejos y que huele que apesta; luego hizo un agujero

en el tabique de la trastienda y esperó la ocasión oportuna.
Por la tarde llegó la chica, e Ichtaber dijo a su aprendiz :

—Oye, Fernando, vete a la trastienda un momento a
arreglar esas hormas que hay en la caja.

Salió Fernando; tomó el fuelle. Miró por el agujero.
Ichtaber estaba besando la mano de la chica; entonces
le apuntó a ella con el fuelle, y metió por el agujero del
tabique una corriente de aire de mal olor. Cuando
Fernando miró después, Ichtaber, el *Chato*, estaba con la
mano en sus diminutas narices, y la muchacha, lo mismo.

Luego Fernando siguió dándole al fuelle con intermi-
tencias, hasta que se cansó.

Dos días después fué de nuevo la chica, y le pasó lo
mismo; y ya no volvió más, porque decía que Ichtaber,
el *Chato*, olía a muerto.

Ichtaber hizo el amor a otra; pero Fernando le jugó la
misma pasada con el fuelle, y el zapatero decía a sus
amigos :

—¡ Arrayua ! En mi tiempo era otra cosa; las chicas
estaban sanas. Ahora, la que más y la que menos huele a
perros.

(from *Zalacaín el Aventurero*, by Pío Baroja.)

LESSON II

THE AUXILIARIES, (I) HABER AND TENER

THE two verbs *haber* and *tener* present no difficulty once
the following brief rules are understood :

Use *haber* in the following cases ONLY :

(*a*) With a Past Participle to make a Perfect tense
(corresponding to the English " I have seen ", " he had
finished ", etc.)—*he visto, había acabado*, etc. Do not
separate the parts of a Perfect tense *¿ Le ha visto Vd ?*
(NOT *¿ Le ha Vd visto ?*).

(*b*) *Haber de* plus Infinitive is one of the ways of saying
" to have to ", particularly with the idea of events which
are scheduled to happen in the near future : *El concierto
ha de empezar a las seis y media.* The Future tense (e.g.,
empezará) is a development from the Infinitive plus the

Present tense of *haber* (e.g., *empezar-he*, *empezar-has*, *empezar-ha*, etc.) and means approximately the same thing.

(c) *Hay*, meaning " there is ", " there are "; *había*, for " there was ", " there were ", and the 3rd person singular of all the other tenses of *haber* give a very useful impersonal form.

Two notes for students of French:

(i) When the past participle is used with *haber* there is no agreement with any subject or object (NOT as in French).

Las casas que he visto en Madrid. (French would, of course, say, " Les maisons que j'ai vues à Madrid.")

(ii) The use of the Perfect tense as a conversational Past, which is so usual in French, does not apply in Spanish. Use the Spanish Perfect exactly where in English we say " I have arrived ", " we have come " (*he llegado*, *hemos venido*). For " I arrived ", " we came ", use the Past Historic (which, of course, is never used in French conversation)—*llegué*, *vinimos*.

For practically all other cases where in English we say " have ", use *tener*.

> *Tengo un sombrero nuevo.*
> *Mi padre tiene un resfriado.*
> *Aquel hotel tiene cincuenta cuartos de baño.*

Remember that there are useful idioms in which *tener* is used with *nouns*. These idioms refer only to *people*, not to things.

> *Tengo frío.*   *Tengo ganas de comer.*
> *Tenemos calor.*   *El niño tiene mucho sueño.*
> *Tiene hambre y sed.*

(Compare these with certain expressions to do with the *weather*, in which *hacer* is used, e.g., *hace frío*, for " the weather is cold "; and note also the use of *estar* when this sort of sentence refers to a *thing*, not a person, e.g., *Mi café está frío, estos platos están fríos—frío* here is an adjective, and therefore agrees with its noun.)

" To have to . . .", when there is external obligation, is *tener que* plus infinitive.

I have to (= must) do a great many things.
Tengo que hacer muchísimas cosas.

Note two special idioms:

(*a*) " To have something done ", meaning " to *get* something done ", is *hacer* plus infinitive.

I am going to have my shoes mended, *Voy a hacer reparar mis zapatos.*

(*b*) " To have *just* done something " is *acabar de* plus infinitive.

I have just posted three postcards. *Acabo de echar al correo tres tarjetas postales.*

And one last note, about meals:

" To have breakfast " (or dinner, or to consume anything to eat or drink) is not *tener*, but expressed differently. *Tomar* is useful here, e.g.,

> *¿A qué hora vamos a tomar el almuerzo?* (or: *¿A qué hora vamos a almorzar?*). " When are we going to have lunch? "
>
> *Tenemos la merienda* implies " We have a packed lunch with us "—presumably ready to eat later.

2 (*a*) Exercise

I have just had a telephone conversation with my wife, who told me to buy a new suitcase for her this morning before I have lunch. She needs one to take to Majorca next month. I shall probably have to get her a leather one. I shall also have to have a new suit made for myself, as I am often too hot in English clothes when the weather is very warm, and I want to buy a light-weight one like those that most Spaniards have for summer wear. I am not afraid of the weather being chilly; when we have been at Palma in the spring in other years I have always found that I have quite enough protection against the weather if I have a waterproof and a scarf.

2 (b) Conversation

(*En el tren. Compartimiento de segunda clase del rápido
desde París; el tren está cerca de Biarritz.*)

ISABEL (*despertándose*) : ¿Qué hora tienes, Martín?

MARTÍN (*que se despertó hace algún tiempo*) : Son las siete.
¿Has dormido bien?

ISABEL : Sí, bastante bien, a pesar de no haber estado muy
cómoda. ¿Cuándo llegaremos a la frontera?

MARTÍN : A las siete y mediã. Tienes todo el tiempo
necesario para lavarte la cara, lo cual te hace mucha
falta; te aconsejo, pues, que vayas en seguida, porque
puede haber cola.

ISABEL : Poco cortés estás, en verdad; pero claro, los
maridos tienen el privilegio de decir tales cosas, y . . .

MARTÍN : Vamos, sí. En Irún podremos tomar café, y
entonces te sentirás mejor. Mira, ¡qué hermoso está!
Allí delante ves los Pirineos, como una enorme muralla.

ISABEL : Sí, y allí al otro lado el mar. Y aquello a lo lejos
¿será la costa española?

MARTÍN : Es la costa cantábrica cerca de San Sebastián.

(ISABEL *se va por el pasillo con su neceser.* MARTÍN
fuma un cigarro y contempla el paisaje.)

UN SEÑOR (*que subió en Bayona*) : ¿Vds van a España, no?
¿Es su primera visita?

MARTÍN : Para mi mujer, sí, es la primera vez que va allí,
pero yo he estado ya varias veces en España, hace
algunos años, de soltero.

EL SEÑOR : Y ¿adónde van Vds? ¿A San Sebastián, a
Madrid, o más al sur?

MARTÍN : Pues quiero enseñarle a mi mujer algo de lo
que yo antes he conocido, y vamos a pasar dos o tres
días en San Sebastián. Luego iremos a Pamplona o a
Burgos, y entonces más o menos directamente a Madrid.
Después puede que demos una vuelta por Andalucía,
pero dentro de cinco semanas hemos de volver a Londres,
pues entonces se acaban mis vacaciones.

EL SEÑOR : ¡Van Vds a hacer todo un viaje! ¡Que lo
pasen muy bien!

MARTÍN : Gracias.
    (*Vuelve* ISABEL.)
ISABEL : ¿Qué estación es ésta?
MARTÍN : Será Hendaya. Aquí la policía francesa puede pedir los pasaportes. Entonces el tren atraviesa el puente internacional sobre el Bidasoa, y llegaremos en seguida a Irún. ¡Qué bien hice en consultar aquella agencia en Londres, que me arregló los pasaportes, todos los billetes y la reserva de asientos! Este viaje es algo largo, pero ha sido muy cómodo.

___

(*En la estación de Irún. Acaba de llegar el tren.* MARTÍN *ha bajado su equipaje de la red.*)

MOZO : ¿Necesitan Vds mozo?
MARTÍN : Sí. Lleve estas dos maletas y este saco. ¿Le acompañaremos a la aduana?
MOZO : Me encontrarán allí, les esperaré. Vds tienen que pasar por aquella puerta para mostrar sus pasaportes y rellenar unas hojas que les darán.

___

(*En la aduana, después de haber revisado los pasaportes.*)

ADUANERO : ¿Son éstas sus maletas? ¿Tienen más equipaje?
MARTÍN : Nada más que estas dos y este saco. No creo que tengamos nada que declarar, todo lo que llevamos es para nuestro uso personal en unas semanas de vacaciones. (*Abre las maletas.*)
ADUANERO : Muy bien. (*Marca su equipaje con tiza.*)
MARTÍN : Ahora podemos ir a buscar el tren para San Sebastián, y como tenemos mucho tiempo, ¡ buscaremos la taza de café que tengo tantas ganas de encontrar !

COMMERCIAL SPANISH, 2

Many of the customs concerning the style of commercial letters are the same in Spanish as in English. The address of the sender is put at the right-hand top corner of the paper, with the date immediately below. A little lower, on the left of the paper, is written the name and address of the person or firm to whom the letter is addressed.

" Dear Sir " is *Muy Señor mío*, or if the letter is written as from a firm or company, *Muy Señor nuestro*. Correspondingly, " Dear Sirs " is therefore *Muy Señores míos* or *Muy Señores nuestros*.

At the end of a letter, to correspond to the English " Yours faithfully " or " Yours truly ", a fairly complicated variety of Spanish expressions will be found to occur. The student will be well advised to memorize two or three of these, and note alternatives in Spanish letters as they turn up.

Here are some typical conclusions to letters :

1. From an individual to a firm—
    Sin otro particular, les saluda atentamente s.s. q.e.s.m.
        Roberto López.

2. From a firm to an individual—
        Somos de Vd, muy attos. y s.s.,
            Hernando y Cía.

3. From one individual to another—
        Se reitera de Vd, afmo s.s.
            José Rodríguez.

The meaning of the abbreviations in the above examples is as follows :

S.S., (plural *SS.SS.*) stands for *seguro servidor* (plural *seguros servidores*), and corresponds roughly to " humble servant ".

Q.e.s.m. stands for *que estrecha su mano*. Sometimes *q.l.e.l.m.* is found, short for *que le estrecha la mano*.

Atto. stands for *atento*, meaning " attentive ".

Afmo stands for *afectísimo*, this in correspondence is not the same thing as the English " affectionate ", its use in example 3 amounts to approximately the same as " Yours very truly ".

For help in writing private letters in Spanish. See page 116.

2 (*c*)

London,
Dear Sirs,   20.4.55
    In reply to your letter of the 16th inst., I am happy to inform you that our representative Mr. Henry Smith

will call on you on or about the 28th inst., to display for your inspection samples of our latest supplies of knitted goods.

We hope that you will find them of interest.

Yours faithfully,

George Johnson & Co.

H. W. B.

2 (d)

Reyes Católicos, 32,
Granada
28 de julio de 19—

Mudarra e Hijos,
Paseo de Gracia, 232,
Barcelona

Muy Señores nuestros,

De acuerdo con su aviso en carta de 20 del corriente, hemos tenido el gusto de recibir la visita de su representante Sr D. José Pérez, a quien hemos ofrecido nuestros servicios para lo que pueda ofrecérsele durante su estancia entre nosotros.

Sentimos que la situación actual no nos anime a hacerles un pedido de mercancías por ahora, aguardaremos mejores tiempos para utilizar sus servicios.

Quedamos de Vds, atts y s.s.

Enrique Alvarez, S.A.

SPANISH LITERATURE, 2

Spanish wit, a national characteristic which has appeared in plenty in all periods of Spanish literature, is to be found in full measure in writings published during this century. Rich examples often occur in short articles in newspapers, sometimes written and signed by the greatest of contemporary authors, a fact which bears witness to the generally high quality of Spanish journalism.

Three writers who have specialized in various forms of humour are Julio Camba (born 1884), many of whose articles have been published under the title of *La Rana Viajera*, collections of sketches dealing with characteristic details of Spanish life—or of life abroad as seen by a Spaniard; Ramón Gómez de la Serna (born 1888), one of whose contributions to Spanish literature has been the invention of a kind of epigram he calls a " *Greguería* "; and Noel Clarasó, a still young writer, whose gallery of comic characters and situations and terse, humorous style of writing bear close affinity to P. G. Wodehouse's writings in English.

Here is an extract from a book by Clarasó :

2 (*e*)

(*Arsenio is Juan Gabriel's elderly valet.*)

Arsenio está completamente seguro de que la llamada a la puerta ha de introducir una modificación en el curso normal de los acontecimientos y que esta modificación será fatal para la cena de amor de su amo. Se acerca de puntillas a la puerta, abre la mirilla sin hacer ruido y mientras el timbre suena por segunda vez se dirige a Juan Gabriel, presa de estupor y de espanto.

—¡ Tu tío Dámaso !

—¿Eh ?

—¡ Tu tío en carne y hueso !

Juan Gabriel se deja caer en una silla y casi rompe a llorar. La presencia de su tío Dámaso interrumpe siempre, por unos días, todas sus costumbres establecidas.

—¿Estás seguro ?

—He visto el sombrero y el cesto.

No cabe el menor duda. El sombrero y el cesto son las dos características inconfundibles del tío Dámaso. No se quita el sombrero de la cabeza ni para dormir, desde hace lo menos cuarenta años, y, al salir de viaje, lleva siempre un cesto con algunas docenas de huevos frescos de sus gallinas, en la seguridad de que todas las gallinas del mundo menos las suyas ponen los huevos con retraso y se les echan a perder en las entrañas. Nunca había probado un huevo de gallinero ajeno, que siempre saben a paja, a cebolla, a alambre o a niño sucio. El timbre suena por tercera vez y Juan Gabriel, antes de dar la orden fatal de abrir la puerta, se atreve a acariciar vagas sospechas consoladoras.

—Quizás sólo viene por algunas horas.

(from *Blas, tú no Eres mi Amigo*, 1946.)

Salvador de Madariaga (born 1886), whose works on Spain, Spanish history, and literature are widely known in English as well as in Spanish—he was for some years Professor of Spanish at Oxford—has contributed much crisp thought to the subject of the psychology of national character. The following extract, containing an attractive theme that he develops at some length, is from *Ingleses, franceses y españoles* :

2(f)

Si rogaseis a un francés (antes de la guerra) que os definiese a un inglés, os contestaría seguramente : " un hipócrita con sentido práctico ". Es curioso observar que la voz popular suele resumir los caracteres nacionales en dos rasgos—un defecto y una cualidad. Así, al *par* esquemático " hipócrita-práctico ", que representa al inglés, corresponden los *pares* "claro-licencioso", para el francés; perseverante-inhábil ", para el alemán; " digno-cruel ", para el español; " ordinario-activo ", para el norteamericano. Es como si en esta aldea de naciones que es el mundo, la fisonomía de cada nación hubiese sido esquematizada en dos rasgos fundamentales, y en esta operación subsistiesen tan sólo una cualidad y un defecto, testigos del doble origen del alma humana.

LESSON III

THE AUXILIARIES, (II) SER AND ESTAR

THE question about when to use *ser* and when to use *estar* is one that English students of Spanish find rather formidable. Firm acquaintance with the rules is the only safe way of avoiding mistakes.

Since the rules for the use of *estar* are fewer than those for using *ser*, it is useful to realize that, if in a given sentence the translation of some part of the verb " to be " does not fit any of the *estar* rules (which are easily memorized), the verb in question is almost certainly the appropriate part of *ser*.

Here are the rules set out in a kind of diagram:

ESTAR		SER
To denote PLACE, situation, or position. (*Madrid está en España; su casa está en la Plaza Mayor.*) I.e., answering the question ¿*DÓNDE?*	1.	To denote TIME. (*Es lunes. Es el día de San Eugenio. Son las seis.*) I.e., in answer to the question ¿*CUÁNDO?*
To denote state of health. (*Mi padre está enfermo. Aquel señor está cojo esta semana*—"he is temporarily lame.") To denote temporary or accidental *state.* (*El suelo está sucio; mi café está caliente.*)	2. WHEN USED WITH ADJECTIVES	To denote permanent characteristics. (*El papel es blanco. Aquella casa es grande.*) To denote nationality, even if this can be or has been changed. (*Somos ingleses; Era alemán, ahora es norteamericano.*) Note that with *rico, pobre, viejo,* and *joven, SER* is always used.
To denote STATE, not action. (*Me mandó una carta que estaba escrita con tinta roja.*)	3. WHEN USED WITH PAST PARTICIPLES	To denote ACTION, not state. (*La carta fué escrita por mi hermano.*)
With a PRESENT PARTICIPLE *estar* makes a progressive form of the verb tense, corresponding to the English "I am thinking", "he was working" (*estoy pensando; estaba trabajando*).	4.	*Ser* is never used with a Present Participle.
Estar is never used with a noun in the predicate.	5.	With a noun in the predicate (i.e., with a noun that depends on the verb "to be" to show its relation to the subject of the sentence.) (*Aquel hombre es mi amigo. Soy periodista, pero durante la guerra fuí soldado. Este edificio es un cine, antes era un teatro.*)

ESTAR		*SER*
With only one impersonal expression, *está bien* (though *está claro* is also occasionally found).	6.	With impersonal expressions. (*Es posible. Es difícil. Es claro*, and all others except *está bien*—" all right ! ")
Alone with a pronoun to denote *place*. (*Estoy yo* means " I am *here* ".)	7.	Alone with a pronoun to denote *identity*. (*Soy yo. Somos nosotros, Eran ellos.*—" It is I " or " it's me ", etc.)

Note : A reflexive construction is very often used in Spanish to replace the use of " Ser + Past Participle " in (3) above : " It is said that . . ." *Se dice que* . . . " This is easily understood." *Esto se comprende fácilmente.*

But if the *agent* is expressed, *ser* and the Past Participle must be used *El palacio fué construido por Felipe Segundo.* "The palace was built by Philip II."

3 (a) Exercise

1. Lieutenant Barno is a very sick man. He has been sent to the seaside for a period of convalescence.

2. Do not touch that tray, the paint is still wet.

3. The lawn is covered with snow this morning. How pretty !

4. The roof is being covered with tiles by the workmen who began the job last week.

5. I used to be a carpenter, but now I am a tobacconist.

6. Wait here for a while. It is only a quarter to four.

7. Who is it ? Who is there ?—It's me.

8. I want some new buttons for my sleeve, these are broken. All right, those will do.

9. My son-in-law is still young. When his father dies he will be rich.

10. The Widow Twankey was very cross with her son.

3 (b) Conversation

(*Vestíbulo de un hotel en San Sebastián.* MARTÍN *e* ISABEL *vienen de la calle; el mozo les sigue con sus maletas.*)

ISABEL : Por fin hemos llegado. ¡ Ay, Dios mío ! ¿ Qué he hecho de mi sombrero ? ¡ Lo habré dejado en el taxi !

EL MOZO : Aún no se ha ido, señora, el chófer está hablando con alguien en la calle. ¿Le digo que busque el sombrero?

ISABEL : Sí, sí, por favor. No he de perderlo. (*Se va* EL MOZO.) Me lo quité porque hacía mucho calor cuando salimos de la estación.

MARTÍN : No importa mucho, en verdad, porque no lo vas a necesitar aquí. Por lo que veo son muy pocas las españolas que llevan sombrero por la calle. Pero más vale que lo recobre el mozo, pues te va a hacer falta cuando volvamos a Inglaterra. ¡ Qué distraída has sido !

ISABEL : Esta vez puedes decir eso, y ¡que pase ! Pero te advierto que algún día de éstos serás tú el que olvide algo, y bien puede ser algo importante.

(EL MOZO *vuelve con el sombrero.*)

ISABEL : Muchísimas gracias. (*Aparte a* MARTÍN.) Mira, Martín, dale al mozo una propina. Tú llevas todo el dinero español que tenemos.

MARTÍN : Claro, se la daré arriba en el cuarto, donde llevará nuestro equipaje. (*Al empleado en la recepción.*) Buenos días. Me llamo Johnson, y tengo reservada una habitación por tres noches. Una habitación con dos camas y sala de baño.

EL EMPLEADO : Sí, señor. ¿Vd nos escribió, no es verdad? Es el número 31, segundo piso, con vistas al mar. ¿Quieren Vds firmar la hoja y el libro de entrada? Mozo, aquí la llave del 31. Suba el equipaje de estos señores.

ISABEL : ¡ Cómo ! ¿Qué tengo que escribir aquí? ¡ Me piden que escriba mi nombre y mis apellidos, mi domicilio, el número de mi pasaporte y otras cosas y no sé para qué !

MARTÍN : No te aflijas, es muy fácil. Yo lo haré esta vez y todo lo que tu tendrás que hacer es firmarlo al pie de la hoja. (*Escribe.*) Ves, ya está acabado. Ahora no tardemos en subir. Cambiaremos los vestidos y nos arreglaremos un poco, luego saldremos a respirar este aire de San Sebastián que dicen es tan puro.

COMMERCIAL SPANISH, 3

Some Useful Expressions

Recibimos oportunamente su carta de 27 del ppdo. We acknowledge receipt of yours of the 27th ult.

Acusamos recibo de su carta del 16 del corriente. We have received yours of the 16th inst.

En nuestro poder su atenta de 22 del pasado . . . Yours of the 22nd ult. to hand . . .

En contestación a la suya de 1 del corriente . . . In reply to yours of the 1st inst. . . .

Nos es grato comunicar a Vds que . . . We are happy to inform you that . . .

Adjunto enviamos a Vds . . . We beg to enclose . . .

El objeto de esta carta es poner en su conocimiento que . . . The purpose of this letter is to inform you that . . .

Mucho les agradeceremos que nos hagan saber . . . We shall be very grateful if you will inform us . . .

Agradeciéndoles anticipadamente este favor . . . Thanking you in anticipation . . .

Dándoles las más expresivas gracias por . . . Thanking you for . . .

Here is a business letter for practice in translation. It is about an agency for second-hand typewriters.

3 (c)

Señor :

     Nos permitimos informarle que somos los agentes de exportación exclusivos de varios fabricantes americanos, y llamamos su atención especialmente hacia nuestras máquinas de escribir reconstruídas. Ciertamente, Vd sabrá que tales máquinas de escribir han sido usadas, pero desarmadas completamente e inspeccionadas, y limpiadas en la fábrica con el mayor cuidado. Nosotros garantizamos absolutamente nuestras máquinas.

Incluimos en esta carta nuestra lista de precios.

Estas máquinas las suministramos con teclado para escribir en español, francés, portugués, italiano, o en cualquier otro idioma, sin recargo alguno sobre el precio.

Le concederemos nuestra agencia exclusiva en esa ciudad y sus alrededores si nos favorece con una orden inicial para cinco máquinas.

Si Vd tuviera interés en comprar además artículos de escritorio, a su indicación tendremos sumo gusto en enviarle listas de precios y muestras.

Esperamos vernos favorecidos pronto con su respuesta y, agradecidos de antemano, le saludamos,

afmos. y ss.ss., q.e.s.m.

X.Y.Z. y Cía.

SPANISH LITERATURE, 3

Poets and dramatists of the present century, like most of the novelists, have usually chosen for their themes subjects concerned with Spain or Spanish life, seen and appreciated all the more keenly for the salutary revolution in thought that took place after the 1898 war.

Among the best of the poets are Juan Ramón Jiménez (1881–1958), an Andalusian who has lived most of his life in Madrid, and whose metrical skill and æsthetic sensitiveness are magnificent; Antonio Machado (1875–1939), who drew the inspiration for much of his best poetry from the vast, stark landscapes of Old Castile; and Federico García Lorca (born 1899 and killed in the Spanish Civil War in 1936), in whose poems and plays it is impossible not to feel the writer's keen affinity with the deepest spirit of the Spanish peasantry.

Some of the best-known dramatists of this period have left masterpieces of dramatic depiction of another sort of Spanish life—calm, middle-class atmosphere, often in country towns, and the problems, frequently of universal interest, that arise there. Such are *Puebla de las Mujeres* and *Doña Clarines*, by the brothers Serafín and Joaquín Quintero; *Canción de Cuna*, a very well-known play about life in a convent, by Gregorio Martínez Sierra, and many works of Jacinto Benavente.

Foreign students wishing to improve their knowledge of Spanish cannot be too strongly recommended to read modern plays, the idiom, vocabulary, and atmosphere are naturally all those of modern Spain, and very many aspects of Spanish life and language are therefore reflected in them.

3 (d)

This is an extract from a one-act play by the brothers Quintero, called *Lo que tú quieras* (" Just as you like, dear ".)

(JOSEFINA *quiere salir al teatro, mientras que su marido* RAMÓN *quiere quedar en casa.* RAMÓN *entra en el salón de su casa en Madrid y ve que su mujer ha puesto un elegante traje de teatro.*)

RAMÓN : ¡ Chica !

JOSEFINA : ¿ Qué ?   ¿ Te parezco muy guapa ?

RAMÓN : No . . .

JOSEFINA : ¿ Cómo que no ?

RAMÓN : Sí, muy guapa ; pero no es eso.

JOSEFINA : Pues ¿ qué es, que has puesto esa cara de asombro ?

RAMÓN : Que me sorprende verte vestida.

JOSEFINA : ¿ Iba a andar desnuda por la casa, Ramón ?

RAMÓN : Medio desnuda vas, no te creas ; porque el escotito. . . .

JOSEFINA : ¡ Ah !   ¿ lo encuentras exagerado ?   No . . . La moda pícara.   Pero si quieres me pondré una flor aquí en medio.

RAMÓN : No discutamos el escote ahora.   ¿ Por qué te has vestido, si nos vamos a quedar aquí ?

JOSEFINA : ¿ Que nos vamos a quedar aquí ?

RAMÓN (*sulfurándose*) : Pero ¿ te haces de nuevas, y de sobremesa lo convinimos ?

JOSEFINA : No te enfades, Moncito ; no te enfades.

RAMÓN : ¡ Adiós mi dinero !

JOSEFINA : ¿ Qué ?

RAMÓN : ¡ Que me llamas Moncito !

JOSEFINA : ¿ Y qué ?

RAMÓN : ¡ Que cuando me llamas Moncito y no Ramón ! . . . ¡ Le temo más a un Moncito tuyo ! . . . ¡ Pobre Moncito !   Yo me entiendo.   (*Pasea.*)

JOSEFINA : ¡ Ay, Moncito, qué pronto te enfurruñas ! y yo
no estoy para desplantes esta noche. ¡ Me ha puesto
más nerviosa el café !

RAMÓN : Y a mí va a ponerme, Finita.

JOSEFINA : ¡ A ti? ¡ Si tú no lo has tomado !

RAMÓN : ¡ El que has tomado tú !

JOSEFINA : ¡ Ah, ya ! . . . ¡ Qué manera más delicada de
decirme que sientes conmigo !

RAMÓN : ¿ Cómo no?

JOSEFINA : ¡ Ea ! pues vamos a ver si nos explicamos.
Empezando porque yo no he de hacer más que lo que tú
quieras . . . (RAMÓN *la mira*) Lo que tú quieras, lo
que tú quieras. Yo entendi que tú, por no sé qué causa,
preferías ir a otro teatro en vez de ir a la Princesa;
pero que no saliéramos, no lo he entendido ni un instante.
(*Vuelve a mirarla él*) Nada, nada; no me eches esos ojos.

RAMÓN : Está bien, Finita, está bien; será que hable yo
en griego y que oigo en chino; porque tú, después de
mis razones, me has dicho que lo que yo quisiera, y que
no saldríamos, y que nos quedaríamos encantados los
dos, y que tú te alegrabas porque yo tenía que
madrugar. . . .

JOSEFINA : ¿ Sí, eh? ¿ Yo he dicho todo eso? ¡ Si seré
distraída ! . . . Y después de decir todo eso me he
vestido para el teatro . . . ¡ Si seré distraída ! . . . ¡ Lo
que es la costumbre de los miércoles !

RAMÓN : No; no es la costumbre de los miércoles; porque
la costumbre de los miércoles es que cenes ya vestida,
pimpollo.

JOSEFINA : O que me vista luego; según. . . .

(*Pero al fin y al cabo, van al teatro.*)

3 (e)

Juan Ramón Jiménez wrote the following short lyric
in 1915.

En aquel beso, tu boca
en mi boca me sembró
un rosal cuyas raíces
me comen el corazón.

Era otoño, el cielo inmenso
arrancaba, con su sol
todo el oro de la vida
en columnas de esplendor.—

Estío, seco, ha venido.
El rosal,—¡ todo pasó !—
ha abierto, tardo, en mis ojos
dos capullos de dolor.

LESSON IV

REMINDERS ABOUT ADJECTIVES

THE feminine forms of adjectives sometimes cause students a little trouble. Remember that all adjectives ending in -o in the masculine change the -o to -a for the feminine, and that adjectives that end in other letters in the masculine do not change.

Thus *un muro blanco y negro; una casa blanca y negra*. But *un médico inteligente y cortés; una enfermera inteligente y cortés*.

NOTE however :

(i) ALL adjectives of *nationality* have the feminine form ending in -*a*, e.g.,

(masc.) *inglés*	(fem.) *inglesa*
francés	*francesa*
alemán	*alemana*
español	*española*

(ii) While comparatives ending in -*or* have no feminine form ending in -*a* (there are ten of these, all useful words : *mayor, menor, mejor, peor, exterior, interior, superior, inferior, anterior, posterior*), all **other** adjectives ending in -*or*, as well as those ending in -*ón* and -*án*, do add -*a* to make the feminine. For instance :

un jardín encantador, but *una casa encantadora*
un chico holgazán, but *su hermana holgazana*

As to the position of adjectives in relation to their nouns, the usual rule is to put them *after*. There are a few, however, which regularly go before, and most of these have that special (known as " apocopated ") form, dropping the final -*o* when they appear before a noun in the *masculine singular*. These are :

bueno *malo*	*primero* *tercero*
alguno *ninguno*	*uno* *postrero*

e.g., *un buen hombre*, but *una buena mujer*, *unos buenos libros*.

Grande (with the meaning of " important ") usually drops its final -*de* before a masculine *or a feminine* singular noun.

In reading Spanish the student will often notice examples of adjectives, other than the nine mentioned just above, which the writers have placed before their nouns. There will also be examples of these nine placed after the nouns to which they belong. The writers' purpose in these instances will be to *emphasize* the adjective—the idea being that if a word is put in an unusual position the reader's attention is directed to it more forcefully than if it is in the expected place.

A few adjectives have one meaning when placed *before* and a different meaning when placed *after* their noun. Note that if the adjective has a more *material* sense, it is placed *after*.

   mi caro padre, my dear, beloved, father; *una mesa cara*, an expensive table
   una pobre mujer, a poor, pitiful, woman; *una mujer pobre*, a poverty-stricken woman
   una gran casa, an important house; *una casa grande*, a large house.

The other adjectives that apocopate are : (i) *Santo*, which drops its final -*to* before the name of a masculine saint, except those beginning with *To*- or *Do*- (e.g., *San José*, *Santa Teresa*; but *Santo Tomás*, *Santo Domingo*), and (ii) *ciento*, which if occurring before any noun (unless a smaller number intervenes) drops its *-to*. Thus: *cien casas, cien cuadros* (but *ciento veinte personas*), and note specially *cien mil páginas*.

Negatives

As to the rules about negatives, they are fairly simple. To make a verb negative, put *no* before it. The other negative words, *nada, nadie, nunca, jamás, ni, tampoco,* and *ninguno* may go before the verb or after, but if they go after, the verb must have *no* before it as well—i.e., there must be *one*, and only one, negative word before the verb in a negative sentence.

You may say *No le veo nunca* or *Nunca le veo*.

> *El no lo cree, y tampoco lo creo yo.*   He does not believe it, and I do not believe it either.   (*Tampoco* is the negative word corresponding to *también* in affirmative sentences.)
>
> *No tengo ningún dinero.*   I have not got any money.

In this last type of negative sentence beware of the temptation to use *alguno* to translate " any ". It is worth remembering that the *alg-* words (*alguno, alguien,* and *algo*) are always wrong in a negative sentence, except in the single and very emphatic use of *alguno* put *after* the noun object :

> *No quedaba periódico alguno.*   There was not a single paper left.

4 (a) Exercise

1. There were no English or American cigarettes left in the shop.

2. Some day I'll find you, but don't give me any more cheese.

3. On the next morning I was awakened by the song of a thrush in the sweet-smelling orange-tree outside my bedroom window.

4. Cordelia was old King Lear's youngest daughter.

5. His mother-in-law is a very superior person; she might almost be the Mother Superior of a convent.

6. The young Andalusians left nothing but a dirty cup and saucer.

7. She went up to him and smacked his face. He is too intelligent to do that again.

8. Three cotton handkerchiefs, two silk shirts, and one leather belt.

9. One lovely evening he and she went to watch the golden sunset over the sea.

10. " This is the oldest rule in the book," said the Queen.

11. The violinist told me that he had never met anyone who could mend his violin.

12. Nobody could do anything that would relieve his pain.

13. No novels, however well they are written, please me as much as the ones I have read by Cervantes.

14. This has nothing to do with that. Take it away !

15. The luggage was so heavy that the porter couldn't help dropping it.

16. You are not to eat ice-cream, or chocolates either, until you have had your tea.

17. Without speaking to either of the ladies, the priest slowly went into the church.

18. At that place by the seaside there were four miles of sand, and we did not see a single soul on the beach.

19. I don't feel tired any more, so I shall go on working. Tell George not to come for me yet.

20. Has he ever been to Barcelona? No? Then it is useless to ask him anything about it.

4 (b) Conversation

(*La misma mañana de su llegada a San Sebastián.*)

ISABEL (*al salir del hotel*) : ¿Adónde iremos primero? Lo único que tengo que hacer es comprarme un cepillo de dientes, he perdido el mío, no sé donde, durante el viaje.

MARTÍN : Aquí al lado hay una droguería. Podremos comprarte uno a la vuelta de nuestro paseo. Vamos ahora a ver esa bahía tan célebre, que se llama la Concha. A esta hora estará llena de gente, y como creo que la

marea está alta seguramente habrá algunos que se
están bañando.

ISABEL : Aquí estamos. ¡ Qué hermoso está! ¡ Y qué
colores tan vivos! Ya veo por qué se llama la Concha,
tiene la forma de una. ¿ Cómo se llaman esos montes,
que con aquella pequeña isla casi parecen cerrar la
entrada del mar?

MARTÍN : El de la derecha es Monte Urgull, y el de la
izquierda es Monte Igueldo. Los dos son parques
públicos, y de ellos hay unas vistas magníficas de todo
el paisaje y del mar alrededor. Podremos dar un paseo
a uno de ellos esta tarde cuando empiece a hacer menos
calor. ¡ Qué sol más estupendo !

ISABEL : Mira, lo que yo quisiera hacer más que nada es
bañarme, el agua realmente invita a ello. ¿ Tenemos
tiempo para tomar un baño antes de almorzar?

MARTÍN : Claro, porque en España no se come temprano.
Podremos quedarnos aquí al sol hasta las dos. Vamos
al hotel a buscar nuestros trajes de baño y luego iremos a
aquel establecimiento allí al lado donde nos guardarán
los vestidos mientras nos bañemos.

———————

(*A las dos y media, en el comedor del hotel.*)

ISABEL : ¡ Mi primera comida en España este año ! ¿ Qué
vamos a tomar?

MARTÍN : Ya veremos. En este hotel, que no es de los
mas importantes, puede ser que no tengamos que escoger.
(EL MOZO *llega.*)

EL MOZO : ¿ Desean sopa?

MARTÍN : Sí, y ¿ quiere Vd buscarnos algún pan? en esta
mesa no hay. (EL MOZO *les sirve la sopa.*)

EL MOZO : En seguida se lo traigo, señor. Y ¿ cómo desean
Vds los huevos, fritos o en tortilla?

ISABEL : Para mí fritos, pero a tí te gustan mucho las
tortillas españolas ¿ no es verdad, Martín ?

MARTÍN : Sí, pero hoy yo también los tomaré fritos.
(*Al* MOZO.) Dos pares de huevos fritos. ¿ Qué le sigue ?

EL MOZO : Pues hoy hay una paella valenciana, o un asado
de ternera con patatas v otras legumbres.

MARTÍN : Tráiganos ternera, otro día probaremos la paella, y como vino, una botella de Rioja, si la hay.

EL MOZO : Sí señor, espere un momento y se la traigo. (*Se va* EL MOZO.)

MARTÍN : Esto parece muy bien. Después del baño tenemos buen apetito. Si la ternera resulta tan bien como olía en el plato que aquel otro mozo acaba de llevar a la mesa de al lado, comeremos muy bien. ¿Tomarás algo como postre?

ISABEL : No sé todavía. Unas frutas, quizás. Me dijo María que las ciruelas son siempre muy buenas por el mes de julio en San Sebastián.

MARTÍN : Aquí viene el mozo con los huevos. ¡ A comer !

COMMERCIAL SPANISH, 4

The following advertisement appeared in a Spanish newspaper.

> SECRETARIO particular necesita el Director Gerente de agencia seguros contra incendios "Alianza española". Buen sueldo. Debe ser buen mecanotaquígrafo, trabajador, inteligente, serio; edad 23 a 28 años, buena letra, buena presencia, práctica en negocios, debe hablar francés. Escribid dando detalles, referencias—Reyes, 38.

A young man who saw this advertisement replied as follows: (in Spanish, of course; try translating it to discover what he really said) :

4 (*c*)

Casares, 45
Madrid
11 de mayo de 19—

Dear Sir,

In today's " A.B.C." I learn that you are requiring a person with knowledge of French and Spanish to undertake the duties of private secretary, and I venture to offer my services.

I am a native of Seville, and five years ago I completed my studies at the School of Commerce there. Since then I have been employed as assistant book-keeper by Messrs. Záuregui, in their Madrid office. They will be happy to supply any necessary references about me. I speak and write English and French perfectly, and I have had considerable practice in translating from these languages. My shorthand is good, and I may add that I work hard and have a good presence. I am 26 and unmarried.

I feel able, therefore, to undertake the post that you offer.

Hoping that you will favour me with a personal interview,
I am
Yours very truly,
Julio Oliver Quintana

El Director Gerente.
Alianza Española, S.A.
Reyes 38, Madrid.

He received the following reply :

4 (d)

Sr D. Julio Oliver Quintana,
Casares, 45,
Madrid

Muy Señor nuestro :

Oportunamente llegó a nuestras manos su carta de Vd de ayer y juzgando que en principio puede interesarnos aceptar su proposición para entrar a formar parte del personal de esta empresa, le rogamos se sirva personarse el próximo lunes, 14 del actual, a las siete de la tarde, en esta su casa, para celebrar una entrevista y contestarle algo definitivo acerca del asunto en cuestión.

Hasta tener el gusto de estrecharle personalmente la mano,
le saludan ss.ss.

" Alianza Española, S.A."

SPANISH LITERATURE, 4

An important novelist who wrote some of his best work before the turn of the century, but who continued to write

interesting books until he died in 1938, was Armando
Palacio Valdés. He was born in Asturias as long ago as
1853, and excelled in describing middle-class people and the
Spanish peasantry. Much of his writing illustrated the
landscapes and simple country customs of his native
province, but his descriptions of other parts of Spain and
the atmosphere there are equally fine. His style is never
exaggerated, he never sought for artificial effects, but his
work has great dignity and virility. The following extract
is from one of his best novels, *La Hermana San Sulpicio*,
published in 1889.

4 (e)

¡ Nos acercábamos a Sevilla ! Sentía mi corazón palpitar
con brío. Sevilla había sido siempre para mí el símbolo
de la luz, la ciudad del amor y la alegría. ¡ Con cuánta
más razón ahora, que iba hacia ella enamorado ! Veíanse
ya algunas huertas de naranjos, y entre sus ramajes de
esmeralda percibíanse como globos de rubíes, según la
expresión de un poeta arábigo, las naranjas que de puro
maduras se derretían. En las estaciones próximas,
Brenes, Tocina y Empalme, observaba cierta animación,
que no podía achacarse al número, harto exiguo, de
viajeros. Algunas muchachas de ojos negros, con claveles
rojos en el pelo, de pie sobre el andén, sonreían a los que
nos asomábamos a las ventanillas. Todas las casetas de
guardas tenían ya en sus ventanas macetas con flores.
Hasta las guardesas, viejas y pobremente vestidas, que,
con la bandera recogida, daban paso al tren, ostentaban
entre sus cabellos grises algún clavel o alelí.

Palacio Valdés was also a master of the art of short-
story writing. In a famous example entitled " El potro
del Señor Cura " he describes how the priest of a village in
Asturias sells his old white horse for a low price, and a few
days later buys from some other dealers a much more
expensive brown one.

4 (f)

Transcurrieron cinco o seis días sin que don Pedro tuviese
necesidad de montar su nuevo caballo, al cabo de los cuales

mandó al criado que lo limpiase y lo enjaezase, pues pensaba
ir a Mieres. El doméstico se le presentó a los pocos
momentos diciéndole :

—¿Sabe, señor cura, que el León (así se llamaba el jaco)
tiene unas manchas blancas que no se pueden quitar?

—Limpia bien, borrego, limpia bien; se habrá rozado
contra la pared.

Por más que hizo no logró que desaparecieran. Entonces el cura, enojado, le dijo :

—Convéncete, Manuel, de que ya no tienes puños.
Vas a ver ahora cómo se marchan en seguida.

Y despojándose de la sotana y echando hacia arriba las
mangas de la camisa, tomó el cepillo y el rascador y él
mismo se puso a limpiarlo. Mas sus esperanzas quedaron
fallidas. Las manchas no sólo no desaparecían, sino que
se iban haciendo cada vez mayores.

—A ver, trae agua caliente y jabón—dijo al fin sudoroso
y despechado.

¡ Aquí fué ella! El agua quedó teñida al·instante de
rojo, y las manchas blancas del caballo se extendieron de
tal modo que casi le tapaban el cuerpo.

En resumen, tanto fregaron por él, que al cabo de media
hora había desaparecido el alazán, quedando en su lugar
un caballo blanco.

Manuel se echó unos pasos atrás, y con la consternación
pintada en el semblante, exclamó :

—¡ Así Dios me mate, si no es el Pichón !

(It was. The rascally horse-dealers had dyed him and
sold him back to the priest.)

LESSON V

SOME USES OF HACER

THERE are several special uses of this verb. Here are
some :

1. The common impersonal use with a noun referring to a
condition of the weather.

> *Hace sol, esta mañana hacía mucho viento.* It is sunny,
> this morning it was very windy.

2. Followed by an infinitive, *hacer* implies " to get something done." E.g.,

> I am going to get my hair cut—*Voy a hacerme cortar el pelo.*

(Both these constructions are mentioned in the Grammar notes to Lesson II.)

3. The impersonal *hace* followed by words expressing a period of time, means " ago "—(similarly *hacía* plus time means " earlier ").

> I arrived two hours ago, but he had arrived a long time earlier. *Yo llegué hace dos horas, pero él había llegado hacía mucho tiempo.*

4. *Hace* plus *time* plus *que* plus *a present tense*, however, is used to express the length of time an action has been going on—the commonest English for which is exemplified thus :

> I have been writing for half an hour. *Hace una media hora que estoy escribiendo.*

The past tense of this construction is similar :

> I had been at home for twenty minutes (when she rang me up). *(Hacía veinte minutos que yo estaba en casa (cuando ella me telefoneó).*

There is a large number of idioms involving *hacer* which will be found in any good dictionary, but the foregoing are the ones which need the greatest care in handling.

5 (a) Exercise

It is cold this morning, but even if it were warmer, I should still be cold. I feel the cold even in my bones. I have been living here for fifteen years, and I do not think it has ever been so cold as this, except once three or four years ago when it froze for six weeks together. After a frost there is always a lot of mud, no matter how powerful the sun is, and that is always very unpleasant. During that frost I had been trying to thaw the water in the pipes in my bathroom for half an hour when suddenly the biggest of the pipes burst, and the resulting confusion was terrible.

How long have you been in this town? Only two years? Then you could not have remembered this. It must have happened before you came. Give me a cup of tea, please, I want to drink it while it is hot.

5 (b) Conversation

(*Un café en la Plaza Mayor de Pamplona. Se sienta* MARTÍN *en la terraza.*)

MARTÍN (*para sí*): ¡ Qué calor esta mañana ! (*A* UN SEÑOR *sentado en la mesa inmediata.*) ¡ Buenos días ! No le había visto. ¿ Qué tal ?

EL SEÑOR : Bien, gracias, ¿ y Vd ? Hace dos días que no le veo.

MARTÍN : Sí : ayer, como hacía un tiempo tan espléndido hicimos una excursión a Roncesvalles. Hoy mi mujer está muy cansada, y no se ha levantado todavía. (*Al* MOZO, *que se acerca*) Un café, solo, por favor. (*Al* SEÑOR) ¿ Está Vd aquí de vacaciones ?

EL SEÑOR : No precisamente eso, porque soy representante de una casa de comercio de Madrid, y tengo unos negocios que ejecutar aquí. Pero como tengo unos tíos en Pamplona, siempre que vengo por aquí me parece que estoy como en mi casa, y de vacaciones. ¿ Qué tal le parece el hotel ?

MARTÍN : A nosotros nos parece muy bueno. Me lo recomendó un amigo mío en Inglaterra, y en verdad nos gusta. Es muy tranquilo, y está bien situado con unas vistas magníficas de los montes, desde el balcón de nuestro cuarto.

EL SEÑOR : ¿ Acababan Vds de llegar, cuando nos vimos la otra noche ?

MARTÍN : Sí, y ¡ qué viaje más extraordinario habíamos tenido !

EL SEÑOR : ¿ Cómo ? ¿ Por qué extraordinario ?

MARTÍN : Pues vinimos desde San Sebastián por aquel ferrocarril de vía estrecha. Una vez fuera de los alrededores de San Sebastián pasa el tren por una serie de túneles que espantan a uno, y cuando no, hay unas vistas estupendas de los montes de Navarra. Tarda menos en subir hasta aquí de lo que se pudiera esperar, pero ¡ lo sucios que estábamos cuando llegamos por fin a la estación de Pamplona !

EL SEÑOR : Hubieran Vds hecho mejor si hubiesen ido por la otra línea, por Alsasua, donde corren trenes más cómodos. Pero claro, todo es buena experiencia.

MARTÍN (*viendo a* ISABEL *que ha salido a la Plaza desde la puerta principal del hotel*) : Aquí viene mi mujer. (*Se levantan los señores y se hacen las presentaciones.*) ¿ Tú que quieres tomar? El mozo volverá dentro de un momento.

ISABEL : Una naranjada, grande y muy fresca. Hace un calor sofocante esta mañana.

MARTÍN : Aguarda a esta tarde. Entonces será mucho peor.

ISABEL : Puede ser. Pero esta mañana quiero ir a cualquier sitio de Pamplona donde haga un poco fresco. ¿ Puede Vd aconsejarnos?

EL SEÑOR : Lo único que puedo sugerir es que vayan Vds a la catedral, que es muy interesante y muy célebre.

MARTÍN : Vamos allí en seguida. (*Al* MOZO *que trae la naranjada.*) ¿ Cuánto le debo? Quiero arreglarlo ahora que tengo un momento libre, nos marcharemos en cuanto mi esposa acabe su naranjada. (*Da un billete al* MOZO, *que le devuelve el cambio.*)

ISABEL : Ya está. Seguramente la he bebido demasiado aprisa, pero por lo menos ya no tengo sed. Vamos ahora a la catedral, allí hará mucho más fresco. ¡ Si no voy allí me derrito ! (MARTÍN *e* ISABEL *se despiden del* SEÑOR *y se van.*)

COMMERCIAL SPANISH, 5

Request for Information; Accepting an Offer to Advertise

Some useful phrases :

> *Me es grato contestar a* . . .   I have pleasure in replying to . . .
> *No tengo inconveniente en* . . .   I have no objection to . . .

Adjuntar }
Incluir } To enclose

Excusado nos parece añadir . . . We need hardly
   add . . .

Debo manifestar a Vds que . . . I should inform you
   that . . .

Me esmeraré en . . . I shall take care to . . .

En la primera ocasión . . . As soon as possible . . .

*Quedando en libertad de cancelamiento en cualquier
   momento.* Subject to cancellation without notice.

En cuanto a, as to, as for

Espero su respuesta a vuelta de correo. Please reply
   by return of post.

A firm taking up a reference offered by another firm or an
individual with whom some sort of business relations are
proposed would write a letter like the following :

5 (c)

Santa Bernarda, 87,
Madrid,
14 de mayo de 19—

José Pérez y Cía,
Encina, 7,
Madrid.

Dear Sirs,
   We beg to request you to supply us with information
concerning the person whose name and address appear on
the enclosed sheet.
   He has quoted your firm as a reference, and we should
be grateful for any information you can supply, which, we
need hardly add, will be treated as fully confidential.

Yours faithfully,
Martínez Rosas y Cía.

The following letter concerns a request to advertise a
garage.

5 (d)

Ramón Campos de Olivera y Cía
Garaje Moderno,
Canfranc
18 de julio de 19—

Sres G. y J. Ramírez,
Adelfas, 38,
Sevilla

Muy Sres míos,

Oportunamente fue en mi poder su estimada de 10 del actual, a la que no he podido corresponder antes, segun mis deseos, por haber estado ausente durante algunos días. Agradezco muy de veras su deferencia para conmigo, y me es grato contestar a la proposición en que se interesan Vds.

No tengo inconveniente en ocuparme de hacer propaganda para su garaje, mediante la entrega de tarjetas que me remitan Vds, a cuantos vehículos entren por esta frontera y sigan su itinerario por esa capital, lo cual ocurre normalmente con los coches de los súbditos franceses residentes en Marruecos que vía Canfranc se reintegran a su domicilio; ellos, como es natural, serán objeto de mi atención preferente.

Como gratificación por este servicio puedo adelantarles que quedaría sujeta a lo siguiente:

150 pesetas mensuales durante los meses octubre a marzo,

250 pesetas mensuales durante los meses abril a septiembre,

ya que éstos últimos registran, como es natural, mayor paso de vehículos.

Sus tarjetas irían marcadas con un sello diciendo: CANFRANC, lo que les permitiría a Vds controlar mi recomendación.

Debo manifestarles que esta operación se realizaría sin compromiso por ambas partes, quedando en libertad de cancelamiento en cualquier momento a conveniencia de cada uno.

Pendiente de sus gratas al respecto, aprovecho la oportunidad para suscribirme suyo affmo s.s.

q.e.s.m.

R. Campos de Olivera

SPANISH LITERATURE, 5

The last half of the nineteenth century in Spanish literature is notable for the appearance of a number of important novelists, of whom the greatest was Benito Pérez Galdós (1843–1920). He wrote many novels, most of them dealing with life in Madrid, of which he gives an immense number of fascinatingly detailed descriptions and pictures. This sort of word-photography is generally termed "realism". But there is much more than mere description of people and places in this author's novels, the very spirit of the city, the conflicts and loves and hates and virtues and failings of the people who lived there in his time are depicted in the liveliest way. Galdós often shows reforming zeal, anxious that the traditional and often obscurantist opinions of Spaniards should give way to a modern and more scientific approach to the problems that life presents. To help in dispelling his readers' ignorance of the century in which they lived, he wrote a series of forty-six short and popular novels called *Episodios Nacionales*, about the main events of Spanish history between 1805 and 1880. Among the best of his works centred in Madrid are *Fortunata y Jacinta, Gloria, Misericordia*, and *La de Bringas*. The extract which follows is taken from *Doña Perfecta*, in which Galdos describes the tension caused by the clash of old and new ideas in a country town.

5 (e)

(Pepe Rey, a keen young scientist on a visit to Doña Perfecta, his aunt, in the remote and violently traditionalist town of Orbajosa, has fallen in love with his cousin Rosario, Doña Perfecta's daughter. After constant disagreements with his aunt, who considers him irreligious, he is forbidden to enter her house, but Rosario remains deeply in love with him.)

Doña Perfecta sintió borbotones de fuego que subían de

su corazón a sus labios. Se contuvo, y sólo con sus ojos negros, más negros que la noche, contestó a su hija.

" ¡ Mamá, mamá mía, yo aborrezco todo lo que no sea él !—exclamó Rosario.—Óigame Vd en confesión, porque quiero confesarlo a todos, y a Vd la primera.

—Me vas a matar, me estás matando.

—Yo quiero confesarlo, para que Vd me perdone . . . Este peso, este peso que tengo encima no me deja vivir . . .

—¡ El peso de un pecado ! . . . Añádele encima la maldición de Dios, y prueba a andar con ese fardo, desgraciada . . . Sólo yo puedo quitártelo.

—No, Vd no, Vd no—gritó Rosario con desesperación. —Pero óigame Vd : quiero confesarlo todo, todo. . . . Después arrójeme Vd de esta casa, donde he nacido.

—¡ Arrojarte yo !

—Pues me marcharé.

—Menos. Yo te enseñaré los deberes de hija, que has olvidado.

—Pues huiré ; él me llevará consigo.

—¿ Te lo ha dicho, te lo ha aconsejado, te lo ha mandado ?—preguntó la madre, lanzando estas palabras como rayos sobre su hija.

—Me lo aconseja . . . Hemos concertado casarnos. Es preciso, mamá, mamá mía querida. Yo amaré a Vd . . . Conozco que debo amarla . . . Me condenaré si no la amo."

Se retorcía los brazos, y cayendo de rodillas, besó los pies a su madre.

" ¡ Rosario, Rosario !—exclamó Doña Perfecta con terrible acento.—Levántate."

Hubo una pequeña pausa.

" ¿ Ese hombre te ha escrito ?

—Sí.

—¿ Has vuelto a verle después de aquella noche ?

—Sí.

—¡ Y tú . . . !

—Yo también le escribí. ¡ Oh ! señora. ¿ Por qué me mira Vd así ? Vd no es mi madre.

—Ojalá no. Gózate en el daño que me haces. Me matas. Me matas sin remedio—gritó la señora con indecible agitación.—Dices que ese hombre . . .

—Es mi esposo . . . Yo seré suya, protegida por la ley . . . Vd no es mujer . . . ¿Porqué me mira Vd de ese modo que me hace temblar? Madre, madre mía, no me condene Vd.

—Ya tú te has condenado; basta. Obedéceme y te perdonaré . . . Responde : ¿cuándo recibiste cartas de ese hombre?

—Hoy.

—! Qué traición ! ¡ qué infamia !—exclamó la madre, antes bien rugiendo que hablando.—¿ Esperábais veros?

—Sí.

—¿ Cuándo?

—Esta noche.

—¿ Dónde?

—Aquí, aquí. Todo lo confieso, todo. Sé que es un delito . . . Soy una infame; pero Vd, que es mi madre, me sacará de este infierno. Consiente Vd . . . Dígame Vd una palabra, una sola.

—¡ Ese hombre aquí, en mi casa ! " gritó Doña Perfecta, dando algunos pasos que parecían saltos hacia el centro de la habitación.

Rosario la siguió de rodillas. En el mismo instante oyéronse tres golpes, tres estampidos, tres cañonazos. Era el corazón de María Remedios que tocaba a la puerta, agitando la aldaba. La casa se estremecía con temblor pavoroso. Hija y madre se quedaron como estatuas.

Bajó a abrir un criado, y poco después, en la habitación de Doña Perfecta, entró María Remedios, que no era mujer, sino un basilisco envuelto en un mantón. Su rostro, encendido por la ansiedad, despedía fuego.

" ¡ Ahí está, ahí está !—dijo al entrar.—Se ha metido en la huerta por la puertecilla condenada. . . ."

LESSON VI

NOTES ON PERSONAL PRONOUNS

FULL rules for using personal pronouns are given in any elementary grammar. Make sure, however, that you know thoroughly the following points :

(1) *Subject* pronouns, (*yo, tú, él, ella, usted, nosotros, nosotras, vosotros, vosotras, ellos, ellas, ustedes*), are seldom used except for clarity or emphasis.

E.g., if *hablaba* stands alone, it is not clear *who* was talking. *Yo hablaba* or *él hablaba*, etc., improve the clarity.

The subject pronouns may be placed either before or after the verb.

(2) *Object* pronouns of *verbs* (*me, te, le, la, lo, nos, os, les, las, los*) must be placed *before* the verb.

EXCEPT when the verb is: (*a*) Infinitive, (*b*) Present Participle, or (*c*) Imperative Affirmative. In these cases the pronoun object goes *after* the verb, and is joined to it. E.g.,

> *Lo compraron para venderlo otra vez.* They bought it in order to sell it again.
> *¡Tráigalo aquí!* Bring it here.

(Note the need of the written accent on the verb, placed on the syllable where the stress would fall if the verb were without the appended pronoun, when the addition of the pronoun would otherwise cause the stress to fall in the wrong place. Note also that no written accent is needed on *venderlo*, because according to the elementary rules of accentuation the stress must fall on the last syllable but one if the word ends in a vowel.)

(3) When the same verb has two pronoun objects, the *indirect* object pronoun (meaning " to me ", " to her ", etc.) goes before the direct :

> *Me lo mostraron.* They showed it to me.
> *Nos los vendieron.* They sold them to us.

If both pronoun objects are 3rd person (i.e., pronouns that would be expected to begin with the letter *l*) the dative one is changed to *se* :

> *¿Van a darle el reloj? Sí, se lo han dado.* Are they going to give him the watch? Yes, they have given it to him.

And if the *se* is not clear, *a él*, or *a ella* or *a Vd*, etc., can be added after the verb.

Note: If the *direct* object is a 1st or 2nd person pronoun, as in the sentence " He introduced us to them ", translate as follows : *Nos presentó a ellos.*

(4) The pronoun objects of *prepositions* are placed after the prepositions that govern them. They are as follows : *mí, ti, él, ella, usted, sí* (meaning " himself " or " herself " or " themselves "), *nosotros, nosotras, vosotros, vosotras, ellos, ellas, ustedes.*

> *Para mí, sin ellos,* etc.

Remember the special forms required with *con* in the singular : *conmigo, contigo, consigo.*

If you have any difficulty in remembering which of these pronouns bears a written accent and which of these and similar adjectives, etc., do not, note the following :

If the accent is ever used to distinguish two parts of speech where the letters in the words are identical, *the pronoun bears the accent* (and the other part of speech does not), e.g.,

> *Esta casa y ésta.*
> *Mi padre lo hizo para mí.*

The word *si,* which does duty for three parts of speech, is accentuated as follows :

> *Sí,* himself, herself
> *sí,* yes
> *si,* if

6 (a) Exercise

Translate into Spanish :

1. Don't tell it to me now, be quiet !
2. Opening the window, I saw that the sun was shining.
3. They did not buy it in order to give it to me, but to my father.
4. Where have you been hiding ?   I want to go for a walk with you at once.
5. The priest cannot give us them today because his brother has not yet returned them to him.

6 (b) Conversation

(Martín e Isabel *atraviesan la Plaza Mayor de Burgos.
Son las nueve y media de una hermosa mañana de julio.*)

Isabel :   Esta ciudad me gusta enormemente, Martín.
Tiene un ambiente interesantísimo.   ¿ Por qué no me
has hablado de ella antes de venir aquí ?

Martín :   No sé.   A mí también me ha gustado siempre
mucho.   Es que hay tantas hermosas ciudades en
España que no se puede hablar de todas a un tiempo.
Vamos ahora a ver un museo pequeño que hay aquí
cerca.   Contiene varios recuerdos del Cid.

Isabel :   ¿ No vamos primero a la Catedral ?   Vi sus torres
esta mañana desde la ventana de nuestra alcoba en el
hotel, y parece magnífica.

Martín :   Luego iremos allí, pero primero has de saber
algo acerca del Cid, que era una de las figuras más
grandes de la España medieval.   Vivía en tiempos de
nuestro Guillermo el Conquistador, y siendo desterrado
por el rey de Castilla fue a Valencia con su especie de
ejército particular, luchando siempre contra los moros.
Les echó de allí y reinó como príncipe en Valencia hasta
su muerte.

Isabel :   Hablas como un profesor.   Pero ¿ qué es aquella
muralla tan fuerte con esa puerta en el medio ?

Martín :   Por allí se sube al museo que te dije, que está
encima de la vieja entrada de la ciudad.   Como sabes,
Burgos en la Edad Media era capital de Castilla, y una
de las ciudades más importantes de toda España.

(*Llegan a la puerta del museo.*)

Martín :   Dos entradas para el museo, por favor.

El Empleado :   Sí, señor.   Pero siento que a esta hora de
la mañana no puedo cambiar ese billete de cinco duros.
¿ No tiene suelto ?

Martín :   Vamos a ver.   Sí, aquí tengo.   (El Empleado
le da los billetes de entrada.)   ¿ Somos los primeros en
venir aquí esta mañana ?

EL EMPLEADO : No, señor. Precisamente han entrado
dos forasteros.

MARTÍN : Subamos, Isabel.

(*En el museo.*)

ISABEL : ! Mira, quiénes están aquí ! ¡ Antonio y María !
¡ Qué casualidad ! No sabíamos que estaban Vds en
Burgos.

MARÍA : ¡ Vds aquí, Isabel ! Mucho me alegro de verles.
Llegamos ayer, y como estábamos algo cansados después
del viaje tan largo por Francia, pasamos aquí un día de
descanso.

ANTONIO : Es el coche más bien que nosotros el que
necesita descanso, lo están reparando en este momento
en el garaje del hotel. ¿Y Vds? ¿Qué tal? ¿Cómo
han pasado el viaje?

MARTÍN : Bien, gracias. De San Sebastián subimos a
Pamplona, porque me gusta mucho Navarra y sur
montañas, y ayer vinimos aquí. Mañana vamos a
continuar hacia Madrid.

ANTONIO : ¡ Qué casualidad ! Nosotros lo mismo. Acabo
de reservar un cuarto en un hotel del Escorial para
mañana noche. ¿Quieren Vds acompañarnos? Habrá
bastante sitio en el coche si arreglamos el equipaje un
poco, y entonces podrán Vds evitar toda la incomodidad
del viaje por tren, y todo eso.

ISABEL : Muchísimas gracias, Antonio. Aceptamos con
gusto. Siempre me parece que es mucho mejor viajar
en auto que por ferrocarril, porque así se pasa por medio
de las ciudades y las aldeas, que son mucho más interesantes que las estaciones.

MARTÍN : Gracias, Antonio. Yo también reservaré por
teléfono un cuarto en el Escorial. Vamos juntos ahora
a tomar un refresco en algún café.

ISABEL : ¡ Poco hemos visto de este museo !

MARTÍN : Yo te lo explicaré después. Bajemos esta
escalera.

COMMERCIAL SPANISH, 6

Banking, Travellers' Cheques

to open an account, *abrir una cuenta bancaria*
current account, *cuenta corriente*
deposit account, *cuenta depósito*
to pay a cheque into an account, *ingresar un cheque*
to cash a cheque, *hacer efectivo un cheque*
to pay by cheque, *pagar mediante un cheque*
to pay by cash, *pagar al contado*
the balance (of an account), *el saldo*
the savings bank, *la Caja de Ahorros*
travellers' cheques, *cheques del viajero*
to sign, *firmar*
the letter of credit, *la carta de Crédito*

6 (c)

Translate into English :

(*Un* EXTRANJERO *entra en un banco madrileño con un* AMIGO *español*.)

EXTRANJERO : ¿Es aquí donde puedo cambiar mis cheques del viajero, no?

AMIGO : Sí. Vaya Vd a aquella ventanilla con el letrero que dice " Giros " y el dependiente le dirá lo que tiene que hacer. En algunos bancos hay una ventanilla con las palabras " Cambio extranjero ", pero como este sucursal no es grande no la hay aquí.

EXTRANJERO (*al dependiente*) : Tengo aquí varios cheques del viajero de mi banco en Inglaterra, y deseo cambiar en pesetas treinta libras esterlinas.

DEPENDIENTE : Sí, señor. ¿Tiene Vd su pasaporte?

EXTRANJERO : Aquí está.

DEPENDIENTE : Bien. Pues firme Vd en los cheques.

EXTRANJERO : ¿Tengo que endosarlos también?

DEPENDIENTE : No, no hace falta.

(*Después de hacer varios cálculos en un papelote el* DEPENDIENTE *le devuelve su pasaporte y los cheques restantes que no cambia este día, y le da una ficha de metal que lleva el número 71.*)

EXTRANJERO (*a su amigo*) : ¿Qué hago con esto?

AMIGO : Ahora tiene que esperar a que el cajero, él que está detrás de aquella ventanilla que lleva el letrero que dice " Caja ", llame el número ése, 71. Es el cajero quien tiene que arreglar así todas las transacciones de pago al contado.

EXTRANJERO : ¿Tardará mucho?

AMIGO : No, no creo, pues su transacción de Vd es muy sencilla.

EL CAJERO : ¡ Número 69 !

EXTRANJERO : Todavía no es mi turno.

AMIGO : No, pero estará muy cerquita.

EL CAJERO (*un minuto más tarde*) : ¡ Número 71 !

EXTRANJERO (*dando al cajero su ficha*) : Soy yo.

EL CAJERO : ¿Le doy su dinero en dos billetes de mil pesetas y el resto en billetes menores?

EXTRANJERO : Sí, eso está muy bien.

    (*Recibe su dinero y sale a la calle con su* AMIGO.)

SPANISH LITERATURE, 6

Another of the great novelists whose work began to appear about 1870, raising the Spanish novel to a literary level worthy of work of successors of Cervantes, was Juan Valera, who was born in Andalusia in 1827 and died in Madrid in 1905. He was of aristocratic family, and spent many years as a young man in the Spanish Diplomatic Service in various parts of Europe and America. His polished prose is what we should expect from a man whose conversation and writings as a diplomat must inevitably have been conducted in clear, but carefully measured style. His best-known novels' have Andalusia as their background, and contain interesting studies of characters that belong to the small towns there. The following extract is from one of his best works, *Pepita Jiménez*, published in 1874. Don Luis, a young man who is studying for the priesthood, has fallen in love with Pepita Jiménez, a wealthy widow of the town, and she with him. He decides that he must leave the neighbourhood at once, take his vows, and become a missionary overseas

as soon as possible. Pepita's old nurse, Antoñona, however, discovering how devastated Pepita is at the news of
this decision, takes matters into her own hands and calls
on Don Luis—to insist that he does not go away, but must
stay and marry Pepita.

6 (d)

Antoñona se había deslizado hasta allí sin que nadie lo
advirtiese, aprovechando la hora en que comían los criados
y don Pedro dormía, y había abierto la puerta del cuarto
y la había vuelto a cerrar tras sí con tal suavidad, que don
Luis, aunque no hubiera estado tan absorto, no hubiera
podido sentirla.

Antoñona venía resuelta a tener una conferencia muy
seria con don Luis; pero no sabía a punto fijo lo que iba
a decirle. Sin embargo, había pedido, no se sabe si al
cielo o al infierno, que desatase su lengua y que le diese
habla, y habla no chabacana y grotesca, como la que usaba
por lo común, sino culta, elegante e idónea para las nobles
reflexiones y bellas cosas que ella imaginaba que le convenía
expresar.

Cuando don Luis vió a Antoñona arrugó el entrecejo,
mostró bien en el gesto lo que le contrariaba aquella visita,
y dijo con tono brusco :

—¿A qué vienes aquí? Vete.

—Vengo a pedirte cuenta de mi niña—contestó Antoñona
sin turbarse—y no me he de ir hasta que me la des.

En seguida acercó una silla a la mesa y se sentó enfrente
de don Luis con aplomo y descaro.

Viendo don Luis que no había remedio, mitigó el enojo,
se armó de paciencia, y, con acento menos cruel, exclamó :

—Di lo que tengas que decir.

LESSON VII

RELATIVE, POSSESSIVE, AND DEMONSTRATIVE PRONOUNS

As this book makes no attempt to provide full grammatical information, this chapter contains notes about

only some of the points that English students of Spanish find tricky.

RELATIVE PRONOUNS. Here are a few points that must not be overlooked:

1. While *que* is used for " who ", " whom ", " which ", and " that " in a relative clause as the subject or object of a verb, the word *quien* can be used interchangeably with *que* to refer to *people*.

> *No interrumpa Vd a ese señor que* (or *quien*) *está hablando*

2. After *prepositions* special care is needed. " Whom " *must* then be *quien*.

> *La señora para quien trabajo.*

3. For avoidance of ambiguity, or for special emphasis, it is very often convenient to use *el cual, la cual, los cuales, las cuales*, or similarly *el que, la que*, etc. (Note that the word *cual* is ALWAYS preceded by the definite article in Spanish, except when it is interrogative, in which case it bears the written accent, and except when it is used as an adverb, meaning *como =* " like ".)

> *Voy a ver a la madre de mi amigo, la cual está en Londres.* (In this sentence, *que* instead of *la cual* would leave doubt as to which, the friend or the mother, was in London.)

NOTE that after *por, sin*, and prepositions of two or more syllables, the *el cual* or *el que* forms of the relative pronoun MUST be used. The reason as far as *por* and *sin* are concerned is obviously that *por que* and *sin que* are commonly used as conjunctions.

4. Remember that *lo cual* and *lo que*, being *neuter*, do not refer to *nouns*, but to some *vague matter, not previously mentioned by name*.

> *No comprendí lo que mi padre me estaba diciendo.*

POSSESSIVE PRONOUNS (*el mío, la mía, los suyos*, etc.). These must always be preceded by the definite article, except when they occur in the predicate after *ser*, when their omission is possible.

Su casa (de él) es mayor que la nuestra.

BUT one may say *Este libro es mío.* " This book is mine, one of mine." Note that *Este libro es el mío* means " This book is mine," the one, probably the only one, that I have.

DEMONSTRATIVE PRONOUNS. The pronouns :

> *éste, ésta, éstos, éstas*
> *ése, ésa,* etc.
> *aquél, aquélla,* etc.

are distinguished by their written accents from the corresponding adjectives. But the NEUTER· words, *esto, eso,* and *aquello never* bear the written accent, there being no adjectives from which they need to be distinguished :

Aquí hay dos campos, éste es más verde que aquél.
No me diga Vd nada más de eso.

To distinguish the meaning of the three demonstrative pronouns, the following may be useful :

1. *éste* means " THIS one " (near me, the person speaking, near the FIRST person).
2. *ése* means " THIS one or THAT one " (near you, the person spoken *to*, near the SECOND person).
3. *aquél* means " THAT one " (near him or them, over there, by the person spoken *of*, near the THIRD person).

INTERROGATIVE PRONOUNS always require the accent, even when they occur in an *indirect* question.

¿Con quién estaba Vd anoche?
Le pregunté con quién había estado.

---

7 (a) Exercise

1. " Where are my bones? " said the dog. " Give them to me at once."
2. I don't like waiting for them to come in to dinner.

3. Bring me six 50-céntimos stamps and four 2-peseta ones when you go to the post office.

4. We do not know Mr. Sánchez yet, introduce us to him, please.

5. Waiting for him for hours in the garden, Elena picked big bunches of honeysuckle and geraniums.

6. "Don't put it down, put it away," said the mother to the untidy child.

7. Have you written to ask them to send it to us?

8. "I am sorry," sobbed the little girl, "I dropped it, but I did not mean to break it."

9. I like that table with the red carpet underneath it.

10. You are to come in after me, but before him.

11. Who is the man with the big red nose?

12. Which are the swans that belong to the queen? The ones swimming on the pond, but you can't see them from here.

13. The bus he is driving was made in the factory we visited last week.

14. That is the door through which you get to the gentlemen's lavatory.

15. Whose is the bunch of bananas that George found in the car?

7 (b) Conversation

En El Escorial

(*Los cuatro amigos están sentados en el jardín de un hotel, debajo de unos árboles. Desde allí hay una hermosa vista muy extensa.*)

MARTÍN : Ya que hemos visto el palacio y recorrido la ciudad, y tomado un almuerzo espléndido, ¿qué vamos a hacer esta tarde?

ANTONIO : Hombre, ¡qué energía tiene Vd! Si después de todo eso yo sólo tengo ganas de echar una siesta.

ISABEL : Sí, claro. Aunque hace mucho calor esta tarde, está muy agradable en este jardín. Prefiero quedarme aquí, de donde tenemos una vista tan espléndida del palacio y de la Sierra, y no volver a dormir en mi cuarto.

ANTONIO : Pues Vds me perdonarán. Yo sí necesito dormir una hora o dos. ¿Vamos al cuarto, Maria?

MARÍA : No, tú estás más cansado que yo, y con razón, porque has conducido el coche muchas horas seguidas desde que salimos de Londres, hace ya una semana. Ve tú a dormir, yo me quedaré aquí con Isabel y Martín.

ANTONIO : Bueno, adiós. (*Se va.*)

MARÍA : ¿Qué parte del palacio le gustó más esta mañana, Isabel? ¿La iglesia, las salas de Felipe Segundo, o las tumbas?

ISABEL : Realmente no sé qué decir. La iglesia se parece mucho a otras que he visto en España, salvo que hay unas cosas muy interesantes en ella, tales como aquellas estatuas tan célebres de Carlos Quinto y su familia. Las salas de Felipe Segundo eran mucho menos tristes de lo que esperaba, alguien me dijo en Inglaterra que no me gustarían nada, porque eran todo negras y severas. Al contrario me impresionaron mucho, pues no son demasiado grandes, como muchas salas en los palacios reales, y están amuebladas con unas mesas y sillas y otras cosas tan bien puestas que bien se puede imaginar al Rey y a su familia como vivían allí y dormían en aquellas mismas camas.

MARÍA : Sí, es verdad. ¿Pero le gustaron las tumbas, y el mausoleo de los reyes allí abajo?

ISABEL : Eso sí fue emocionante. Aquella capilla redonda, con las urnas de todos los reyes de España desde el siglo xvi, tan imponentes en mármol, no la olvidaré nunca. Pero claro es que tal sitio no puede ser precisamente alegre. El monumento que más me gustó era la tumba de Don Juan de Austria, tan hermosamente esculpida en mármol blanco que parece que está durmiendo. Era él de quien dijo el guía que había luchado contra los turcos, ¿no es verdad, Martín?

MARTÍN : Sí. La flota española bajo su mando destruyó la flota turca, que entonces amenazaba la Europa cristiana, en Lepanto, cerca de la costa de Grecia, en 1571.

ISABEL : Mira que buena cabeza tienes para las fechas. A mi se me olvidan en seguida.

MARTÍN : ¿A qué hora piensan Vds salir mañana, María?

MARÍA : No sé, pero será probablemente cerca de las diez.

Antonio quiere pasar unos días en un sitio que conoce en la Sierra de Guadarrama, antes de ir a Madrid. No se puede ver desde aquí, está más a la izquierda, pero es muy hermoso. Allí fuimos juntos una vez hace muchos años, se sube por la carretera desde Cercedilla a la cumbre del Puerto de Navacerrada, y allí en el mismo puerto está el hotel, a dos mil metros de altura. Llegaremos a tiempo para almorzar, espero. ¿ Y Vds, salen temprano para Madrid?

MARTÍN : Sí, iremos en cualquiera de los trenes. Ahora que este trozo del ferrocarril se ha electrificado el viaje de aquí a Madrid es muy agradable. Quisiera llegar a Madrid bastante temprano, porque tenemos que hallar una pensión que nos convenga. Ya he telefoneado a una que conozco, pero su teléfono no funcionaba, o por lo menos no pude comunicar.

ISABEL : Pero en esta temporada del año es cierto que encontraremos sitio en alguna pensión sin dificultad, porque hay mucha gente fuera, de veraneo.

MARTÍN : Claro. Y ahora, si no se necesita más tiempo mi presencia aquí, voy a dar un paseo. Tengo ganas de ver aquella " silla de Felipe II " de la cual tanto he oído hablar.

MARÍA : ¡ Eso a estas horas ! ¡ Bien dijo alguien que sólo los ingleses y los perros rabiosos salen al sol de mediodía !

(*Pero* MARTÍN *se va, a dar su paseo.*)

COMMERCIAL SPANISH, 7

Useful phrases :

a vuelta de correo, by return of post

cumpliendo con sus órdenes, in fulfilment of your instructions

Obra en nuestro poder, we have to hand

Esperando sus instrucciones al respecto . . . Awaiting your instructions on this matter . . .

Celebraríamos . . . We should be pleased . . .

Nos pesa . . . We regret . . .

Quedamos impuestos de que . . . We note that . . .

(*hacer*) *todo lo que esté de su parte*, (to do) everything
you can
Para su gobierno, for your guidance

7 (*c*)

Translate the following letter, dealing with an order to a
Spanish firm, and invent a suitable reply.   A model letter
of reply (7(*d*)) is given in the Key at the end of this book.

284, Newgate St.,
London, E.C.3
15 de abril de 19—

Sr D. Juan Rodríguez,
San Gabriel, 97,
Madrid

Distinguido colega,
      Se espera que, a partir del 25 del próximo mes, las
tarifas de importación en productos de cerámica obtengan
un aumento del cinco por ciento (5%) sobre las actuales.
Por lo cual sería conveniente, antes de que esta nueva
disposición se lleve a cabo, importar mercanderías que
en el futuro próximo pudiéramos necesitar.
      Habiendo consultado nuestro libro de almacén he sacado
un extracto, el cual le adjunto, por valor de £400, que le
cargaré en su cuenta a su favor.
      Permítame repetirle que es completamente necesario
que estas mercancías entren en Inglaterra antes del día
25 de próximo mes, pues de no ser así, se verían sujetas al
nuevo aumento de derechos de importación y por con-
siguiente este pedido carecería de valor.
      En espera de sus gratas noticias se despide de Vd suyo
afmo,

s.s. q.e.s.m.
(Henry Smith)

SPANISH LITERATURE, 7

Pedro Antonio de Alarcón (1833–91), a journalist and
politician, a native of Andalusia, is particularly famous
for having written a number of charming and very neat
short stories, as well as some longer novels, which include

the very well-known *El Sombrero de Tres Picos*. The story of the latter is the basis of Manuel de Falla's famous ballet.

His descriptions of different kinds of life in nineteenth-century Spain are excellent, particularly when he describes scenes and people in Andalusia. The following extract from the *Three-cornered Hat* occurs towards the end of the novel, when the Corregidor, after his unsuccessful amorous adventure with the miller's wife, returns to his town house to discover that the miller has arrived there before him. Since the miller has disguised himself in the Corregidor's clothes, the Corregidor can only fear that the miller will be taking his vengeance by assailing the Corregidor's wife.

7 (e)

¡ Ave María Purísima ! ¡ Las doce y media y sereno !

Así gritaba por las calles de la ciudad quien tenía facultades para tanto, cuando la molinera y el Corregidor, cada cual en una de las burras del molino, el Sr. Juan López en mu mula, y los dos alguaciles andando, llegaron a la puerta del Corregimiento. La puerta estaba cerrada. Dijérase que para el Gobierno, lo mismo que para los gobernados, había concluido todo por aquel día.

—¡ Malo ! pensó Garduña. Y llamó con aldabón dos o tres veces.

Pasó mucho tiempo, y ni abrieron ni contestaron. La Señá Frasquita estaba más amarilla que la cera. El Corregidor se había comido ya todas las uñas de ambas manos. Nadie decía una palabra.

¡ Pum ! ¡ Pum ! ¡ Pum !, golpes y más golpes a la puerta del Corregimiento, aplicados sucesivamente por los dos alguaciles y por el Sr. Juan López. ¡ Y nada ! ¡ No respondía nadie ! ¡ No abrían ! ¡ No se movía una mosca !

Sólo se oía el claro rumor de los caños de una fuente que había en el patio de la casa. Y de esta manera transcurrían minutos, largos como eternidades. Al fin, cerca de la una, abrióse un ventanillo del piso segundo, y dijo una voz femenina :

—¿ Quién ?

—Es la voz del ama de leche—murmuró Garduña.

—¡ Yo !—respondió D. Eugenio de Zúñiga—.   ¡ Abrid ! Pasó un instante en silencio.

—¿ Y quién es Vd ?—replicó luego la nodriza.

—¿ Pues no me está Vd oyendo ?   ¡ Soy el amo !   ¡ El Corregidor !

Hubo otra pausa.

—¡ Vaya Vd mucho con Dios !—repuso la buena mujer.— Mi amo vino hace una hora, y se acostó en seguida. ¡ Acuéstense Vds también, y duerman el vino que tendrán en el cuerpo !

Y la ventana se cerró de golpe.

LESSON VIII

RADICAL-CHANGING VERBS

STUDENTS of Spanish very often find that those verbs which change their stem in conjugation present serious difficulty. If it is realized, however, that all three classes of radical-changing verbs follow a relatively simple system, much of the difficulty disappears. To memorize the following diagrams is a considerable help :

Class I.   This class contains all the verbs with infinitives ending in *-AR* and *-ER* that ever do change their stem in conjugation. (There is no method, of course, for re-cognizing for certain which of the *-AR* and *-ER* verbs do and which do not make this change. This is the only snag. These *-AR* and *-ER* verbs have to be learned by practice.)

Present Indicative.	Past Historic.	Present Subjunctive.
....	*	....
....	*	....
....	*	....
*	*	*
*	*	*
....	*	....
Present Participle *		

In this diagram a change from a stressed *e* to *ie*, or a stressed *o* to *ue*, is denoted by ....; while if there is never any change of stem, the part is denoted by *.

It should be remembered that the other verb tenses which do not appear in the diagram, such as the Imperfect and the Future, never change in this way; the Past Subjunctive always adopts the stem of the 3rd person plural Past Historic; and the 2nd person singular of the Imperative always has the form of the 3rd person singular of the Present tense.

Class II. This contains only verbs ending in *-ERIR*, *-ENTIR*, *-ERTIR*, along with *hervir*, *morir*, and *dormir*. No others.

Present Indicative.	Past Historic.	Present Subjunctive.
....	*	....
....	*	....
....	———	....
*	*	———
*	*	———
....	———	....
Present Participle———		

In this diagram, the persons marked .... and * change as in Class I, while the line ——— denotes that these parts change the *e* or *o* of the stem (an unstressed *e* or *o*) to *i* and *u* respectively.

Class III. This class contains only verbs ending in *-IR*, mostly those ending in *-EDIR*, *-ESTIR*, *-EGIR*, *-EBIR*,

Present Indicative.	Past Historic.	Present Subjunctive.
———	*	———
———	*	———
———	———	———
*	*	———
*	*	———
———	———	———
Present Participle———		

-*ETIR*, and the -*ERVIR* verbs except *hervir*. All the parts which in either of the previous classes made any radical change, change in this class also, but with the difference that all changes are now from *e* (whether a stressed or an unstressed *e* in the stem) to *i*.

Exceptions to this scheme are almost too rare to bother about. *Jugar* and *adquirir* are almost the only common verbs which are radical changing but which do not exactly conform to the types shown above, and their irregularities should be treated separately and learned as exceptions. (Both follow Class I.)

For practice, try the following exercise. If you find that you need to consult the diagram frequently, work the the same exercise again a day or two later, until you remember the changes easily.

8 (*a*) Exercise

1. Write the 3rd person singular and the 1st person plural of the Present Indicative, Past Historic, and Present Subjunctive of *MOSTRAR*, *CONSENTIR*, and *DORMIR*.

2. Write the 1st person singular and the 3rd person plural of the same tenses of *PENSAR*, *PREFERIR*, and *CORREGIR*.

3. Write the 2nd persons, singular and plural, of the same tenses of *COMENZAR*, *VESTIR*, and *SERVIR*.

4. Write the 3rd person singular and the 3rd person plural of the same tenses of *SUGERIR*, *PEDIR*, and *ATRAVESAR*.

5. Write the Present participles of *MORIR*, *CONTAR*, and *GEMIR*.

6. Write the 2nd person singular of the Imperative of *DORMIR* and *VOLVER*.

7. Write the 1st person singular and 1st person plural of the Past Subjunctive of *SENTIR*, *ENCONTRAR*, and *IMPEDIR*.

8 (*b*) Exercise

Translate into Spanish :

1. Begin to put up the net now, before it starts to rain, so that we can perhaps play tennis this afternoon.

2. She asked for a better dictionary, and he suggested that she should follow the usual custom and buy a copy of this big one.

3. The wretched schoolmaster corrected the pupils' exercises the same evening, and returned them to them the following day.

4. " I am sorry; I prefer to go a different way," said the Archbishop.

5. " I am very sorry indeed that you prefer that, because there is no other way," replied his sister.

6. Laugh, and the world laughs with you; weep, and you weep alone.

7. The queen crosses the road, looking to the left to see if there is a car coming, and then smells the orange-blossom on the tree by the pond.

8. They water the streets several times a day in Madrid to prevent there being too much dust; unless, of course, it rains.

9. " Shut your eyes and go to sleep at once, you naughty child," repeated the nurse.

10. As soon as the train had left Granada, the children started quarrelling violently about which of them should sit by their mother.

8 (c)

Translate into English :

(The Drive from the Escorial to the Puerto de Navacerrada)

El sol se levantaba detrás de Peñalara cuando dejamos el Escorial, y como estábamos a fines de julio el calor era mayor del que podíamos soportar cómodamente. Sin embargo sopló una brisa fresca del norte poco después que alcanzamos el campo abierto, y llegamos al pie del ferrocarril de la montaña, en Cercedilla, cerca de las diez sin sentirnos demasiado calurosos ni cansados. El ferrocarril sube a la izquierda del valle, mientras que la carretera sube serpenteando por la derecha, entre los pinares y las peñas que se hallan a lo largo de la falda más baja de la ladera escarpada de esta montaña. En la mitad de la subida, la carretera pasa por medio del pequeño grupo de casas conocido como el Ventorrillo, en un punto expuesto, desde el cual hay una vista magnífica sobre toda la parte inferior del valle, y a cualquier hora del día el sol juega sobre los Siete Picos, a la derecha, la Maliciosa a la izquierda, y sobre las llanuras abiertas de Castilla con su indistinto horizonte de color bermejo allá a lo lejos al oeste. Llegamos al hotel a la cabeza del valle a tiempo para tomar el último almuerzo.

COMMERCIAL SPANISH, 8

Postal Communications

Essential vocabulary for arranging despatch, etc., of letters, postcards, parcels, and other matters accepted by the Post Office :

la carta, the letter
la tarjeta postal, the postcard
la Dirección General de Correos, the General Post Office
la estafeta, the branch post office
la carta urgente, the express letter
la correspondencia certificada, registered correspondence
sellado con lacre, sealed with sealing-wax
el sello postal, the postage stamp
el timbre, the (revenue, etc.) stamp
la lista de correos, the Poste Restante
el apartado (*Número 248*), the post-box (No. 248)
la correspondencia asegurada, insured correspondence
impresos, printed matter
muestras de comercio, business samples
envíos contra reembolso, cash on delivery service
el paquete postal, parcel
el giro postal, the postal order
por correo marítimo, by surface mail
por avión, by air mail
el buzón, the posting box
el franqueo, postage
el impreso (*de cablegrama*), the (cable) form
el reparto, the delivery
el remitente, the sender
el destinatario, the addressee
la dirección, las señas, the address

8 (d) Exercise

Translate the following phrases :

(a) Se lo enviamos por correo, bajo sobre certificado.

(b) He sabido por este mismo correo que nuestros clientes desean tenerlas dentro del mes próximo.

(c) Le agradeceré me conteste a vuelta de correo.

(d) El Apartado de Correos es la caja en la que la oficina de Correos del lugar de residencia de un comerciante o particular va depositando toda su correspondencia con objeto de que por sus empleados pueda ser retirada en las horas que mejor le convengan, con lo que consigue tener el correo con mayor antelación, toda vez que al llegar a la Administración es distribuído inmediatamente a los apartados, mientras que al tener que llevarlo a domicilio, siempre ha de sufrir un pequeño retraso, puesto que el cartero, al salir de la oficina, ha de seguir una ruta muy extensa.

SPANISH LITERATURE, 8

Poets of the Later Nineteenth Century

At least three of the poets of the last half of the nineteenth century are well worth the attention of anyone who enjoys reading Spanish. The nearest in point of time is Rubén Darío (1867–1916), who was born in Nicaragua, and in his intensely colourful verse and prose struck a new note that has greatly influenced later poets. He lived much in Paris, and some of his work reflects the influence of the French Symbolist school. Probably his best-known poem is " Sonatina ", to be found in most anthologies of modern Spanish verse.

Ramón de Campoamor (1817–1901) reflects the domestic serenity of the nineteenth century in his arm-chair philosophy and neat, simple thoughts on commonplace situations, out of which, however, he extracts material for much pleasing poetry. Two of his best-known poems are " El Tren Expreso " and " ¡ Quién supiera escribir ! "

Gustavo Adolfo Bécquer (1836–70) reflects some of the passionate but colourful and melodious woe of the Romantic school of poets which preceded him. He was an unhappy man but a brilliant artist, and his poetic output consists of seventy-six "Rimas", which, though each is a separate poem, full of melody and subtle thought, together tell the tale of the sad career of his artistic spirit. The following, "Rima no. LIII", is the best known, and refers to the love affair which was perhaps the chief reason for his unhappiness.

8 (e)

Volverán las obscuras golondrinas
En tu balcón sus nidos a colgar,
Y otra vez, con el ala a sus cristales
    Jugando, llamarán.

Pero aquéllas, que el vuelo refrenaban
Tu hermosura y mi dicha a contemplar,
Aquéllas que aprendieron nuestros nombres,
    Ésas, no volverán.

Volverán las tupidas madreselvas
De tu jardín las tapias a escalar,
Y otra vez a la tarde, aun más hermosas
    Sus flores abrirán.

Pero aquéllas, cuajadas de rocío,
Cuyas gotas mirábamos temblar
Y caer, como lágrimas del día,
    Ésas, no volverán.

Volverán del amor en tus oídos
Las palabras ardientes a sonar,
Tu corazón de su profundo sueño
    Tal vez despertará.

Pero mudo, y absorto, y de rodillas,
Como se adora a Dios ante su altar,
Como yo te he querido . . ., desengáñate,
    ¡ Así no te querrán !

LESSON IX

ORTHOGRAPHIC-CHANGING VERBS

THE fact that the Spanish letters *c* and *g*, when followed by *e* or *i* have different sounds from those they have if followed by any other letters causes certain verbs to vary their spelling in conjugation (in order to preserve the sound of the *c* or *g* that occurs in the infinitive).

The verbs in question are those ending in *-car*, *-cer*, *-cir*, and *-gar*, *-ger*, *-gir* (with a very few less common ones ending in *-guar*, *-guir*, and *-quir*).

The following table illustrates the changes :

Spelling of syllable.				
Infinitive ending {	*-car* *-quir*	*-zar* *-cer* * *-cir*	*-gar* *-guir*	*-ger* *-gir*
Following vowel :				
a . . .	*-ca*	*-za*	*-ga*	*-ja*
e . . .	*-que*	*-ce*	*-gue*	*-ge*
i . . .	*-qui*	*-ci*	*-gui*	*-gi*
o . . .	*-co*	*-zo*	*-go*	*-jo*

* Verbs ending in *-ecer* and *-ocer*, however, have a special conjugation. The commonest are *conocer* and *parecer*, and their 1st singular Present tense and all persons of the Present Subjunctive contain *-zc-* (e.g., *conozco*, *parezcamos*).

The only parts liable to be affected by these rules are the 1st singular of the Present tense OR the 1st singular of the Past Historic (not both in the same verb), and all persons of the Present Subjunctive.   Remember not to use a *j* when the guttural sound can be spelled by using *g* in these verbs, and similarly, economize in *z*s.

The very few verbs ending in *-guar*, and some other uncommon ones, require a diæresis over the *u* before a flectional *e*. They present no real difficulty, but they are not common enough to be dealt with here.

Note also the invariable appearance of the letter *Y*

instead of *I* in certain verbs with infinitives ending in a vowel followed by *-er* or *-ir*. As an invariable rule, AN UNSTRESSED *I* CANNOT STAND BETWEEN TWO OTHER VOWELS, it must be replaced by *y*.

In *leer*, for example, the parts affected are :

> Present Participle : *leyendo* (for *leiendo*)
> Past Historic—
> > 3rd person singular : *leyó* (for *leió*)
> > 3rd person plural : *leyeron* (for *leieron*)

and the Past subjunctives, derived from *leyeron*, are therefore *leyese* and *leyera*.

No other parts of this type of verb make this change.

Finally, it is worth noting that the verbs ending in *-uir* (other than those mentioned already, ending in *-guir* and *-quir*) need special attention in conjugation. Two common ones are *huir* and *construir*. They require a *y* in certain parts—four in the Present tense, two in the Past Historic, six in the Present Subjunctive, and in the Present Participle. These parts are exactly the same ones as those which, in the case of radical-changing verbs, ever require a radical change. See the diagram for Class 3 of the radical-changing verbs, Lesson 8, above.

9 (a) Exercise

Write the following verb parts :

1. 1st and 3rd persons singular of the Present Indicative of *REZAR*, *PAGAR*, *SACAR*, *VENCER*, *ESPARCIR*, *CORREGIR*.

2. 1st and 3rd singular Past Historic and 1st and 3rd singular Present Subjunctive of the same verbs.

9 (b) Exercise

Translate into Spanish :

1. Pay me what you owe me as soon as you can.

2. I took all my money out of my pocket, and then she took all hers out of her handbag.

3. Collect those oranges before the children scatter them all over the floor.

4. Let us distinguish clearly between this and that.

5. Our old gardener built himself a beautiful wall fifty yards long at the end of the orchard.

6. I know Martin, and he knows me, but I shan't wait here until he appears.

7. Look in the encyclopædia and verify all the dates you are not sure of.

8. I hit him, because he hit me first.

9. "When we reach Barcelona I will buy you a white chrysanthemum," said the baker.

10. We hope to finish our work before night falls.

9 (c) Conversation

(*Madrid. Vestíbulo de un inmueble de la calle de Goya. MARTÍN e ISABEL acaban de bajar del taxi que les ha conducido de la estación.*)

MARTÍN : Al fin estamos aquí. (*Al portero que se asoma de la portería*) Buenos días. ¿ Me hace el favor de decirme en qué piso está la pensión, el tercero o el cuarto ?

PORTERO : Está en el cuarto, señor. Pero por desgracia hoy no funciona el ascensor, y tendrán Vds que subir a pie.

MARTÍN : ¿Cómo que no funciona? En mi última visita aquí casi nunca funcionaba. Pero no importa, yo me cargaré con las maletas. (*A* ISABEL) ¿ Puedes tú llevar aquel saco tuyo y mi maletín ?

ISABEL : Claro que sí. Subamos.

(*En la puerta de la pensión.*)

MARTÍN (*a la criada que les abre*) : Buenos días. ¿ Puedo hablar con la señorita ?

CRIADA : Sí, señor. ¿ De parte de quién ?

MARTÍN : Johnson. Tal vez la señorita se acuerde de mí. Pasé una temporada aquí hace seis años, y estoy aquí ahora con mi mujer. Deseamos saber si hay un cuarto libre, para quedarnos un par de semanas.

CRIADA : Voy a ver, señor. Se lo diré a la señorita. Siéntese aquí, por favor. (*Se va la criada.* MARTÍN *e* ISABEL *pasan adentro.*)

———

(*Unas horas más tarde, después de arreglar su estancia en la pensión,* MARTÍN *e* ISABEL *se hallan en su cuarto, que es grande, y tiene un balcón sobre la calle.*)

ISABEL : ¡ Cuánto me alegro de estar aquí al fin de esta parte del viaje! Me gusta ver los lugares nuevos, pero no me gusta tanto viajar. Aquí podremos deshacer nuestras maletas y estar como en casa. ¿ Crees que esa criada pueda hacer lavar alguna ropa? Me hace grandísima falta.

MARTÍN : Sí, claro. El servicio del lavado en España es magnífico y muy rápido. Es porque con este sol toda la ropa lavada se seca en seguida, y además las lavanderas españolas saben muy bien planchar. Yo también tengo camisas y un pijama que lavar. Vamos ahora a arreglar nuestras cosas un poco, y luego daremos un paseo, porque son las seis y media, y ya va haciendo más fresco.

ISABEL : ¿ A qué hora se sirve la cena en esta casa?

MARTÍN : Si no me acuerdo mal, no se sirve antes de las diez. En Madrid siempre se come muy tarde.

ISABEL : Luego tenemos mucho tiempo para nuestro paseo. Vamos a salir.

COMMERCIAL SPANISH, 9

Spanish newspapers and periodicals can usually be obtained through agencies abroad. Sometimes, however, it is desired to subscribe directly for them to the publishing office in Spain. The following letters indicate a useful form of procedure and a possible answer from a Spanish publisher.

9 (*d*)

Casa Editorial " Rango ",
Madrid

Muy Sres míos,

Siendo mi deseo subscribirme a su revista titulada " Rango " por un período de tres meses, es por lo que les ruego tengan a bien de informarme del precio de dicha subscripción, así como la forma de pago más conveniente.

Sin otro particular, y en espera de sus gratas noticias se despide de Vd, suyo afmo.

Peter Brown

9 (e)

Peter Brown, Esq.,

Dear Sir,

In reply to your letter of the 3rd inst., we regret to have to inform you that the minimum subscription to this review is for a period of six months. The price of a six months' subscription is sixty pesetas, and payment should be made in advance. Payment may be made in any way convenient to you.

We are, Sir,
Yours very truly,
Casa Editorial " Rango "

SPANISH LITERATURE, 9

Poetry of the Romantic Movement of the Nineteenth Century

José de Espronceda (1808–42) is usually considered to be the greatest of the Spanish poets of the Romantic school (though two others, the Duque de Rivas (1791–1865) and José Zorrilla (1817–93), must not be overlooked—their treatment in verse of old Spanish legends is especially attractive and important). Espronceda's work contains much that is very characteristic of this type of verse: magnificent melody and command of words, the spirit of revolt against imposed conventions and the restrictions of society (reflecting in literature something of the same spirit that had imbued the French revolutionaries in the sphere of politics), passionate love, frustration, and eventual despair. He drew much inspiration from Byron and Victor Hugo.

One of his greatest works is " El Estudiante de Salamanca ", a poem on the theme of Don Juan—a theme well known throughout western Europe since its creation in the seventeenth century by Tirso de Molina in his play *El Burlador de Sevilla*. The arrangement of the four sections of Espronceda's poem gives the form of the

whole work a close resemblance to a work of music in
Sonata form.

The following extract is from the first part, and shows
something of Espronceda's skill in creating mysterious
atmosphere, of which this poem is full.

9 (f)

Súbito rumor de espadas
cruje, y un ¡ ay ! se escuchó ;
un ¡ ay ! moribundo, un ¡ ay !
que penetra el corazon,
que hasta los tuétanos hiela
y da al que lo oyó temblor.
Un ! ay ! de alguno que al mundo
pronuncia el último adiós.

El ruido
cesó,
un hombre
pasó
embozado,
y el sombrero
recatado
a los ojos
se caló.
Se desliza
y atraviesa
junto al muro
de una iglesia,
y en la sombra
se perdió.

Una calle estrecha y alta
la calle del Ataúd
cual si de negro crespón
lóbrego eterno capuz
la vistiera, siempre obscura
y de noche sin más luz
que la lámpara que alumbra
una imagen de Jesús,

atraviesa el embozado
la espada en la mano aún,
que lanzó vivo reflejo
al pasar frente a la cruz.

LESSON X

IRREGULAR VERBS

SPANISH irregular verbs are much less difficult to master than is sometimes supposed. There are in fact only twenty-three to be considered. But because the verbs that are irregular are almost all extremely common and essential ones, students must know them thoroughly. The following series of hints will help to clear up difficulties where the verb conjugations have seemed puzzling.

The verbs are: *asir, andar, caber, caer, dar, decir,* the verbs ending in *-ducir, estar, haber, hacer, ir, oir, poder, poner, querer, saber, ser, salir, tener, traer, valer, venir,* and *ver*.

THE PRESENT INDICATIVE. Of the above verbs, *andar* is quite regular in this tense. *Poder* and *querer* behave like radical-changing verbs of the first class.

The following are irregular in the 1st person singular only, the rest of the tense being quite regular: *asir (asgo), caber (quepo), caer (caigo), dar (doy), -ducir (-duzco), hacer (hago), poner (pongo), saber (sé), salir (salgo), traer (traigo), valer (valgo),* and *ver (veo)*.

Only eight, therefore, are thoroughly irregular, thus:

> *decir:* digo, dices, dice, decimos, decís, dicen
> *estar:* estoy, estás, está, estamos, estáis, están
> *haber:* he, has, ha, hemos, habéis han
> *ir:* voy, vas, va, vamos, vais, van
> *oir:* oigo, oyes, oye, oímos, oís, oyen.
> *ser:* soy, eres, es, somos, sois, son
> *tener:* tengo, tienes, tiene, tenemos, tenéis, tienen
> *venir:* vengo, vienes, viene, venimos, venís, vienen

THE IMPERFECT. All Imperfects throughout the language are regular, except the following: *ir (iba, ibas, iba, íbamos,* etc.); *ser (era,* etc.); and *ver (veía,* etc.).

THE PAST HISTORIC. Seventeen of these are irregular, and are best learned in groups, thus :

(i) *dar* (*di, diste, dio*, etc.) : an -*AR* verb which in this tense takes the endings of the regular -*ER* or -*IR* conjugation.

$$\left.\begin{array}{c} ser \\ ir \end{array}\right\} (fui, fuiste, fue, \text{ etc.})$$

These two verbs have identical Past Historics. Note that *fue* is the only 3rd person singular Past Historic in the language that does not end in -*ó* or -*o*.

(ii) The -*UV*- group : *andar* (*anduve*), *estar* (*estuve*), *tener*, (*tuve*) (note compounds, e.g., *detener* (*detuve*).

(iii) The -*U*- group : *caber* (*cupe*), *haber* (*hube*), *poder* (*pude*), *poner* (*puse*), *saber* (*supe*).

(iv) The -*I*- group : *hacer* (*hice*), *querer* (*quise*), *venir* (*vine*).

(v) The -*J*- group : *decir* (*dije*), -*ducir* (-*duje*), *traer* (*traje*). People who know some Latin will recognize that the Latin Perfect *dixi*, *duxi*, and *traxi* have given rise to these three Spanish Past Historics, changing the *x* to *j*, as happens also in other familiar words, such as *Quijote* and *Méjico*.

Note that in the 3rd person plural of these three Past Historics the forms are *dijeron*, -*dujeron*, and *trajeron* (not *dijieron*, etc.).

Note that throughout the above groups of Past Historics NO verb part bears any written accent.

The Past Historics of the rest of these verbs are regular, but remember that *caer* and *oir* have to follow the rule set out in the preceding chapter; an unstressed *i* between two other vowels never occurs in Spanish, and must be written as *y* (*oí, oíste, oyó*, etc.).

THE FUTURE. All futures are regular, except twelve.

(i) *caber* (*cabré*)   *haber* (*habré*)   *poder* (*podré*)
    querer (*querré*)   *saber* (*sabré*)

(Here the *e* of the infinitive stem is omitted.)

(ii) *poner* (*pondré*)   *salir* (*saldré*)   *tener* (*tendré*)
    valer (*valdré*)   *venir* (*vendré*)

(Here the *e* or *i* of the infinitive stem is replaced by a *d*).

(iii) *decir (diré)*   *hacer (haré)*

(These two are quite irregular in stem.)

THE CONDITIONAL always follows the Future stem, with the regular endings (*-ía, -ías, ía, íamos*, etc.).

THE PRESENT SUBJUNCTIVE. The stem of this tense always follows the 1st person singular of the Present Indicative with the ending appropriate to the conjugation (i.e., in *-AR* verbs, the Present Subjunctive ending is *-e, -es, -e*, etc.; and in *-ER*, or *-IR* verbs it is *-a, -as, -a*, etc.).

The exceptions are six. These are the verbs in which the 1st person singular of the Present Indicative does not end in *-o* (*doy, voy, soy, estoy, he*, and *sé*): *dar (dé), estar (esté), ir (vaya), haber (haya), ser (sea)*, and *saber (sepa)*.

THE IMPERATIVE. *2nd person Singular*. This throughout the language has the same form as the 3rd person singular of the Present Indicative, except in the following eight verbs: *decir (di), hacer (haz), ir (ve), poner (pon), salir (sal), ser (sé), tener (ten), venir (ven)*.

The 1st person plural is always identical with the 1st person plural present subjunctive except in the verb *IR*, which has the form 'vamos', (not vayamos).

The 2nd person plural is never irregular. Simply take the infinitive and change the final *-R* to *-D* (*poner* produces *poned, ir* produces *id*).

IMPERFECT SUBJUNCTIVES (*-SE* or *-RA* forms). These are always formed by taking the 3rd person plural of the Past Historic, and replacing the final *-RON* by *-se, -ses, -se*, etc., or *-ra, -ras, -ra*, etc. There are no exceptions to this rule.

PARTICIPLES. Present Participles of all these verbs are regular, except the following:

(i) *decir (diciendo), ir (yendo), poder (pudiendo)*, and *venir (viniendo)*;

(ii) The few where the rule about the unstressed *-i-* between two other vowels has to be enforced, e.g., *caer: cayendo* (not *caiendo*).

Past Participles are regular except :

(i) *decir* (*dicho*), *hacer* (*hecho*), *poner* (*puesto*), and *ver* (*visto*) ;

(ii) there are a few verbs not otherwise irregular which do not form their Past Participles regularly. These are : *morir* (*muerto*), *abrir* (*abierto*), *cubrir* (*cubierto*), *escribir* (*escrito*), *romper* (*roto*), *imprimir* (*impreso*), *prender* (*preso*), and the verbs ending in *-olver* (*volver, resolver*, etc.—*vuelto, resuelto*, etc.).

There are virtually no other irregularities of any importance in the conjugation of any Spanish verb.

10 (*a*) Exercise

Translate into Spanish :

1. Not being able to open the tin, he put it back on the shelf in the cupboard.
2. " Come here and tell me the truth, Johnny," said his grandmother.
3. If I drove that car too fast, I should probably fall out of it.
4. I'll try to see the duchess now, before she goes to Australia.
5. Would you like George to know what we are doing ?
6. " Listen ! Go out at once, and wait in the garden until I'm ready," said the boy to his sister.
7. We can't get on that tram, there isn't room for us.
8. He walked slowly, but eventually reached the market-place.
9. She told me to bring no money, but I had my wallet in my pocket.
10. When you have finished your work, you may go out, but not until then.

10 (*b*) Conversation

Translate into English :

(*Una hora después del último episodio, habiendo dado unas vueltas por el Paseo de la Castellana y el de Recoletos, se sientan* MARTÍN *e* ISABEL *en la plaza de la Cibeles, delante del Palacio de las Comunicaciones.*)

ISABEL : Desde aquí veremos todo. Aquí hay tanto que
ver : mucha gente, muchos coches, edificios imponentes,
y alguna sombra para sentarnos. ¿Qué tomaremos?

MARTÍN : Tengo ganas de comer algo ligero. En la
pensión, como te dije, no cenaremos antes de las diez.
Pediré al mozo dos paquetes de patatas fritas y beberé
cerveza. ¿Y tú?

ISABEL : Me basta con un vasito de aquel vino dulce que
probamos ayer en el Escorial. ¿Era de Málaga, no?

(MARTÍN *pide lo que desean cuando viene el mozo, y
éste se lo trae.*) (*Media hora después.*)

MARTÍN : Mira, Isabel, me veo en un apuro. ¿Tienes
dinero contigo?

ISABEL : No. Como tú pagas siempre y no quería ir de
compras esta tarde dejé lo poco que tengo en la pensión.
¡Cómo! ¿Has dejado allí el tuyo también? ¡Pero
qué vamos a hacer? ¡No tenemos dinero para pagar al
mozo! Tú siempre tan correcto, ¿cómo has podido
hacer una cosa tan tonta?

MARTÍN : Sí. Tonto fui, lo admito. Sólo que ahora
acabo de recordar que dejé el dinero en mi cartera,
encerrado en el maletín. Poco es, tendremos que cambiar unos cheques de viajero mañana en un banco.
Pero por ahora lo que importa es ¿cómo salir de aquí
sin dinero?

ISABEL : Pues, si nos vamos sin pagar y el mozo nos ve,
va a armar un lío tremendo y la policía nos llevará a la
cárcel. ¡Buen principio para nuestras vacaciones en
Madrid!

MARTÍN : Hija, no. No exageres. Lo que podemos hacer
es esto : Como no conozco a nadie a quien pueda pedir
prestado dinero, yo volveré ahora a la pensión para
coger mi cartera, y tú permanecerás aquí hasta que esté
de vuelta.

ISABEL : ¡Yo permanecer aquí! ¡Pero si tengo miedo!
Nunca he quedado sola en una ciudad extranjera a tal
hora. ¿Y si algún hombre me habla?

MARTÍN : Nadie te dirá nada. Además, si quieres, te
haces entender bastante bien en español para explicar
nuestro apuro a quienquiera que sea. Pero oye. Lo que

puedes decir si alguien viene es esto : " Mi marido viene."
Nada más. Lo mismo al mozo si pregunta si quieres
algo más para beber, como a otra persona cualquiera.
Y no te molestará nadie. Yo me voy. Pero ¡ ay !
¡ ni una peseta para pagar el tranvía ! Hay que ir
andando. Adiós. Acuérdate bien : " Mi marido
viene."

(*Tres cuartos de hora después vuelve* MARTÍN *triunfante en
taxi, con la cartera.* MARTÍN *paga, y vuelven los dos
hacia la pensión. Y no ha tenido* ISABEL *que explicar
nada a nadie, ni aun decir, por esta vez, las palabras
mágicas* " *Mi marido viene* ".)

COMMERCIAL SPANISH, 10

10 (*c*)

Telephoning

One of the things that travellers to Spain, either for business or pleasure, often find that they have to do is to make
use of the telephone. Telephoning in a foreign language
can be a difficult experience at first, and it is not always
easy to find the vocabulary that is conventionally used.
Study of the following conversation, which contains a great
many of the normal telephoning terms, will prevent much
confusion and save the traveller much time, besides giving
him that feeling of independence that is so valuable when
we are abroad.

(*Desde su hotel en Madrid,* MARÍA *desea poner una conferencia
telefónica con una amiga en Londres.*)

ANTONIO : Como no encuentro la guía telefónica y no sé
el número que hay que marcar para solicitar la con-
ferencia, creo que lo mejor sería llamar a Informaciones,
cuyo número es 03.
MARÍA : De acuerdo. ¿ Puedo usar el teléfono ?
ANTONIO : Sí, claro.
MARÍA : Gracias.
(MARÍA *descuelga el aparato y marca cero, tres.*)
TELEFONISTA : Compañía telefónica Nacional de España.
Informaciones. ¿ En qué puedo servirle ?

MARÍA : Quisiera poner una conferencia con Londres.
TELEFONISTA : Ah, sí. Número 09, Conferencias.
MARÍA : Gracias.
(MARÍA *cuelga el aparato, y seguidamente lo descuelga y marca* 09.)
TELEFONISTA : Compañía telefónica nacional de España, Conferencias. ¿ En qué puedo servirle ?
MARÍA : Desearía poner una conferencia con Londres.
TELEFONISTA : Número, por favor.
MARÍA : DWC 1989.
TELEFONISTA : Londres, Inglaterra, DWC 1989.
MARÍA : Exacto.
TELEFONISTA : Su número, por favor.
MARÍA : 37 75 51.
TELEFONISTA : Bien, cuelgue, ya le llamaremos.
MARÍA : Por favor, ¿ me podría decir cuánto tardará ?
TELEFONISTA : Una media hora.
MARÍA : Gracias.
(MARÍA *cuelga el teléfono.*)
MARÍA : Ahora, lo que tenemos que hacer es esperar.
ANTONIO : ¿ Cuánto tardará ?
MARÍA : Dijo que una media hora, pero ya sabes, nunca hay seguridad en esto.
ANTONIO : Depende de lo ocupada que esté la línea. Algunas veces . . .
(*Suena el teléfono.*)
MARÍA : ¡ Ya está aquí ! ¡ Qué pronto !
(*Descuelga el aparato.*)
MARÍA : Diga.
VOZ : 36 85 64.
MARÍA : Lo siento, se ha equivocado de número.
VOZ : Perdone.
(MARÍA *cuelga el aparato.*)
MARÍA : ¡ Que fastidio ! Esto de esperar me crispa los nervios.
(*Suena el teléfono.*)
MARÍA (*descolgando*): Diga.
TELEFONISTA : 37 75 51.
MARÍA : Sí, diga.

Telefonista : No cuelgue, por favor.
> (*Se oyen varias voces a través del auricular. Después se oye una voz clara y concisa.*)

La Voz clara : London, Hello !

María : At last ! Hello ! . . .

SPANISH LITERATURE, 10

10 (*d*)

The Romantic Drama

One of the most interesting features of the Romantic movement was its drama. In 1833, on the death of the oppressively conservative king, Fernando VII, many Liberals who had been exiled for political reasons returned to Spain. Most of them had spent years abroad; and many had been influenced by English, French, German, and Italian writers, notably Byron, Scott, and Victor Hugo. The best Spanish plays of the succeeding period include *Don Alvaro*, by the Duque de Rivas *El Trovador*, by García Gutiérrez (two of Verdi's best-known operas are based on these), and *Don Juan Tenorio*, by Zorrilla. The vogue for this kind of drama was brief, all the above plays appeared within ten years, 1835–44.

The plots are invariably melodramatic and somewhat improbable; the interest of these plays lies rather in the passionate, lyrical verse, the character studies of ill-fated, gradually disillusioned young men and woebegone, forsaken young women, and a studied picturesqueness of staging that is usually scholarly and well worth attention. The following extract is from one of the best : *Los Amantes de Teruel*, by Juan Eugenio Hartzenbusch (1837).

The plot is from a mediæval legend bearing some relation to that of *Romeo and Juliet*. In the extract the hero, Marsilla, is explaining his origin and story to a Moorish queen in whose care he is near the beginning of the play.

Marsilla :

Mi nombre es Diego Marsilla,
y cuna Teruel me dió,
pueblo que ayer se fundó
y es hoy poderosa villa,
cuyos muros, entre horrores
de lid atroz levantados,

fueron con sangre amasados
de sus fuertes pobladores.
Yo creo que al darme ser
quiso formar el Señor,
modelos de puro amor,
un hombre y una mujer,
para hacer la igualdad
de sus afectos cumplida,
les dió un alma en dos par-
    tida,
y dijo : " Vivid y amad."
Al son de la voz creadora,
Isabel y yo existimos,
y ambos los ojos abrimos
en un día y una hora.
Desde los años más tiernos

fuimos ya finos amantes ;
desde que nos vimos, antes
nos amábamos de vernos ;
porque el amor principió
a enardecer nuestras almas
al contacto de las palmas
de Dios, cuando nos crió :
y así fué nuestro querer,
prodigioso en niña y niño,
encarnación del cariño
anticipado al nacer,
seguir Isabel y yo,
al triste mundo arribando,
seguir con el cuerpo amando,
como el espíritu amó.

LESSON XI

POR AND PARA

THE translation of the English word " for " into Spanish
often causes difficulty—the uses of the Spanish prepositions
por and *para* need care and practice.

It should, of course, be remembered that the *conjunction*
" for " (meaning " because ") is neither *por* nor *para*, but
porque or *como*.

If the word " for " is a preposition, decide whether :

(*a*) the meaning is " for the sake of ", " on account
of ", or " in exchange for "—in which cases use
POR ; or

(*b*) the implication is *purpose* or *destination*—in
which case use *PARA*.

Study these examples :

Hizo grandes sacrificios por su familia. He made great
sacrifices for his family. (" For the sake of ".)

Nos castigaron por no haberles dicho la verdad. They
punished us for not having told them the truth.
(" On account of.")

Pagamos muchísimo dinero por esta casa. We paid a great deal of money for this house. (" In exchange for.")

Mañana vamos a salir para Barcelona. Tomorrow we are going to leave for Barcelona. (" Destination " implied.)

Compró un regalo para su madre. He bought a present for his mother. (" Purpose " and " destination " are implied here.)

Note that *por* also means " through ", " by ", or " per " :

Salió por la ventana. He went out through the window.

Esta silla fué rota por Juan. This chair was broken by Juan.

Veinte por ciento. 20%.

And when translating expressions of *time,* no equivalent of the English word " for " is needed, unless *futurity* is implied :

He vivido un año en Madrid; ahora voy a América por seis meses. I have lived *for* a year in Madrid; now I am going to America *for* six months.

It is a very good practice to collect as many examples of the different uses of *por* and *para* as possible from any Spanish texts read. Such examples are certain to be very valuable as models for future use in Spanish conversation or composition.

11 (*a*) Exercise

Translate into Spanish :

1. How much did you pay for that car?
2. I think he did that just to deceive me.
3. This house was built by a good architect.
4. Tomorrow evening I am going to leave for Seville.
5. I stayed in the cinema for two hours.
6. I am going to Buenos Aires for six or eight months.
7. Through having saved so much money, he had now become a very rich man.
8. I want you to go to post for me; I am very busy and can't go out.

9. He bought this book for * me, but it will be quite useless.

10. I looked for him in the garden, for we had to set out for the station at five o'clock.

11 (b) Conversation

Translate into English :

(MARTÍN e ISABEL, *saliendo de la pensión, encuentran a* ANTONIO *y* MARÍA, *a las diez de la mañana.*)

ISABEL : ¡ Qué estupendo ! No sabíamos que estaban Vds en Madrid.

MARÍA : Sólo llegamos anoche, y como Antonio tiene algunos asuntos que hacer esta mañana en esta misma calle, yo vine con él para saludarles   Pero ¿ van Vds de paseo ?

ISABEL : Ibamos a ver si encontrábamos algunos artículos de regalo para llevar a nuestras familias en Inglaterra. ¿ Quisiera Vd acompañarnos ?   Nos haría un favor muy grande, pues claro está que Vd conoce las tiendas mucho mejor que nosotros. ¡ Mira, Martín ! (MARTÍN, *que ha estado hablando con* ANTONIO, *se vuelve.*)   María va a acompañarnos a las tiendas ; dice que Vd, Antonio, tiene que hacer algunos asuntos por aquí, y que ella puede venir con nosotros.

MARTÍN : ¡ Qué magnífica idea ! Entonces, es claro que las dos señoras no necesitarán mi presencia en esta expedición.   Se divertirán mucho mejor sin mí, y como me aburre algo el tener que andar vagando de tienda en tienda en busca de no se sabe qué, les dejaré, y nos veremos a la hora de comer. A propósito, ¿ quisieran Vds almorzar con nosotros en nuestra pensión ? Se come bien aquí, y además el comedor es mucho más fresco y tranquilo que cualquier restaurante.

ANTONIO : Con mucho gusto, ¿ no es verdad, María ? Con que ¿ nos veremos aquí de nuevo a eso de las dos ?

---

* If the meaning of " for " were " for my sake "—i.e., to prevent anyone else from buying it—the Spanish would be *por mí*. Here the implication is rather " destined for me ", and the translation must be *para mí*.

MARTÍN : Digamos en el café de enfrente a la una y media para tomar un aperitivo. Yo subiré a la pensión para avisar a la señorita.

ISABEL : ¿ Y adónde irás luego, Martín ?

MARTÍN : No te preocupes. Tengo muchas cosas que hacer. Una de ellas es ir al banco para cambiar unos cheques; de seguro vamos a necesitar más dinero si tú vas de compras. ¡ Adiós! ¡ Que lo paséis bien!

(*Se separan, y las señoras van bajando la calle. En la esquina toman un autobús que las lleva hasta una parada cerca de la Gran Vía, donde se apean, y poco después entran en uno de los grandes almacenes que hay allí.*)

MARÍA : En este almacén estoy segura de que hallará Vd todo lo que desee para regalos. Hay toda clase de artículos en todas las calidades.

ISABEL : Sí, se parece a algunos de los almacenes muy bonitos que he visto en París. Y a algunos de los que hay en Londres, también, claro.

MARÍA : ¡ Qué desea Vd comprar, Isabel ? ¿ Háy algo especial que busca ?

ISABEL : Sí. Unos pañuelos de encaje español para mi madre, algún brazalete de plata para mi hermanita, unas muñequitas vestidas de bailadoras españolas como las que he visto en algunos escaparates para dos amiguitas que tengo, y otras cosas—¡ ah, sí ! Allí hay muchas tarjetas postales con vistas de Madrid. Tengo que comprar por lo menos una docena para mandar a mis amigas inglesas.

MARÍA : Aquí hay unos pañuelos de encaje muy bonitos.

ISABEL (*a la dependienta*): Me hace el favor, ¿ valen lo que indica en esta etiqueta ?

LA DEPENDIENTA : Sí, señora, todos los precios están marcados.

ISABEL : Bien, pues me quedaré con estos cinco. ¿ Se puede cambiar este billete de cien pesetas ?

LA DEPENDIENTA : Sí, señora.

(*Envuelve los pañuelos en papel, y se los da a* ISABEL. *Las dos señoras siguen andando por el almacén en busca de las otras cosas que* ISABEL *necesita comprar.*)

COMMERCIAL SPANISH, 11

Claims Concerning Missing or Damaged Goods

costo, flete y seguro, cost, freight and insurance (c.i.f.)
el consignatario, the consignee
el consignador, the consignor
el embarcador, the shipper
flete de retorno, inward freight
término medio, average
seguro marítimo, marine insurance
a todo riesgo, against all risk
asegurar por el viaje redondo, to insure out and home
salvamento, salvage
géneros averiados, damaged goods
los aseguradores, the underwriters
asegurar, to insure
póliza nula, invalid policy
ferrocarril P.V. (= *Pequeña Velocidad*), (slow) goods train.

11 (c)

Domínguez y Cía,
San Blas, 12,
Madrid
12 de mayo de 19—

Sr D. Juan García,
Paseo de Málaga 10,
Sevilla

Muy señor mío,
Con referencia a su atenta carta fecha 27 de abril,
hemos de comunicarle que las mercancías que nos reclama
fueron mandadas por ferrocarril P.V. con fecha 10 de abril
del corriente, segun acredita nuestro talón de ferrocarril
no. 3257.
Por tanto, y puesto que Vd no las ha recibido, creemos
conveniente hacer la reclamación correspondiente al caso,
para lo cual rogamos nos dé su consentimiento.
En espera de sus gratas noticias se despiden de Vd,
s.s.q.e.s.m.
José Domínguez

SPANISH LITERATURE, 11

The eighteenth century was not a very fruitful period in Spanish literature. The great Golden Age of Spanish history, when Spain had led the world in politics as well as in literature, was over by about 1680, and the Habsburg dynasty of Spanish kings, which had ruled in Spain for nearly two centuries, died out in 1700. A branch of the French royal family replaced it, and French taste consequently became the fashion in Spanish aristocratic circles throughout the following century. In matters of drama it was inevitable that the plays of Molière should attract the notice of Spanish playwrights sooner or later, and of these writers the finest was Leandro Fernández de Moratín (1760–1828).

Although in form and type of theme Moratín followed the pattern set by Molière, the background and atmosphere of his plays is very Spanish. In language and style he was a purist, and devoted to the highest ideals of straightforwardness and simplicity. As a result, his plays are models of careful, economical construction and restraint, and directly or indirectly many Spanish dramatists of the century and a half since his time have derived much valuable inspiration from his work.

He wrote only a very small number of plays, the best of which had a current social topic as their theme. The following extract is from the opening scene of *El Sí de las Niñas* (first performed in 1806, just two years before Spain was plunged into the Peninsular War). In it Moratín deals with the theme of " May and September " marriages, and here we find don Diego, an elderly, wealthy bachelor, in a discussion with his confidential servant, Simón, on the subject of a marriage. Simón at first does not understand don Diego's intentions.

11 (d)

DIEGO : Pues ya ves tú. Ella es una pobre. . . . Eso sí. . . . Pero yo no he buscado dinero, que dineros tengo; he buscado modestia, recogimiento, virtud.

SIMÓN : Eso es lo principal. . . . Y sobre todo, lo que usted tiene, ¿ para quién ha de ser ?

DIEGO : Dices bien. . . . ¿Y sabes tú lo que es una mujer aprovechada, hacendosa, que sepa cuidar de la casa, economizar, estar en todo? . . . Siempre lidiando con amas, que si una es mala, otra es peor, regalonas, entremetidas, habladoras, llenas de histérico, viejas, feas como demonios. . . . No, señor, vida nueva. Tendré quien me asista con amor y fidelidad, y viviremos como unos santos. . . . Y deja que hablen y murmuren y . . .

SIMÓN : Pero, siendo a gusto de entrambos, ¿qué pueden decir?

DIEGO : No, yo ya sé lo que dirán; pero. . . . Dirán que la boda es desigual, que no hay proporción en la edad, que . . .

SIMÓN : Vamos, que no me parece tan notable la diferencia. Siete u ocho años, a lo más.

DIEGO : ¡Qué, hombre! ¿Qué hablas de siete u ocho años? Si ella ha cumplido dieciséis años pocos meses ha.

SIMÓN : Y bien, ¿que?

DIEGO : Y yo, aunque gracias a Dios estoy robusto y . . . con todo eso, mis cincuenta y nueve años no hay quien me los quite.

SIMÓN : Pero si yo no hablo de eso.

DIEGO : ¿Pues de qué hablas?

SIMÓN : Decía que. . . . Vamos, o usted no acaba de explicarse, o yo lo entiendo al revés. . . . En suma, esta doña Paquita, ¿con quién se casa?

DIEGO : ¿Ahora estamos ahí? Conmigo.

SIMÓN : ¡Medrados quedamos!

DIEGO : ¿Qué dices? . . . Vamos, ¿qué?

SIMÓN : ¡Y pensaba yo haber adivinado!

DIEGO : ¿Pues qué creías? ¿Para quién juzgaste que la destinaba yo?

SIMÓN : Para don Carlos, su sobrino de usted, mozo de talento, instruído, excelente soldado, amabilísimo por todas sus circunstancias. . . . Para ése juzgué que se guardaba la tal niña.

DIEGO : Pues, no, señor.

(*During the play we meet doña Paquita's mother, doña Irene, a vulgar, foolish old woman, doña Paquita herself, and don Carlos. The two latter have, unknown to their elders,*

already made each other's acquaintance and fallen in love.
There is a fine scene in Act 3 when don Diego and doña
Irene discover this impediment to their plans, but don Diego
eventually relents, and permits Carlos and Paquita to marry.)

LESSON XII

VERBS REQUIRING CERTAIN
PREPOSITIONS BEFORE INFINITIVES

" WHICH preposition, if any, has to be used between the
verb and the dependent infinitive in these sentences? :
' I wanted to see him ', ' I consented to see him ', ' I
decided to see him ', ' I began to look for him ', ' I forgot
to look for him '."

The student will often require to know the answer to
these and similar questions, and a complete list of all verbs
and the prepositions that they take before a dependent
infinitive is obviously beyond the scope of this book.
Below, however, is a list of about thirty of the commonest,
with which it is well worth while to become as familar as
possible, as they are met with extremely frequently.

BUT note that where the main verb of a sentence is a
verb of wishing or of emotion, and the subject of the main
verb is *not the same* as that of the subordinate infinitive
(e.g., " I want *him* to drink this ") the infinitive construction
must be replaced in Spanish by a subjunctive (e.g., *Quiero*
que él beba esto), although of course " I want to drink this "
(myself—no change of subjects being implied) would be
Quiero beber esto. For more on this topic, see the next
grammar section, Lesson XIII.

alegrarse de, to be glad to

apresurar(se) a, to hurry to

arriesgarse a, to risk

atreverse a, to dare to

ayudar a, to help to

cesar de, to cease to

comenzar a, to begin to

conseguir, to manage to

consentir en, to consent to

convidar a, to invite to

decidir ⎫
decidirse a ⎭ to decide to

desear, to desire to

elegir, to choose to

empezar a, to begin to

esperar, to hope to

fingir, to pretend to

impedir, to prevent from

jurar de, to swear to

lograr, to succeed in

negar, to deny

negarse a, to refuse to

obligar(se) a, to oblige (one-self) to

estar obligado de, to be obliged to

oler a to smell of

olvidarse ⎱ to forget to
olvidarse de ⎰

pensar, to intend to

pensar en, to think of

prohibir, to forbid

querer, to want to

rehusar(se) ⎱ to refuse to
rehusar(se) a ⎰

soñar con, to dream of

tardar en, to be a long time in

tratar de, to try to

12 (*a*) Exercise

Translate into Spanish :

1. Luis invited Juana to go with him to the cinema.
2. Her mother refused to allow it.
3. They succeeded in leaving Juana's house while her mother was upstairs.
4. They decided to sit in the back row of the stalls.
5. Juana wanted to smoke Luis's cigarettes.
6. They were a very long time returning home.
7. Juana had forgotten to take her latchkey.
8. She did not dare to ring the bell.
9. Luis helped her to get in through the dining-room window.
10. She was terrified at seeing her father, who was waiting for them.

Translate into English :

12 (*b*) Conversation

(*El Paseo del Prado.* Martín e Isabel, *que van a pasar una hora o dos en el* Museo, *se acercan a la entrada.*)

Isabel : ¿Es aquí donde vamos a pasar la mañana, no? Muchas ganas tengo de ver estas pinturas de que tanto he leído.

Martín : Sí.   Yo también siento siempre un placer enorme al entrar en este museo, en donde hay una de las mejores colecciones de obras maestras de pintura del mundo entero.   Sobre todo de las escuelas españolas.

Isabel : ¿Me vas a mostrar todo lo que hay que ver?

MARTÍN : No. Eso sería imposible en una mañana.
Lo mejor será ir a las salas en donde están los cuadros
de los pintores más importantes, El Greco, Velázquez y
Goya, y estudiarlos primero. Si tratamos de ver
mucho más en nuestra primera visita sólo guardaremos
una idea muy confusa de lo que hemos visto. (*Al
portero*) ¿Cuánto hay que pagar? (*Paga lo necesario
y pasan adentro*).

MARTÍN : Pasemos primero por estas salas a la izquierda
donde hay muchos cuadros italianos, que son por cierto
muy hermosos e interesantes, y pronto llegaremos a las
salas de Velázquez.

ISABEL : Pero ¡qué maravillosos son! ¡Podría pasar
aquí muchos días enteros sin cansarme de ver tantos
cuadros hermosos!

MARTÍN : Volveremos el domingo.

(*Recorren cuatro o cinco salas a la izquierda del
museo.*)

MARTÍN : ¡Ah, sí! Aquí está el cuadro que siempre me
encanta. La ponen siempre en esta sala pequeña
donde no existe ningún otro.

ISABEL : Sé que se llama " Las Meninas ", pero no recuerdo
lo que me has dicho acerca de él. ¿Quién es aquella
figura a la izquierda, que parece que está pintando algún
retrato?

MARTÍN : Es el autoretrato de Velázquez. Se dice que
una mañana del verano del año 1655, Velázquez estaba
retratando, en su estudio del antiguo palacio real de
Madrid, a los reyes, Felipe Cuarto y a su esposa, doña
Mariana. En un momento de descanso entró su hija,
la infanta Margarita María, a verles, seguida de dos
damas de honor—que son las meninas—dos enanos y
otras tres personas de la corte. Después de esta visita,
Velázquez tuvo la idea de pintar, no lo que él vió en
aquel momento, sino lo que veía el rey. Así lo hizo, y
aún en el fondo de la sala pintó un espejo, en que se ven
reflejados el mismo rey y la reina. Se dice también
que cuando el rey vió este cuadro por primera vez
—Velázquez lo había pintado en secreto—lo miró en
silencio durante algún tiempo, y luego, tomando un

pincel, añadió, en el pecho de la figura de Velázquez,
la cruz roja de la Orden de Santiago, indicando así sin
una palabra, cómo le premiaba por haber hecho una
obra tan magnífica.

ISABEL: ¡Qué magnífico es, en verdad! Me gustan los
colores tan delicados, casi transparentes, la luz que cae
así tan naturalmente de la derecha. ¿No te parece
que nosotros estamos allí, en el cuarto? A mí me
parece tan verdadero que casi puedo percibir el olor de
aquella sala.

MARTÍN: Pues ¡dicen los historiadores que aquel palacio
olía muy mal!

ISABEL: ¡Qué prosáico eres! ¿Es allí donde iremos
mañana? Dijiste que me llevarías a ver el Palacio
Real.

MARTÍN: No. El que está allí ahora es muy hermoso, y
reemplazó el antiguo en el siglo xviii. Pero ocupa el
mismo sitio, al oeste de Madrid, mirando hacia el valle
del Manzanares.

ISABEL: Vamos ahora a la próxima sala. ¿Son todas
estas pinturas de Velázquez?

MARTÍN: Sí, y aquí también hay muchas muy célebres.
Allí están "Las Lanzas" y "Las Hilanderas", por
ejemplo.

(*Y les dejamos pasar el resto de la mañana en el museo,
estudiando los cuadros.*)

COMMERCIAL SPANISH, 12

Payment Overdue

Here is a type of letter concerning payment which is
overdue for goods despatched.

el plazo, term, period, time
abonar, pay, credit, compensate (*abonar en cuenta*, to
credit with)
cuenta corriente (*c/c*), current account
la cubierta, cover
cumplir con los pedidos, to fill the orders
demandar, to claim, demand
girar, to draw, remit

la queja, complaint
el poder, power, faculty, power of attorney
llegar a nuestro poder, to reach us, to come to hand
prefijado, agreed upon, stated

12 (c)

González y Cía,
San Martín, 45,
Bilbao
14 de marzo de 19—

Sr. D. Javier Hernández,
Henares, 12,
Burgos

Muy Señor nuestro,

Hace algún tiempo que cumplió el plazo de pago de
su cuenta de mercancías no. 3105, y comoquiera que aun
no hemos recibido noticias suyas referente a ello, es por lo
que le rogamos tenga a bien abonar el resto de 1525 ptas.
en nuestra cuenta corriente en el Banco de Vizcaya en
ésa, con lo cual quedará cubierta.

Sin otro particular le saludamos atentamente,

González y Cía.

SPANISH LITERATURE, 12

Cervantes (í)

The greatest of Spanish prose writers, Miguel de Cervantes
(1547–1616), wrote when the greatness of Spain was at its
height. His career is fascinating. As a young man he
served in the Spanish Army in Italy, and under the famous
Don Juan de Austria he fought in the naval battle of
Lepanto, when an alliance of Christian forces defeated
the Turks. On his way back to Spain in 1575 he was
captured by pirates, and spent five years in captivity in
Algiers. On his return to Spain he found it difficult to
obtain congenial employment, and after writing a few
plays and one minor novel he was appointed tax-collector
for a district in Andalusia, a post which involved much
travelling up and down the southern half of the country.
Through no fault of his own, he was involved in a financial

swindle in 1592, and in consequence he spent some years in and out of prison. In 1601 he and his sisters, with whom he lived, transferred their home to Valladolid when King Philip III moved the royal Court there, and it was there that he put the finishing touches to the first part of *Don Quijote*, which he published in 1604. He was fifty-seven. Fate now seemed to have smiled on him, as the book was immediately popular, but in spite of his fame, he made little more than a bare living from this and his later books.

El Ingenioso Hidalgo Don Quijote de la Mancha, full of entertaining incident, reflects many of the experiences that Cervantes had had in his varied career, and embodies also the philosophy of a mature, kindly author who in a hard life had learned how to face and overcome most of life's fears and disappointments. Through the adventures of his famous hero and of Sancho Panza, his faithful rustic squire, Cervantes seems to show to his readers that man must do with the utmost faith what he believes to be right, permitting no defeat to daunt him. Don Quijote, who is mad, is often mistaken about what is or is not right, but we cannot but admire his immense, dauntless courage. And across the pages of this novel there moves a vast crowd of minor characters, over six hundred of them, who illustrate superbly the everyday life of the Spanish countryside in Cervantes' time. His prose style is unsurpassed.

The best known of Don Quijote's adventures follows here. The familiar English expressions " quixotic " and " tilting at windmills " are taken, of course, from this work.

12 (*d*)

En esto, descubrieron treinta o cuarenta molinos de viento que hay en aquel campo, y así como don Quijote los vio, dijo a su escudero :

—La ventura va guiando nuestras cosas mejor de lo que acertáramos a desear ; porque ves allí, amigo Sancho Panza, donde se descubren treinta, o pocos más, desaforados gigantes, con quien pienso hacer batalla y quitarles a todos las vidas, con cuyos despojos comenzaremos a enriquecer ; que ésta es buena guerra, y es gran servicio de Dios quitar tan mala simiente de sobre la faz de la tierra.

—¿Qué gigantes?—dijo Sancho Panza.

—Aquéllos que allí ves—respondió su amo—de los brazos largos, que los suelen tener algunos de casi dos leguas.

—Mire vuestra merced—respondió Sancho—que aquéllos que allí se parecen no son gigantes, sino molinos de viento, y lo que en ellos parecen brazos son las aspas, que, volteadas del viento, hacen andar la piedra del molino.

—Bien parece—respondió don Quijote—que no estás cursado en esto de las aventuras : ellos son gigantes; y si tienes miedo, quítate de ahí, y ponte en oración en el espacio que yo voy a entrar con ellos en fiera y desigual batalla.

Y diciendo esto, dio de espuelas a su caballo Rocinante, sin atender a las voces que su escudero Sancho le daba, advirtiéndole que, sin duda alguna, eran molinos de viento, y no gigantes, aquéllos que iba a acometer. Pero él iba tan puesto en que eran gigantes, que ni oía las voces de su escudero Sancho, ni echaba de ver, aunque estaba ya bien cerca, lo que eran; antes iba diciendo en voces altas :

—Non fuyades, cobardes y viles criaturas; que un solo caballero es el que os acomete.

Levantóse en esto un poco de viento, y las grandes aspas comenzaron a moverse, lo cual visto por don Quijote, dijo :

—Pues aunque mováis más brazos que los del gigante Briareo, me lo habéis de pagar.

Y en diciendo esto, y encomendándose de todo corazón a su señora Dulcinea, pidiéndole que en tal trance le socorriese, bien cubierto de su rodela, con la lanza en el ristre, arremetió a todo galope de Rocinante y embistió con el primer molino que estaba delante; y dándole una lanzada en el aspa, la volvió el viento con tanta furia, que hizo la lanza pedazos, llevándo tras sí al caballo y al caballero, que fué rodando muy maltrecho por el campo. Acudió Sancho Panza a socorrerle, a todo el correr de su asno, y cuando llegó halló que no se podía menear : tal fué el golpe que dio con él Rocinante.

—¡Válame Dios !—dijo Sancho. —¿No le dije yo a vuestra merced que mirase bien lo que hacía, que no eran sino molinos de viento, y no lo podía ignorar sino quien llevase otros tales en la cabeza ?

—Calla, amigo Sancho—respondió don Quijote; —que las cosas de la guerra, más que otras, están sujetas a contínua mudanza; cuanto más que yo pienso, y es así verdad, que aquel sabio Frestón, que me robó el aposento y los libros, ha vuelto estos gigantes en molinos, por quitarme la gloria de su vencimiento: tal es la enemistad que me tiene; mas al cabo al cabo, han de poder poco sus malas artes contra la bondad de mi espada.

LESSON XIII

THE SUBJUNCTIVE (I)

THE Subjunctive mood is required so frequently in Spanish that no apology is needed for repeating here a statement of the basic rules that govern its use.

It should first be remembered that this mood is *never* required in a *main clause*,

EXCEPT when it is a mere substitute for the Imperative, e.g.,

> *¡Que calles!* Be quiet!
> *No nos levantemos.* Let us not stand up.

Its uses are conveniently grouped under nine headings, of which four appear in this lesson, four in the next, and one (the use in Conditional sentences, mostly involving the word IF) in Lesson XV.

GROUP I. After verbs of *wishing, commanding, forbidding*:

> *Quiero que Vd compre las entradas para el teatro.* I want you to buy the theatre tickets.
> *Me dijeron que llegase temprano.* They told me to arrive early.

(BUT note that, as stated in the Grammar section to Lesson XII, if the subject of the main verb is the same as the subject of the dependent verb, no Subjunctive is needed, and the Infinitive is all that is required, as in English:

> *Quiero comprarlas.* I want to buy them.)

AND note also that if the verb *decir* is followed by an *Indicative*, as in the second example above, the meaning implies *information*, not instruction, e.g.,

> *Me dijeron que llegaba temprano.*   They told me that I was arriving early.

Note that *¡Ojalá (que) . . .!*, an expression that means "Would that . . .", since it stands for a whole clause implying a wish, is followed by the Subjunctive:

> *¡Ojalá cese de llover!*   I wish it would stop raining.

GROUP 2.   After verbs implying *doubt, denial,* and those of *thinking or believing when used negatively or interrogatively* :

> *Niega que lo haya dicho.*   He denies that he has said it.
> *¿Cree Vd que esto sea la verdad?*   Do you think that this is the truth?

(BUT *Creo que José llegó esta tarde,* "I believe that José arrived this afternoon", requires the Indicative because the main verb is *not* a negative or interrogative verb of thinking, etc.)

GROUP 3.   After a verb of *emotion* (when the subject of the main verb is different from the subject of the dependent verb, as in Group 1). For this purpose there are five emotions, Joy, Sorrow, Fear, Hope, and Surprise.

> *Me alegro de que Vd pueda venir a vernos.*   I am glad you can come and see us.
> *Siento que su hermano esté enfermo.*   I am sorry that your brother is ill.
> *Temo que tarde mucho en restablecerse.*   I am afraid that he may be a long time getting better.
> *Espero que pueda venir a Inglaterra este año.*   I hope that he will be able to come to England this year.

(N.B. It is permissible to put the future indicative in a subordinate clause after *esperar* : *Espero que podrá . . .*)

> *Me sorprende que no lo sepan.*   I am surprised that they do not know it.

(BUT, of course, if the subjects of the main and dependent verbs are the same, the Infinitive is used, e.g.,

Me alegro de aprender que Vd vendrá a Inglaterra este año. I am glad to learn that you will be coming to England this year.)

GROUP 4. After expressions of necessity, and impersonal verbs *which do not stress a* FACT :

Es necesario (preciso, menester, fuerza) que hable Vd más despacio. It is necessary for you to talk more slowly.

(THOUGH, if the necessity is *general*, and does not refer to a particular person, the Infinitive is used :
Es necesario hablar despacio. It is necessary to speak slowly.)

Es absurdo que me diga tales cosas. It is absurd for him to tell me such things.
Es posible que no me haya oído. It is possible that he did not hear me.

(BUT if a *fact is stressed*, the Indicative is used :

Es verdad que lo hizo. It is true that he did it.
Era claro que habían perdido el tren. It was obvious that they had missed the train.)

Many examples of the Subjunctive occur in the grammar exercises earlier in this book. The following exercise, however, contains *exclusively* sentences in which the uses of the Subjunctive that have been described in the above Groups 1–4 are exemplified.

13 (a) Exercise

Translate into Spanish :

1. I am glad you have remembered that I don't like sugar in my tea.
2. The author is very sorry that he did not send his manuscript to the publisher in time for publication.
3. Lock the conservatory door, let the cat out, and go up to bed quietly.
4. Perhaps it is true, perhaps not. It is most important, however, for us to know exactly what did happen.

5. The old Irishman sat up in bed and told them to bring him some soup.

6. His mother forbade him to go out with that girl.

7. She knew that his mother did not like him to smoke.

8. He said that he would take her home after the performance.

9. You can't deny that you understand it completely.

10. Do you think you can reach here by two o'clock?

Note : In sentence 5 the expression *incorporarse en la cama* is needed to translate " sit up in bed ". *Sentarse* will clearly not do, as it means " sit down ".

13 (b)

Translate into English :

La Leyenda del Santo Cristo de la Vega (i)

A mediados del siglo dieciseis en la bella y antiquísima ciudad de Toledo vivía un gallardo y joven hidalgo llamado don Fernando de Medina del Ríoseco. Era muy rico y habitaba un palacio espléndido que había heredado de sus abuelos y que estaba lleno de suntuosos tapices, espléndidos muebles y magníficas armas. Pero pese a todas sus riquezas este palacio era triste; por sus grandes salas, pasillos o escaleras no se oían las voces dulces de mujeres o niños, sólo reinaba un silencio profundo quebrantado de vez en cuando por el paso lento de algún servidor, que vestido de negro andaba tranquilamente por aquellas salas sombrías.

No lejos de este palacio, en una choza pequeña, al pie de la roca sobre la cual se levanta el Alcázar, vivían dos mujeres, María del Valle, una viuda pobre, y su hija Catalina, una muchacha muy hermosa de diez y ocho años. La vida no les era fácil, pues tenían que trabajar mucho para ganar el dinero suficiente con que cubrir las necesidades de la vida. Dos veces al día, por la mañana muy temprano y al anochecer, Catalina bajaba con su borrica al río Tajo en busca de agua, y más tarde, ya llenas las ollas que llevaba la borrica, volvía a subir la cuesta.

Una mañana al amanecer, cuando ya los primeros rayos del sol doraban las altas torres del Alcázar y de la Catedral, el joven hidalgo, Fernando de Medina del Ríoseco, montado

en un hermoso alazán, bajaba por la misma senda que
Catalina solía bajar, y en este mismo momento ella con su
borrica empezaba a ascender, con las ollas llenas de agua.
Justamente cuando iban a encontrarse, el caballo de Fernando tropezó con la raíz de un alcornoque que estaba allí
al lado de la senda, e hizo caer a Fernando al pie del árbol.
Catalina se acercó temerosa de que hallase muerto a este
joven tan gallardo, pues notó que tenía la cara bañada de
sangre y que no se movía. Estaba claro que necesitaba
ayuda, y como no había nadie más que ella en aquella
senda, se quitó el pañuelo que llevaba anudado al cuello
y lo mojó en el agua que llevaba la borrica. Entonces
suavemente bañó el rostro del joven, quitándole poco a
poco la sangre, y cuando vio que ésta hubo ya acabado de
correr, ató el pañuelo alrededor de la cabeza de Fernando
de manera que conservase limpia la herida. En este
momento Fernando abrió los ojos y vio a Catalina, como
si fuera un ángel, arrodillada a su lado, con los rayos del sol
ya levantado, reflejados en sus ojos y cabellos de oro.
Se miraron, y se enamoraron en seguida. Media hora más
tarde, cuando Fernando se sintió completamente restable-
cido, volvieron los dos juntos a subir aquella senda que les
conducía de nuevo a la ciudad. A la mañana siguiente
Fernando y Catalina se encontraron otra vez en aquel
mismo sitio, y así ocurrió durante muchos otros días.
Cuanto más tiempo pasaban juntos más se amaban. Y se
creyeron felices.

Una tarde, sin embargo, vino una nube a oscurecer este
cielo tan rosáceo bajo el cual habían vivido estos dos
jóvenes tan felices. Paseándose con Catalina al lado del
Tajo, bajo los álamos a la orilla del río, Fernando le dio
a la muchacha la mala noticia de que a la mañana siguiente
tendría que marcharse con su tercio de soldados para la
guerra en Flandes, y que probablemente tendría que estar
ausente dos o tres años.

—Pero te amo, Catalina, te amo con todo mi corazón.
Y cuando vuelva, te haré mi esposa.

—Yo también te amo a ti, como bien sabes, respondió
Catalina. Pero ¿juras, verdaderamente, que te casarás
conmigo cuando vuelvas?

—Sí, lo juro, por supuesto, dijo Fernando.

—Sin embargo aquí no tenemos testigos. ¿Quién será el testigo de nuestro juramento?

Con esto vieron que no estaban lejos de una capilla pequeña que hay allí en el medio de la hermosa vega de Toledo, la que ahora se llama la del Cristo de la Vega. Entrando en ella, Catalina le dijo a Fernando :

—Allí está Nuestro Señor Jesucristo, crucifijado en aquella cruz de madera. Él será nuestro testigo. Juremos ante Él que nos vamos a casar cuando tú vuelvas.

Y en las tinieblas de aquella capilla tranquila, llena del olor a incienso y a cera apagada, los dos lo juraron.

Y a la mañana siguiente partió Fernando camino de Madrid, para juntarse con su tercio.

(*A seguir.*)

COMMERCIAL SPANISH, 13

The following letters deal with a request from a private subscriber to the Spanish National Telephones Company, asking for the installation of an extension to his existing line, and the negative answer from the Company. They are models for many similar types of formal business requests, and translations are, as usual, to be found in the Key at the end of this book.

13 (c)

Santa Marta, 14,
Salamanca
18 de noviembre, 19—

Sr Jefe de Centro,
Cía Nacional Telefonica de España,
Salamanca

Muy Señor mío,

Mucho le agradeceré que previos los trámites reglamentarios, se digne conceder autorización con el fin de que me sea concedida una derivación de un supletorio con línea de prolongación a mi teléfono número 4763 a las señas y nombre a continuación detallados :

Ildefonso de las Morenas Gaztambide, con domicilio en
Santa Marta, 14, de esta capital.*

En espera de verme favorecido en la petición que les
formulo, aprovecho esta ocasión para saludarle atentamente,
s.s., q.e.s.m.

Ildefonso de las Morenas Gaztambide

13 (d)

The reply :

Muy Sr. mío,

Acusamos recibo de su atta. carta fecha 18 del
corriente, en la que solicita una derivación de su supletorio
con línea de prolongación a su teléfono número 4763 a las
señas arriba indicadas, y sentimos manifestar a Vd que
por dificultades de órden técnico no nos es posible llevar a
cabo de momento esta instalación.

No obstante, registramos su petición para cuando
nuestras disponibilidades nos permitan llevarla a efecto.

Atentamente le saluda,

Joaquín Llopis,

(Jefe Grupo)

SPANISH LITERATURE, 13
Cervantes (ii)

The following episode occurs in Chapter 45 of the Second
Part of the *Quijote*, published in 1615.

Sancho Panza's chief ambition, when he took service as
Don Quijote's squire, was to be made governor of some
island as reward for his services.   In the Second Part
Don Quijote and Sancho spend some time as guests of a
certain Duke, and they provide him and the Duchess with
much entertainment.   Hearing of Sancho's desire, the Duke
arranges for him to be made governor not of an island, but of
a village in the ducal domain.

* " Capital ", because Salamanca is the chief town of the province
of the same name.

The substance of this incident was not new in Spanish, but Cervantes tells it with great artistry.

13 (e)

A este instante entraron en el juzgado dos hombres, el uno vestido de labrador y el otro de sastre, porque traía unas tijeras en la mano, y el sastre dijo :

—Señor gobernador, yo y este hombre labrador venimos ante vuestra merced en razón que este buen hombre llegó a mi tienda ayer (que yo, con perdón de los presentes, soy sastre examinado, que Dios sea bendito), y poniéndome un pedazo de paño en las manos, me preguntó : ' Señor, ¿habría en este paño harto para hacerme una caperuza? ' Yo, tanteando el paño, le respondí que sí; él debióse de imaginar, a lo que yo imagino, e imaginé bien, que sin duda yo le quería hurtar alguna parte del paño, fundándose en su malicia y en la mala opinión de los sastres, y replicóme que mirase bien si habría para dos; adivinéle el pensamiento, y díjele que sí; y él, caballero en su dañada y primera intención, fué añadiendo caperuzas, y yo añadiendo síes, hasta que llegamos a cinco caperuzas; y ahora en este punto acaba de venir por ellas : yo se las doy, y no me quiere pagar la hechura; antes me pide que le pague o vuelva su paño.

—¿ Es todo esto así, hermano?—preguntó Sancho.

—Sí, señor—respondió el hombre;—pero hágale vuesa merced que muestre las cinco caperuzas que me ha hecho.

—De buena gana—respondió el sastre.

Y sacando encontinente la mano de debajo del herreruelo, mostró en ella cinco caperuzas puestas en las cinco cabezas de los dedos de la mano, y dijo :

—He aquí las cinco caperuzas que este buen hombre me pide, y en Dios y en mi conciencia que no me ha quedado nada del paño, y yo daré la obra a vista de veedores del oficio.

Todos los presentes se rieron de la multitud de las caperuzas y del nuevo pleito. Sancho se puso a considerar un poco, y dijo :

—Paréceme que en este pleito no ha de haber largas dilaciones, sino juzgar luego a juicio de buen varón; y así, yo doy por sentencia que el sastre pierda las hechuras, y el labrador el paño, y las caperuzas se lleven a los presos de la cárcel.

(*The prisoners to whom these little caps were given would no doubt be expected to use them as bags to dangle from the window of the jail, so that passers-by could put alms into them.*)

LESSON XIV

THE SUBJUNCTIVE (II)

FURTHER types of sentence in which the subjunctive must be used are as follows :

GROUP 5. In adverbial clauses of TIME, when *Future* time is implied :

> *Mientras que Vd duerma, iré al mercado.*   Whilst you are asleep, I shall go to market.
> *Cuando vaya al mercado, compraré café.*   When I go to market, I shall buy coffee.

ALSO :

> *Dijo ella que cuando fuese al mercado, compraría café.* She said that when she went to market she would buy coffee.

(The Subjunctive is required after *cuando* even in this sentence in past time, because the *cuando . . .* clause implies future time in relation to the time of the main clause *Dijo*.)

If no futurity is implied, the indicative is used :

> *Mientras que dormía Vd, fui al mercado.*   While you were asleep, I went to market.

Other common conjunctions of time that require the same construction are : *hasta que*, " until "; *luego que*; *tan pronto como*; and *así que*, " as soon as "; *después (de) que*, " after ".

Note that *antes (de) que*, " before ", ALWAYS requires the Subjunctive, whether futurity is implied or not:

Lo haré antes (de) que él lo descubra.   I will do it before he finds out.

Lo hice antes (de) que él lo descubriese.   I did it before he found out.

GROUP 6.   After certain conjunctions implying purpose, etc., if the subordinate verb *does not state an accomplished fact.*

Gritó para que le oyéramos.   He shouted so that we should hear him.

Con tal que Vd no lo pierda, le prestaré mi reloj.   Provided that you will not lose it, I will lend you my watch.

Llegó ayer, sin que lo supiésemos.   He arrived yesterday, without our knowing.

Other such conjunctions are : *a fin de que,* " in order that "; *a condición de que,* " on condition that "; *suponiendo que,* " supposing that "; *dado que,* " given that "; *de modo que, de manera que,* " so that ".

NOTE that *aunque,* " although ", perhaps the commonest of all these conjunctions, requires the same careful consideration :

Aunque buscase mucho tiempo, no lo hallaría.   Even if I looked for it for a long time, I should not find it. (No accomplished fact stated, therefore Subjunctive.)

Aunque busqué mucho tiempo, no lo descubrí.   Even though I looked for it for a long time, I did not find it. (Accomplished fact stated, therefore indicative.)

GROUP 7.   In adjective clauses (describing " someone who . . ." or " something which . . .") the Subjunctive is required if the antecedent to the relative pronoun is indefinite or negative.

Busco un hombre que tenga un sombrero verde.   I am looking for a man who has a green hat. (No particular man is implied, anyone with a green hat will do. Note the omission of the personal *a* before the indefinite *hombre*.)

BUT *Busco a un hombre que tiene un sombrero verde*

here the personal *a* and the Indicative verb are required
because it is implied that a *particular man* is sought, whose
identity is fully known to the speaker.)

> *No encuentro a nadie que sepa esto.* I do not find
> anyone who knows this. (Note that *nadie* as the
> object of a verb always requires the personal *a*.)

GROUP 8. The following indefinite expressions formed
by the addition of *-quiera* require the Subjunctive:

quienquiera que, whoever	*dondequiera que,* wherever
cuandoquiera que, whenever	*comoquiera que,* however
cualquiera que (plural: *cualesquiera*), whatever	

Note that this last word may drop its final *-a* before a
noun, and that if used with a noun the noun precedes the
que.

> *Quienquiera que sea, y dondequiera que vaya, le seguiré.*
> Whoever he is, and wherever he goes, I will follow
> him.
> *Cualquiera que sea su opinión de Vd . . .* Whatever
> your opinion may be . . .
> *Cualesquier libros que busque Vd . . .* Whatever
> books you are looking for . . .

BUT note that if an accomplished fact is referred to, the
Indicative is needed:

> *Cuando* (or *cuandoquiera que*) *venía aquí, yo le esperaba
> en la estación.* Whenever he came, I always waited
> for him at the station.

AND note these two idioms:

> *Por bueno que sea . . .* However good he is . . .
> *Por mucho dinero que tenga . . .* However much
> money he has . . .

14 (a) Exercise

Translate into Spanish:

1. You can't accuse me of crimes I haven't committed.
2. Show me where I can find a hotel where I can spend
the night.

3. I shan't forget her as long as I live. No more will you.

4. " As soon as the post comes, let me know, please," said the visitor.

5. As soon as it had come, we took him his letters.

6. The writing-table is placed so that you will get the light from the left.

7. Wherever you go, you will find no better bicycles on the market.

8. Stumbling among the bare rocks, and losing our way again and again, we went on until we reached the summit.

9. Passengers who alight before the train stops at a station will be heavily fined.

10. Even although he is my best friend, I shall have to thrash him if he does that again.

11. In the afternoons, while Granny is asleep, I knit or darn socks.

12. Shut the bathroom door so that the steam won't fill the house.

13. Yes, I will come to your party, on condition that you won't make me sing.

14. Although the girl seemed quite grown up, she was only fifteen.

15. The Prime Minister ought to have consulted Parliament before doing such a thing.

14 (b)

Translate into English :

Leyenda de Santo Cristo de la Vega (ii)

Dos años después, en una hermosa tarde de otoño cuando los rayos del sol poniente ya empezaban a dorar la faz de las aguas del río, y se ponían aún más amarillos que nunca los caminos polvorientos que atravesaban la Vega una muchacha ya de veinte años subió hasta la torre de la Puerta de Visagra, aquel punto de las murallas de la ciudad desde donde se ve más claramente el camino de Madrid. Esto lo hacía todas las tardes, pero hoy con más ansia que nunca, porque habían venido noticias de la llegada en Madrid de un tercio de soldados que habían combatido en Flandes. Y esta tarde, al caer el sol, vio Catalina acercarse a la Puerta, por el camino de Madrid, una nube pequeña, que al acercarse más y más se distinguió como una nube de polvo hecha por un hombre a caballo que avanzaba a galope.

Sí, no cabía duda, era él, era Fernando. En seguida bajó Catalina de lo alto de la torre a aquella plaza pequeña que hay delante de la puerta. Cuando llegó a ella el caballero, Catalina gritó : —¡ Fernando, Fernando mío ! ¡ Aquí estoy !

Pero él, apenas refrenando el caballo, no se dignó de observar a esta mujer, pobre al parecer, que le estorbaba en su marcha.

—¡ Fuera, vil mujer ! dijo, y sin reconocerla, o más bien sin querer reconocerla, atravesó la plazuela y siguió calle arriba hacia su palacio, dejando a Catalina desmayada de dolor allá al pie de la torre.

Sin embargo, Catalina era una muchacha de espíritu, y no quiso dejar las cosas así. Se quejó, dos o tres días más tarde, al corregidor de la ciudad, y su queja se oyó delante de todos los miembros del gran tribunal de justicia.

—¿ Pero afirmas, Catalina del Valle, dijo el corregidor, que don Fernando de Medina del Ríoseco, antes de marcharse para Flandes, juró que se casaría contigo al volver ? ¿ Y que ahora que ha vuelto, rehusa a cumplir con su promesa ? ¿ Háy algún testigo de este juramento ?

—Sí, lo afirmo. Y tengo un testigo, también.

—Pues, ¿ quién es ? ¿ Por qué no le has hecho venir aquí a este tribunal ?

—Es Nuestro Señor, el Santo Cristo de la Vega, respondió Catalina.

—Entonces hay que ver si Él afirma lo mismo que tú, dijo el corregidor.

Así se trasladó todo el tribunal a aquella capilla en el fondo de la Vega, que olía a incienso y a cera apagada. Con ellos fué también don Fernando, a quien el corregidor había mandado buscar, pero él entró orgulloso y altanero, mientras que los demás todos andaban humildes, no atreviéndose a figurar lo que pudiera suceder en esta ocasión tan inusitada.

Aguardaron todos a que hablase el corregidor, y con voz suave y gentil él repitió, delante de la cruz donde pendía el santo imagen de Jesucristo, la historia que le había contado Catalina. Por fin añadió:

—¿Afirmas Tú que hubo tal juramento?

Para que jurase, un notario levantó hasta la imagen el libro de los Evangelios. Y en aquel momento se oyó por el aire de la capilla un susurro como de alas invisibles, y luego una voz delicadísima que dijo:

—Sí, juro.

Y en el mismo instante cayó el brazo derecho de la imagen sobre el libro de los Evangelios, quedando pendiente del hombro, tal como ha quedado desde aquel día hasta hoy. Todos los asistentes en la capilla se arrodillaron, santiguándose. Aun Fernando, ya al lado de Catalina, se arrodilló, y le dijo en voz baja:

—¿Me quieres perdonar, Catalina? Lo que he hecho ha sido malo, malísimo, pero ahora, ¿quieres casarte conmigo?

—Sí, por supuesto me casaré contigo, así como juré, respondió ella.

A la caída de aquella hermosa tarde de otoño, cuando ya los del tribunal hubieron partido, los dos amantes se pasearon largo tiempo a orillas del río Tajo bajo los álamos. Y a la mañana siguiente se casaron, en la pequeña capilla de Nuestro Señor Jesucristo, allá en el fondo de la Vega.

Private letters.

A useful guide for foreigners writing private letters to friendly Spaniards is to copy or vary slightly the opening and closing phrases from letters which their friends have sent to them. This further help may be useful, however:

(Some opening phrases, in order of familiarity.)

1. Mi distinguido Sr. Sánchez, (= " Dear Mr. Sánchez.")
2. Apreciado amigo Sánchez,
3. Estimado y querido amigo Juan,
4. (Mi) querido amigo Juan,

(And some closing phrases, all of which correspond to " Yours sincerely ". The alternatives are similarly in order of familiarity.)

1. Con un afectuoso saludo, queda a su disposición su incondicional amigo . . .

2. Recibe un cordial saludo de su afmo. amigo . . .

3. Sin otro particular le abraza afectuosamente . . .

4. Sin más por ahora, recibe (reciba) un fuerte abrazo de tu (su) amigo . . .

COMMERCIAL SPANISH, 14

14 (c)

Complaint Concerning Goods Arriving in Bad Condition

Muy Señores nuestros,

Con fecha de hoy han sido en nuestro poder las mercancías correspondientes a su envío no 3253. Sentimos comunicarles que han llegado a nuestras manos en pésimas condiciones; cerca de un 10% de las lámparas han llegado rotas y del resto un 5% no funcionan.

Sabemos muy bien que no tenemos derecho a reclamación alguna ya que las mercancías no estaban aseguradas contra riesgos del viaje, pero puesto que los daños recibidos se deben en su mayor parte al mal estado del embalaje se lo hacemos constar por que si en lo sucesivo ocurriera de nuevo, nos veremos precisados a importar nuestros productos de otra casa exportadora.

Sin otro particular, quedamos de Vds afmos s.s. q.e.s.m.

Baltasar Flores y Cía.

(Reply to the above.)

14 (d)

Dear Sirs,

In reply to your letter of the 28 ult. we are happy to inform you that in respect of the goods you have received, as per our invoice no. 3253, which reached you in a damaged condition, we shall be happy to compensate you in any way you find suitable.

We understand that the damage was caused chiefly by poor packing, due no doubt to temporary difficulties caused by a change of operatives in our packing department.

Fortunately this difficulty has now been overcome, thanks to the appointment of a more competent employee.

We trust that you will accept our apologies for any inconvenience you have been caused, and we assure you of our best attention at all future times.

Yours very truly,

John Harrison, Lambert & Co.

SPANISH LITERATURE, 14

Cervantes (iii)

Cervantes' most famous work after the *Quijote* is a collection of a dozen short stories written between 1597 and 1611, and published in 1613 under the title of *Novelas Ejemplares*.

The whole collection makes extremely good reading, not only for the author's magnificent style but also for the varied pictures they present of sixteenth-century life and taste.

The extract which follows is taken from one of the shortest, " El Licenciado Vidriera "—" The University Graduate Who Thought He Was Made of Glass ", and here Cervantes is almost certainly drawing upon his personal recollections of his departure for Italy with Spanish troops in 1567.

Tomás Rodaja, the hero of the story, after some years as a student at the University of Salamanca, is persuaded by an army captain whom he meets on a journey in Andalusia to join the colours.

14 (*e*)

Llegaron aquella noche a Antequera, y en pocos días y grandes jornadas se pusieron donde estaba la compañía, ya acabada de hacer, y que comenzaba a marchar la vuelta de Cartagena, alojándose ella y otras cuatro por los lugares que les venían a mano. Allí notó Tomás la autoridad de los comisarios, la comodidad de algunos capitanes, la solicitud de los aposentadores, la industria y cuenta de los pagadores, las quejas de los pueblos, el rescatar de las boletas, las insolencias de los bisoños, las pendencias de los

huéspedes, el pedir bagajes más de los necesarios, y finalmente, la necesidad casi precisa de hacer todo aquello
que notaba y mal le parecía. Habíase vestido Tomás
de papagayo, renunciando los hábitos de estudiante, y
púsose a lo de Dios es Cristo, como se suele decir. Los
muchos libros que tenía los redujo a unas *Horas de Nuestra
Señora*, y un *Garcilaso* sin comento, que en las dos faltri-
queras llevaba.

Llegaron más presto de lo que quisieran a Cartagena,
porque la vida de los alojamientos es ancha y varia, y
cada día se topan cosas nuevas y gustosas. Allí se em-
barcaron en cuatro galeras de Nápoles, y allí notó también
Tomás Rodaja la extraña vida de aquellas marítimas
casas, adonde lo más del tiempo maltratan las chinches,
roban los forzados, enfadan los marineros, destruyen
los ratones y fatigan las maretas. Pusiéronle temor las
grandes borrascas y tormentas, especialmente en el golfo
de León, que tuvieron dos : que la una los echó en Córcega,
y la otra los volvió a Tolón, en Francia. En fin, tras-
nochados, mojados, y con ojeras llegaron a la hermosa y
bellísima ciudad de Génova, y desembarcándose en su
recogido Mandrache, después de haber visitado una iglesia,
dio el capitán con todos sus camaradas en una hostería,
donde pusieron en olvido todas las borrascas pasadas,
con el presente gaudeamus.

LESSON XV

THE SUBJUNCTIVE (III) "IF" SENTENCES

STUDY the following examples of " if " sentences and note
the constructions that they require. All are straightforward and easy enough until nos. 4 and 5, when the
MAIN verb is Conditional. Then, and only then, is the
Subjunctive required in the dependent clause.

1. If I have time, I go to the theatre.
   Si tengo tiempo, voy al teatro.
2. If I had time, I used to go to the theatre.
   Si tenía tiempo, iba al teatro.

3. If I have time, I shall go to the theatre.
   Si tengo tiempo, iré al teatro.
4. If I had time, I SHOULD go to the theatre.

   $Si \left\{ \begin{matrix} tuviese \\ tuviera \end{matrix} \right\} tiempo, \left\{ \begin{matrix} iría \\ fuera \end{matrix} \right\} al teatro.$

5. If I HAD HAD time, I SHOULD HAVE gone to the theatre.

   $Si \left\{ \begin{matrix} hubiese \\ hubiera \end{matrix} \right\} tenido tiempo, \left\{ \begin{matrix} habría \\ hubiera \end{matrix} \right\} ido al teatro.$

The English sentence sometimes avoids the word "if", for example :

Had I seen you, I should have given you this.

$Si le \left\{ \begin{matrix} hubiese \\ hubiera \end{matrix} \right\} visto, le \left\{ \begin{matrix} habría \\ hubiera \end{matrix} \right\} dado esto.$

Note two things to avoid :

(1) Do not put *si* meaning "if" before a Spanish verb in the Future or Conditional Indicative, unless the meaning is "whether", e.g.,

   Le pregunté si podrá acompañarme al cine.   I asked him whether he could go to the cinema with me.

(2) It is never in any circumstances correct to use the Present Subjunctive after *si*.

15 (a) Exercise
Translate into Spanish :

If I lived in the country I should buy most of my provisions at the village shop, but once or twice a month I should have a stock of tinned goods sent from one of the stores in the nearest town.   Then if friends came to see me I should always have enough to eat in the house, even if more friends came than I expected.   Last year when my wife and I rented a small cottage on the east coast for the summer months we used to leave a key with an old woman who lived near by, so that if we sent her a postcard from London telling her the time of our arrival, she could go in and light fires if the house felt damp. Then if we arrived in the middle of the night we had not much to do before going to bed.

We liked that cottage so much that we may buy it next year if I do not find another that suits me better. There was a very charming one that we discovered ten miles from the sea, but it had no bathroom, and the agent was such an unpleasant man that I did not want to have anything to do with him.

If you are motoring near those villages next year and we are there at the same time, you must come and see us. All you will have to do is to ask the man in the village shop if he knows whether we have come, and he will give you our address as if he had known us all our lives.

15 (b) Conversation

(*En un café en la plaza principal de Toledo, a las diez de la mañana. ANTONIO y MARÍA han salido de Madrid camino de Córdoba, y sus dos amigos ingleses les han acompañado hasta Toledo. Éstos volverán a Madrid por ferrocarril la misma tarde.*)

ANTONIO : Usted, Martín, conoce Toledo mejor que yo, y como sólo tenemos unas horas aquí, me parece que Vd debiera organizarnos para que con el tiempo disponible podamos visitar cuanto más sea posible de lo que hay que ver.

MARTÍN : Es verdad que de estudiante en Madrid hace muchos años venía aquí a menudo, y como casi todo Toledo es un monumento histórico, no creo que lo hayan cambiado mucho desde mi última visita. Con que si quieren mirar este plano de la ciudad, les explicaré lo que podremos hacer. Primero iremos a la Catedral, por una de estas calles a la izquierda. Claro es que allí hay bastante para ocuparnos no sólo todo el día, sino muchos días seguidos, pero como hoy tenemos que ver por lo menos una media docena de iglesias tendremos que limitarnos a una visita de media hora.

MARÍA : Claro. Pero ¿son todas las calles estrechas como ésta, o hay alguna ancha y nueva?

MARTÍN : No, en Toledo no hay ninguna calle verdaderamente ancha, todas son muy viejas y estrechas.

ISABEL : ¿A dónde iremos después de ver la Catedral?

MARTÍN : Daremos una vuelta a la derecha para ver una
pintura muy importante del Greco, aquel pintor tan
célebre del siglo xvi; la veremos en la iglesia de Santo
Tomé. Se llama " El entierro del Conde de Orgaz ", y
estoy seguro que habrán visto muchas fotografías de
ella. Se la explicaré después. Entonces seguiremos
bajando la cuesta, dirigiéndonos a la casa del mismo
pintor, el Greco, donde él vivía. Ahora es un museo,
pero completamente restaurada y amueblada, y es muy
interesante no sólo por su estilo sino también por su
situación. De su jardín hay unas vistas magníficas a
través del río. Luego cerca hallaremos dos pequeñas
iglesias interesantísimas, el Tránsito y Santa María
la Blanca. Las dos eran antiguamente sinagogas de la
Edad Media.

ANTONIO : El camino que Vd dice lo sigo bastante bien en
el plano de la ciudad. ¿No es allí cerca donde está
aquella fábrica tan célebre, de cuchillería y otras cosas
con decoraciones de arte toledana?

MARTÍN : Sí. En efecto está al lado de Santa María la
Blanca, y quisiera pasar unos minutos allí, como quiero
comprar para Isabel un par de tijeras, porque hace poco
tiempo yo perdí un buen par suyo. El método de
grabar el metal con el oro en dibujos y arabescos se
puede estudiar allí de cerca, si se quiere.

ISABEL : Gracias, Martín. No esperaba esto. Yo también
quisiera comprar algún regalo para ti. ¿Y entonces,
qué?

MARTÍN : La iglesia de San Juan de los Reyes está allí
cerca, en una extremidad de la colina. De allí se ve
toda la Vega, con el río Tajo y el Puente de San Martín,
que lo cruza. Podemos buscar allí un sitio en donde
merendar, ya que hemos traído con nosotros desde
Madrid estas buenas meriendas hechas.

MARÍA : Seguramente entonces tendremos ganas de
merendar.

MARTÍN : Después de merendar, si tenemos fuerzas todavía

y si no hace demasiado calor, podremos ir a ver la pequeña capilla al pie de la colina que se llama el Cristo de la Vega, de la cual ya conocen la leyenda. Las murallas y las antiguas puertas de la ciudad son muy interesantes desde aquel lado. Finalmente, entrando otra vez en la ciudad por la Puerta de Visagra, subiremos la cuesta hasta la Puerta del Sol (que es una verdadera puerta medioeval, y no una plaza como la Puerta del Sol de Madrid.) Detrás de ella hay otra iglesia precio-sísima que se llama el Cristo de la Luz, que en tiempos de los moros era una mezquita. Entonces no sé si tendremos tiempo para subir al Alcázar, para ver los destrozos hechos durante la guerra civil, cuando fué sitiado por los rojos setenta y siete días. Son muchas las historias que se cuentan acerca de este episodio.

ISABEL : Y entonces, querido Martín, estaré cansadísima y no desearé más que sentarme tranquila en un café hasta el momento de coger nuestro tren. Pero vamos, si no queremos perder tiempo debemos ir ahora a la catedral, ¿ no?

COMMERCIAL SPANISH, 15

Repairs to a Car

15 (c)

Garaje " Excelsior "
Castellón de la Plana
1 de marzo 19—

Sr D. Leandro Ferraz,
Puente Mayor,
Segorbe

Muy Señor nuestro,

Esta mañana nos comunica su mecánico la urgencia con que necesita el coche, y demás instrucciones acerca de los frenos, de todo lo cual tomamos buena nota.

En cuanto a la pintura, nuestro pintor nos ha proporci-onado un catálogo de colores publicado por la casa O.U.E. de Madrid (Sta Lucía, 38, tfno 03854) y creemos que el color más aproximado al de su coche es el denominado

" Gris Acero ", marcado en dicho catálogo con el número *nueve*. Mucho le agradeceremos instrucciones urgentes acerca de este extremo, rogándole, para el caso de diferir la numeración en el catálogo que Vd vea, nos especifique también la denominación del color.

En espera de sus instrucciones, le saludan atentamente sus afmos. y ss.ss. q.e.s.m.

Por " Garaje Excelsior ",
Lucas Fernández

SPANISH LITERATURE, 15
Lope de Vega

The famous Spanish drama of the Golden Age owes much of its greatness to Lope de Vega (1562–1635), probably the most prolific dramatic author in the whole of the world's history (his writings include about 1,800 " *comedias* " and 400 religious plays called " *autos sacramentales* "). Clearly there was an insistent public demand for plays which Lope and other contemporary writers supplied, and for many years the Madrid theatres received, from his and other pens, a new play twice a week. His " *comedias* " (a generic term, a very few of them are in fact tragedies) are masterpieces of entertainment.

Some of them are magnificent by any standards, in conception, theme, and craftsmanship. His characterization is often stereotyped, and dramatic situations in his plays tend to be repetitive, but with his superb dramatic technique he could always produce the unexpected note that kept the audience's interest. He made particularly his own the type of play known as " *comedia de capa y espada* ", using again and again familar devices such as characters assuming disguises, mistaken identities, people overhearing conversations not intended for them, lost keys found by the wrong people, letters delivered to the wrong hands, and above all the constantly recurring theme of " *honor* ".

No brief extract can do justice to the charm and versatility of his genius, but several of his best plays are readily accessible in English educational editions. The language, although now well over 300 years old, does not present great difficulty to the general reader who knows some Spanish. Among these are *Fuenteovejuna, El Remedio en la Desdicha, Peribáñez y el Comendador de Ocaña, El mejor Alcalde, el Rey* and *El Caballero de Olmedo* (the last is a tragedy).

The following sonnet gives an example of his lyrical powers, in a religious vein.

15 (d)

El Pastor Divino

Pastor, que con tus silbos amorosos
me despertaste del profundo sueño;
tú, que hiciste cayado dese leño
en que tiendes los brazos poderosos;
    vuelve los ojos a mi fe piadosos,
pues te confieso por mi amor y dueño,
y la palabra de seguirte empeño
tus dulces silbos y tus pies hermosos.

    Oye, Pastor, que por amores mueres,
no te espante el rigor de mis pecados,
pues tan amigo de rendidos eres;
    espera, pues, y escucha mis cuidados;
pero, ¿cómo te digo que me esperes,
si estás para esperar los pies clavados?

LESSON XVI

THAN

THE word " than " requires much care in translation into Spanish.

1. Normally—when there is no clause after the word " than "—it is *que*:

   *Tiene más naranjas **que** yo.*
   *María es más alta **que** Juana.*

2. If a *number* follows (and if the meaning is " a greater number than " or " a smaller number than ") then use *de*:

   *Tenemos más **de** veinte botellas vacías.*

(But beware of elliptical sentences such as *Esta mujer*

*trabaja más **que** tres hombres*—here " than " does not imply
" a greater number than . . .")

3. If the comparison is with a CLAUSE (i.e., if there is a
VERB among the words after " than ") use *de lo que* :

*Este señor sabe más **de lo que** yo creía.*

4. But if the comparison is between a NOUN (placed
between the comparative word *más*, *menos*, etc., and the
" than ") then use *del que, de la que, de los que, de las que*,
to agree with the noun in question :

*Aquellas vacas dan más leche **de la que** daban el año
pasado.*

16 (*a*) Exercise

Translate into Spanish :

It was clear that this house was older than we at first
thought. More than one of the ancient oak doors was
rotten and green with age, and more damage had been
done by rats than we could see in the photograph that the
former owner had sent us. In the grounds was an old
lake, bigger than the one we used to swim in when we
lived in that hotel more than twenty miles nearer to
London. The present owner wants to sell it, but he asks
much more for it than it is worth. It has certain advan-
tages, of course. There are more cows in the dairy-farm
than there were in the one we went over last week. If
we took this farm we could send more milk to the dairy in
Maidstone than we used to do. We do not have to decide
at once, the agent permits us more than three weeks to
make our decision.

16 (*b*) Conversation

(*A los dos o tres días después de su llegada a Córdoba*, ISABEL
y MARTÍN *vuelven a la casita de campo de la familia de
Antonio, habiendo pasado la mañana recorriendo la
ciudad. Están en el coche de* ANTONIO *con él, que
conduce, y con* MARÍA.)

ANTONIO : ¿ Qué tal le ha parecido Córdoba, Isabel ? ¿ Cuál
de las cosas que ha visto por aquí le ha gustado más ?

ISABEL : Pues, no sé, Antonio. Hay tantas cosas interesantes que no puedo decidir. Claro que la Mezquita
es lo que más me ha asombrado. No tenía idea alguna
de lo enorme que es. Por dentro, con tantas columnas
unidas por aquellos arcos del tipo especial de los moros,
se parece a un bosque denso. ¡ Y pensar que la con-
struyeron los moros hace más de mil años !

MARTÍN : Sí, y aunque en el centro hay aquel coro del
siglo diez y seis, de estilo tan diferente, me parece que
los dos estilos forman un maravilloso conjunto.

MARÍA : ¿ Sabe, Vd, Martín, Vd que es arquitecto, por
qué se puso allí el coro de aquel estilo ?

MARTÍN : Dicen que el emperador Carlos V, queriendo
convertir la Mezquita de los moros en una catedral digna
del Dios cristiano, y no queriendo que se sirviese de
aquel hermoso Mihrab como capilla mayor, hizo derribar
la parte central de la mezquita para construir el coro que
está allí actualmente.

MARÍA : Pero en efecto no hizo derribar una gran parte,
porque oí decir a alguien que aun hoy hay más de
quinientas columnas.

ISABEL : También me ha gustado la parte de afuera, el
Patio de los Naranjos, donde todo parecía sol y paz.

ANTONIO : Sí, han tenido suerte con el tiempo, aunque,
claro, aquí en Córdoba a fines de julio hace siempre mucho
sol, y muchísimo, calor, también. A mí me gusta mucho
el calor, y no tendré ganas de volver a Inglaterra cuando
nos marchemos de aquí la semana que viene.

ISABEL : ¡ Ay ! Y mañana mismo nosotros también
tenemos que empezar nuestro viaje de vuelta. ¡ Qué
triste !

MARTÍN : Sí. Pero ha sido un gusto enorme el ver otra
vez esta parte de Andalucía. No sólo la mezquita y la
ciudad, que son por cierto interesantísimas, sino también
la vida del campo. Muy bonita es, de veras, la casita
de campo de tu hermana, Antonio.

ANTONIO : Sí, le gusta mucho a ella vivir en el campo, y
para sus hijos la vida en el campo es mucho más sana
que tener que vivir todo el año en Córdoba. A los chicos
les interesa mucho el cortijo de mi cuñado que está al

lado. ¿Les ha dicho mi hermana que el mayor de los hijos se va a hacer Ingeniero Agrónomo? Va a ingresar en su curso en la Universidad de Madrid en octubre.

MARÍA : Sí, es muy inteligente este chico. Y me alegro de que haya escogido esta carrera. Según lo que su padre me explicó, carecemos de especialistas agrícolas en España.

ISABEL : Pues con lo muy aprisa que nos ha conducido el coche, Antonio, aquí estamos en la casita. ¡ Qué magnífica vista de la Sierra hay desde aquí !

(*Bajan los cuatro del coche en la puerta de la casita, y entran en la grata penumbra del salón, donde la hermana de* ANTONIO *espera la vuelta de sus huéspedes.*)

COMMERCIAL SPANISH, 16

Offer of Business from a Shipping Agency

16 (*c*)

Combustibles, S.A.
Plaza Mayor,
Almería
30 de abril de 19—

Sr D. Fernando Jiménez,
Montesinos, 33,
Madrid

Muy Sr. nuestro,

Al estar informados de su calidad como exportador de corcho, nos permitimos dirigirnos por vez primera a Vd, con el deseo de ofrecerle nuestros servicios y colaboración en este puerto de Almería.

Para su gobierno, le informamos que somos agentes de varias compañías navieras, nacionales y extranjeras, de toda solvencia, y por lo tanto contamos con servicios de buques para todo el mundo.

Además estamos dedicados activamente al negocio de fletamentos, y con toda seguridad podemos manifestarle que estamos en posición de ofrecerle buque para cargar en cualquier puerto de España, para cualquiera del extranjero.

En la confianza de que estudiará nuestra propuesta con todo interés, y que pronto podremos contarle entre nuestros mejores clientes, quedamos a su entera disposición para lo que guste mandar de sus affmos.   y ss.ss.

q.e.s.m.

Por " Combustibles, S.A."

Juan José Alcover

SPANISH LITERATURE, 16

Calderón (1600–81)

Lope de Vega established lines which the Spanish dramatists of the Golden Age followed closely throughout the seventeenth century. Calderón, more than a generation younger than Lope, at first wrote plays very much in Lope's style, and won much praise which established him as an accepted playwright in Madrid and at the Court of Philip IV. Some of his finest works, however, contain religious or philosophical themes which are deeper and greater than any written by Lope, and have a wider universal appeal. Such are *La Vida es Sueño*, *El Mágico Prodigioso*, and *El Príncipe Constante*. He frequently employed the " *honor* " theme, in plays where terrible vengeance is wrought by the injured party to remove some stain on his or his family's reputation. As a careful constructor of plays Calderón shows the greatest artistic genius, and the lyrical poetry that most of them contain is magnificent of its kind, in the mannered style (*estilo culto*) of his time.

One of his best and most famous plays is *El Alcalde de Zalamea*. In it an Army Captain, billeted for a short time with his band of soldiers in the village of Zalamea, carries off Isabel, the unwilling daughter of the village mayor, Pedro Crespo. The Captain, after dishonouring Isabel, is wounded in a fight in a wood near the village, and returns to his lodgings in Zalamea for medical attention. Pedro Crespo enters and endeavours to persuade him to marry Isabel to redeem the Crespo family honour. The Captain will not consent, considering that it would be beneath him, as one of noble family, to marry a girl of peasant stock, and he is at the same time sure that since as a soldier he is not subject to civilian tribunals, a military tribunal will take a light view of his misdemeanour.

16 (d)

CRESPO:
> . . . Mirad
> Que a vuestros pies os lo ruego
> De rodillas, y llorando
> Sobre estas canas, que el pecho,
> Viendo nieve y agua, piensa
> Que se me están derritiendo.
> ¿Qué os pido? Un honor os pido,
> Que me quitasteis vos mesmo;
> Y con ser mío, parece,
> Según os le estoy pidiendo
> Con humildad, que no es mío
> Lo que os pido, sino vuestro.
> Mirad que puedo tomarle
> Por mis manos, y no quiero,
> Sino que vos me le deis.

CAPITÁN:
> Ya me falta el sufrimiento,
> Viejo cansado y prolijo.
> Agradeced que no os doy
> La muerte a mis manos hoy,
> Por vos y por vuestro hijo;
> Porque quiero que debáis
> No andar con vos más cruel,
> A la beldad de Isabel.
> Si vengar solicitáis
> Por armas vuestra opinión,
> Poco tengo que temer;
> Si por justicia ha de ser,
> No tenéis jurisdicción.

CRESPO:
> ¿Que en fin, no os mueve mi llanto?

CAPITÁN:
> Llanto no se ha de creer
> De viejo, niño y mujer.

CRESPO:
> ¿Que no pueda dolor tanto
> Mereceros un consuelo?

CAPITÁN:
> ¿Qué más consuelo queréis
> pues con la vida volvéis?

CRESPO :	Mirad que echado en el suelo
	Mi honor a voces os pido.
CAPITÁN :	¡ Qué enfado !
CRESPO :	Mirad que soy
	Alcalde en Zalamea hoy.
CAPITÁN :	Sobre mí no habéis tenido
	Jurisdicción : el consejo
	De guerra enviará por mí.
CRESPO :	¿ En eso os resolvéis ?
CAPITÁN	Sí,
	Caduco y cansado viejo.
CRESPO :	¿ No hay remedio ?
CAPITÁN :	Sí, el callar
	Es el mejor para vos.
CRESPO :	¿ No otro ?
CAPITÁN :	No.
CRESPO :	Pues ¡ juro a Dios
	Que me lo habéis de pagar ! (*Levántase,*
	y toma la vara de Justicia) —¡ Hola !
	(*Salen labradores.*)
UN LABRADOR :	¡ Señor !
CAPITÁN (*aparte*) :	¿ Qué querrán
	Estos villanos hacer ?
LABRADOR :	¿ Qué es lo que mandas ?
CRESPO :	Prender
	Mando al señor Capitán.
CAPITÁN :	¡ Buenos son vuestros extremos !
	Con un hombre como yo,
	Y en servicio del Rey, no
	Se puede hacer.
CRESPO :	Probaremos.
	De aquí, si no es preso o muerto
	No saldréis.

Crespo duly has the Captain garrotted. When the King,
Philip II, appears in Zalamea shortly afterwards, on his
way to invade Portugal, Crespo presents him with a fully
certified record of the case and satisfies him entirely as to
the justice of the measures he has taken. Isabel enters
a convent. This theme of virtuous peasantry versus

tyrannical aristocracy has always been very popular among Spanish audiences, and *El Alcalde de Zalamea* is still frequently revived.

LESSON XVII

MAY, MIGHT, AND OUGHT

THE English auxiliary verbs " may " and " might " usually contain the idea of " possibility ", and require a Spanish translation that reflects this.

" She may have forgotten " implies " It is possible that she has forgotten ", and needs in translation *Es posible que* . . . or *Puede que* . . . or *Tal vez* . . . or *Quizás* . . .

> *Tal vez lo haya olvidado.*

The verb *poder* will very often convey this idea :

> May I come in ? *¿ Puedo entrar ?*
> Father said we might (could) go to the cinema. *Papá dijo que podíamos ir al cine.*

" Ought " is invariably the conditional of *deber* (for which the Past Subjunctive form in -*ra* is very often substituted, even in a main clause).

> You ought to go and see him. *Debería Vd (debiera Vd) ir a verle.*
> They ought not to have done this. *No hubieran debido hacer esto.*

Translate :

17 (a) Exercise

1. Don't be long, we may start without you.
2. May I eat an apple, please ?
3. It is possible that the train may arrive before it is expected.
4. I can't help thinking that you might have broken your leg in that accident.
5. He works so hard that he may make a lot of money.
6. Long may he live !

7. Their mother said that they might stay at the party until seven o'clock.

8. He ought not to go out this morning, he has a bad cold.

9. The traveller did not know that he ought to have raised his hat.

10. They ought to have given me a clean towel.   This is filthy.

17 (b) Exercise

El tesoro del albañil cordobés

Translate into Spanish :

Ricardo, a workman who lived in a humble street in Córdoba, was visited late one night by two mysterious priests, who asked him whether he was willing to work for them.   Ricardo consented, as he was poor, and the priests offered him good payment.   He was surprised,[1] however, that the work had to be done at night, and that the priests covered his eyes with a handkerchief during their walk so that [2] he should not see where he was going.   When the priests uncovered his eyes Ricardo saw that he was in the middle of a small courtyard, where they gave him what he needed for the work, which was to build a wall which would [3] close up a space behind the staircase of the house.   He worked hard all night, but before he finished,[4] one of the priests came to him and said : " Do not close the opening yet, we have seven bodies to bury behind that wall.   You must help me to carry these bodies into the space."   Very frightened, Ricardo followed the priest into another part of the house, where they found seven large boxes, which were very heavy.   All of them were very firmly closed, but Ricardo was able to see through cracks in the lids that they did not contain corpses, but gold coins. They placed them in the space; the priest then helped him to finish the wall, after which Ricardo was paid well for his work, and again blindfolded, he was led back to his home.

Several years passed without Ricardo hearing [5] anything of the priest or of the buried treasure.   One day, however, the proprietor of some old houses came to him and said : " I want you [6] to repair a house which the neighbours say is haunted by two old priests who used to live there." Ricardo went with him to see it, and as soon as he had reached the courtyard he recognized it and the wall which he himself had built under the staircase. " Now," he said to the landlord, " I will repair this house, and as I like it I will rent it from you and live in it. I am not afraid of the ghosts." The landlord consented, and before long the neighbours were much surprised [7] to see the great prosperity of Ricardo and his family, who lived happily in that old house for many years.

Notes : This passage contains several common uses of the Subjunctive, and it is worth while to check your Spanish translation by referring to the Grammar notes to Lessons XIII and XIV.
(1) See Lesson XIII, Group 3. (2) See Lesson XIV, Group 6. (3) See Lesson XIV, Group 7. (4) See Lesson XIV, Group 5, and note the special rule about *antes que.* (5) See Lesson XIV, Group 6, the third example quoted. (6) See Lesson XIII, Group 1. (7) See Lesson XIII, Group 3, but note that as the subjects of the main and dependent verbs are the same, no subjunctive is required.

COMMERCIAL SPANISH, 17

The following model letter contains several very useful phrases, and concerns the purchase of garage equipment from a firm of wholesale suppliers.

17 (c)

Ramón Serrano y Cía, S.A.
México, 148,
Barcelona
30 de diciembre de 19—

Garage Autocar,
Av. Generalísimo, 13,
Cuenca

Muy señor nuestro :
        Tenemos preparado en nuestro almacén el equipo compresor de aire RATMA que tuvo la amabilidad de

solicitar a nuestro representativo, D. Andrés Alcover, pero antes de proceder a su envío debemos comunicarle que este aparato, procedente de la última serie que nos ha entregado nuestro taller, ha resultado a un precio superior al que teníamos catalogado, y hemos de venderlo en lo sucesivo a Ptas 1235, con un 10% de descuento, en lugar de 1150 que costaba anteriormente.

Por lo expuesto, nos hemos permitido dejar en suspenso el envío del equipo de engrase, rogándole tenga la amabilidad de prestarnos su conformidad al nuevo precio, recibida la cual procederemos a expedirle seguidamente el aparato.

Pendientes de sus gratas noticias, atentamente le saludan,

Autoaccesorios Ramón Serrano y Cía, S.A.

SPANISH LITERATURE, 17

Religious Poets of the Sixteenth Century

The sixteenth century produced some of the finest poets that have ever written in Spanish, and many of them wrote on religious subjects, as befitted a century in which strife born of religious differences filled a large part of men's minds in all parts of Europe.

Fray Luis de León (1537–91), one of the greatest of these poets, was a famous teacher at the University of Salamanca, and his poems, full of the desire to escape from the paltry things of this world to a deeper knowledge of God through fuller acquaintance with the wonders of the universe, have irresistible charm. The most famous of his poems is the one beginning " Qué descansada vida ", and in it the poet compares the unhappiness and insecurity that result from the search for worldly wealth with the beauty and charm of his own quiet garden—" por mi mano plantado ", as he says.

The finest of the purely religious poets were the mystics Santa Teresa (1515–82) and San Juan de la Cruz (1542–91), both of whom led exceedingly active lives as reformers in the Carmelite monastic order, but who found time for the deepest and purest form of religious contemplation, and this is reflected to the full in their verse.

The following poem of San Juan de la Cruz owes some of its atmosphere and inspiration to the Old Testament love song usually called the Song of Solomon. (San Juan de la Cruz used this source much more fully in another and perhaps more famous poem, his " *Cántico Espiritual* ".) The poet, however, is not writing here about worldly love, but about the search of the soul of man for God.

17 (*d*)

En una noche obscura,
Con ansias en amores inflamada,
¡ Oh dichosa ventura !
Salí sin ser notada,
Estando ya mi casa sosegada.

A escuras, y segura,
Por la secreta escala disfrazada,
¡ Oh dichosa ventura !
A escuras, y en celada,
Estando ya mi casa sosegada.

En la noche dichosa,
En secreto, que nadie me veía,
Ni yo miraba cosa,
Sin otra luz y guía,
Sino la que en el corazón ardía.

Aquesta me guiaba
Mas cierto que la luz del mediodía,
A donde me esperaba
Quien yo bien me sabía,
En parte donde nadie parecía.

¡ Oh, noche, que guiaste,
Oh noche amable más que el alborada :
Oh noche, que juntaste
Amado con amada,
Amada en el Amado transformada !

En mi pecho florido,
Que entero para él sólo se guardaba,

Allí quedó dormido,
Y yo le regalaba,
Y el ventalle de cedros aire daba.

El aire de la almena,
Cuando ya sus cabellos esparcía,
Con su mano serena
En mi cuello hería,
Y todos mis sentidos suspendía.

Quedéme, y olvidéme,
El rostro recliné sobre el Amado,
Cesó todo, y dejéme,
Dejando mi cuidado
Entre las azucenas olvidado.

LESSON XVIII

WILL, WOULD, SHOULD, AND COULD

1. NOTE that "will" and "would" are not always merely the sign of the Future and Conditional tenses, but often imply *willingness*, and consequently require, probably, the verb *querer* or some other verb of wishing for an accurate translation.

Will you please close the door?   *¿Quiere Vd cerrar la puerta, por favor?*

2. "Will not" may mean "refuse":

He would not look at it. *Se negó a mirarlo* or *No quiso mirarlo.*

3. "Would" is sometimes merely a sign of the imperfect indicative:

He would go to sleep every afternoon. *Todas las tardes se dormía.*

4. If "should" means "ought", translate accordingly:

He should have sent it to me sooner. *Hubiera debido mandármelo más temprano.*

5. " Could ", like its Present tense " can ", is always some part of *poder*. Some care is necessary, however, to distinguish between sentences where " could " is Conditional, and where it is some other past tense.

I could do it if I tried (meaning " I should be able . . .").
Si tratase de hacerlo; lo podría.

He told me that he could not do it (meaning ". . . he was not able to do it "). *Me dijo que no lo podía hacer.*)

18 (*a*) Exercise

Translate :

1. I should speak more politely, if I were you.
2. You should not try to do too many things at once.
3. I knew that I should soon have to buy a new dictionary.
4. Every evening at half-past six he would go to the shop and buy a newspaper.
5. Will you tell me how to get to the Post Office, please ?
6. The taxi-driver would not accept a tip from the old lady.
7. She said she would be back late.
8. I could not read that, even if I had my spectacles.
9. My friends invited me to spend a month in Barcelona, but I could not go.
10. I shouldn't like to think that you could have done such a thing.

18 (*b*) Conversation

(*La última noche de la estancia de* MARTÍN *e* ISABEL *en la casita de la hermana de* ANTONIO. *De sobremesa.*)

MARTÍN : Según parece, tendremos un día sólo para ver todo lo que se puede de Sevilla, pues nos marchamos de aquí mañana por la mañana, llegaremos a Sevilla a eso de las nueve y media, y tendremos entonces casi exacta-mente veinte y cuatro horas disponibles. ¿Qué nos aconseja Vd que tratemos de ver en aquel tiempo?

ANTONIO : Pues a ver. Irán primero a su hotel, que

está en la Plaza de San Fernando, que está bastante
cerca de la Catedral, y ésta es uno de los mejores monu-
mentos del gótico español. Para verla, y para ver el
Patio de los Naranjos y la Giralda, hace falta a lo menos
una hora y media o dos horas. Si quieren subir a lo
alto de la Giralda, lo cual aconsejo, porque desde allí
hay una vista magnífica, necesitarán una media hora
más.

ISABEL: Según las fotografías que he visto de ella debe
de ser altísima, pero como desde el avión al día siguiente
tendremos una vista semejante, tal vez fuera mejor
prescindir de esta subida.

ANTONIO : Claro. Pues entonces pueden ir a ver el museo
de pinturas. Hay una cantidad de cuadros magníficos
que por cierto deben ver. El museo está a unos quinientos
metros de su hotel, no muy lejos de la estación.

MARTÍN : Entonces será la hora de almorzar, o por lo
menos para descansar un poco.

ANTONIO : Sí. Con el calor que seguramente va a hacer
no sé si tendrán fuerzas para pasar la tarde andando.
Pero no deben dejar de ver el Alcázar y sus jardines, y
allí podrán sentarse en la sombra si encuentran que el
calor es sofocante. El Alcázar, como tal vez saben, es
el antiguo palacio de los reyes moros, y aunque se ha
modernizado considerablemente bien vale la pena de
verse. Un poco más tarde, cuando haga menos calor,
Vds pueden dar un paseo por los jardines de María
Luisa, siguiendo hasta el lado del Guadalquivir, donde
verán la Torre del Oro, que también es árabe, y que
antiguamente formaba parte de las murallas de la
ciudad.

ISABEL : ¿ Tendremos tiempo para dar una ojeada a las
tiendas ? Se dice que las de Sevilla son preciosísimas.

MARÍA : Sí, especialmente las de la calle de las Sierpes,
donde no se permite que pase ningún coche, para dejar
paso libre a los peatones. Las tiendas allí son bellísimas
y muy célebres.

ANTONIO : En un día apenas podrán ver más que estos
sitios de interés especial. Claro que se necesita mucho
más tiempo para ver una ciudad tan magnífica como

Sevilla. Tampoco tendrán tiempo en un día para ir a los toros.

ISABEL : Fuimos a una corrida en Madrid. Era bastante buena, pero a mí no me interesan mucho los toros. A Martín, sí.

MARTÍN : Es verdad que me gustan mucho la animación y los colores vivos, y la habilidad y la destreza de los toreros, pero como es el único día que podremos pasar en Sevilla no iremos a los toros, sino que nos pasearemos viendo los edificios y jardines que Antonio nos ha dicho. ¿ Pero no va Vd a recomendarnos que veamos el barrio de Santa Cruz ? Recuerdo en mi última visita el encanto de aquellas calles tortuosas, cada casa con su patio de tipo distinto y muchos con fuente.

ANTONIO : Sí, por supuesto deben ir allí si es posible con el poco tiempo que tendrán.

ISABEL : Bueno, muchas gracias, Antonio, por habernos explicado tan bien lo que podremos hacer. Y ahora que va haciéndose tarde, y que tengo que hacer mis maletas, me parece que Martín y yo debiéramos subir a nuestro cuarto, pues mañana nos hemos de levantar muy temprano para coger el tren. Conque ¡ adiós, y buenas noches !

(MARTÍN e ISABEL *suben a su cuarto.*)

COMMERCIAL SPANISH, 18

Railway Regulations

The following extract from the official Spanish railway guide contains a number of useful terms concerning passenger trains and the conveyance of passengers' luggage.

18 (*c*)

El transporte de equipajes de los viajeros en los ferro-carriles españoles está sujeto a las siguientes condiciones :

Trenes corrientes :—(Se entienden por tales, los expresos, rápidos, correos-expresos, correos, correos-ómnibus, directos o semi-directos, sean arrastrados por tracción a vapor o tracción eléctrica).

En estos trenes el viajero tiene derecho a 30 kilogramos de equipaje facturado gratuítamente (15 kilos los niños que pagan medio billete). La facturación se hace sólo hasta 15 minutos antes de la salida del tren respectivo, pudiéndose hacer con anticipación incluso de varios días en la consigna de la estación pagando los derechos de consigna.

Además del equipaje facturado, el viajero puede llevar bultos de mano, siempre que por sus dimensiones excesivas no molesten a los demás viajeros. No se admiten como tales bultos de mano las sustancias explosivas, armas de fuego o aquellos objetos que por su mal olor o peligro para los viajeros sean inadmisibles.

Los equipajes deben retirarse hasta tres horas después de la llegada del tren y son conducidos en el mismo tren que el viajero. Pasado dicho plazo devengan almacenaje. El exceso de equipaje se paga por fracciones de 10 kilogramos al precio de la tarifa correspondiente.

SPANISH LITERATURE, 18
Lazarillo de Tormes and the Picaresque Novel

In 1554 there was published in Spain, anonymously, the novel *Lazarillo de Tormes*. It describes in straightforward, completely unsentimental style, various episodes in the life of appalling hardships led by a small boy, Lazarillo, who at the age of about ten was put to serve a series of masters, all of whom were very unsatisfactory characters for one reason or another. Throughout his career in the service of these masters the boy was led to exercise his wits and cunning to obtain enough to eat, as his masters were nearly all either poverty-stricken or extremely stingy; and this earned him the epithet of " *pícaro* "—" rascal "— a word that has given the name to this type of novel. Other famous Spanish picaresque novels are Mateo Alemán's *Guzmán de Alfarache* (1599) and Quevedo's *El Buscón* (1626).

It cannot be assumed, from this and the other contemporary evidence, that *Lazarillo de Tormes* gives a complete or even characteristic picture of Spanish life at the time, but the descriptions that this book contains of various forms of beggary, particularly in Toledo, as seen through the eyes of a young boy, are marvellously realistic.

The episode quoted occurs at the outset of the boy's career, just after he leaves his home by the River Tormes in Salamanca, in the company of his first master, a blind beggar.

18 (d)

Salimos de Salamanca, y llegando a la puente, está a la entrada de ella un animal de piedra, que casi tiene forma de toro, y el ciego mandóme que llegase cerca del animal, y allí puesto, me dijo : " Lázaro, llega el oído a este toro, y oirás gran ruido dentro de él." —Yo simplemente llegué, creyendo ser así, y como sintió que tenía la cabeza par de la piedra afirmó recio la mano y dióme una gran calabazada en el diablo del toro, que más de tres días me duró el dolor de la cornada, y díjome : " Necio, aprende que el mozo del ciego un punto ha de saber más que el diablo,"—y rió mucho de la burla. Parecióme que en aquel instante desperté de la simpleza en que como niño dormido estaba, y dije entre mí : " Verdad dice éste, que me cumple avivar el ojo y avisar, pues solo soy, y pensar como me sepa valer."

LESSON XIX

MEASUREMENTS

NOTE the following model ways of expressing length, breadth, height, etc. :

1. *Esta calle tiene más de cien metros de largo* (or *de longitud*). This street is over 100 yards long.

2. *La carretera tiene 15 metros de ancho* (or *de anchura*). The roadway is 15 yards wide.

3. *Aquella iglesia tiene 30 metros de alto* (or *de altura*). That church is 30 metres high.

4. *Aquel pozo tiene 30 metros de profundidad* (NOT *de profundo*). That well is 30 metres deep.

Other ways can be seen in the following examples :

This room is 4 metres high.
La altura de este cuarto es de cuatro metros.
Este cuarto es alto de cuatro metros.
Éste es un cuarto de cuatro metros de alto.

The Metric System

The rapid conversion of Spanish weights and measures to the English system inevitably presents travellers with mental arithmetic. The following notes, not pretending to be exhaustive or 100% accurate, will be helpful.

1 kilometre is five-eighths of a mile, thus five miles are equal to eight kilometres.

100 kilometres is just over 62 miles.

1 metre is a little more than a yard. $5\frac{1}{2}$ yards equal 5 metres.

1 kilogramme is a little less than $2\frac{1}{4}$ pounds.

100 grammes is thus about $3\frac{1}{2}$ ounces, 250 grammes is rather more than half a pound.

For calculating temperatures, Spain uses the Centigrade thermometer.

0 degrees Centigrade equals			32	degrees Fahrenheit	
10 ,,	,,	,,	50	,,	,,
20 ,,	,,	,,	68	,,	,,
30 ,,	,,	,,	86	,,	,,

and so on; boiling point (100 degrees Centigrade) is 212 degrees Fahrenheit; and a rise of 5 degrees Centigrade equals a rise of 9 degrees Fahrenheit.

As to money, since the value of the peseta and the pound sterling are liable to fluctuation, the currently quoted rates of exchange must be consulted to obtain a correct idea of the comparative values of Spanish and British currency.

There are 100 céntimos in a peseta; 25 céntimos are

sometimes referred to by the old term *un real*; 5 pesetas are sometimes called *un duro*—it is common to see printed prices of some commodities calculated in *duros*. The English word " dollar " is found in dictionaries as the equivalent of *duro*.

19 (*a*)
A Medieval Legend from Seville

Pedro el Cruel, rey de España a mediados del siglo catorce, tenía muchos palacios y otras residencias en varias partes de sus dominios, pero el que más le gustaba era el Alcázar de Sevilla. Situado en un lugar muy apacible de la gran ciudad andaluza, y en medio de unos jardines hermosísimos, aun hoy día puede verse con mucho de la gloria de su esplendor medioeval, que ilustra tan bien la mezcla de las civilizaciones española y árabe.

Sus salas, ornadas de azulejos y de relieves intrincados, pintados de colores muy vivos, son las mismas salas en donde holgaba don Pedro y su corte, a la cual pertenecían muchos hombres y muchas mujeres cuya corrupción era tan notoria.

Tan mala era la corte, y tantos eran los asesinatos y duelos que de día en día se descubrían, que don Pedro se vio obligado a hacer un decreto, por el cual mandaba que a quienquiera luchase en duelo se le cortara la cabeza en el mismo sitio en que el duelo hubiese tenido lugar.

Una noche poco después, de esto, el rey, a quien le gustaba dar paseos nocturnos, muchas veces con algún fin amoroso, paseaba por el Barrio de Santa Cruz, estas calles tortuosas y estas plazuelas que aun hoy constituyen una de las partes más típicas de Sevilla. La noche era tenebrosa, y don Pedro andaba embozado en su capa. Pero pronto, al pasar por una calle solitaria, entre un convento abandonado por un lado y unas chozas decrépitas en el otro, notó el rey que alguien le seguía. Era su rival, un duque, quien iba, sin duda, a la casa de la misma mujer a la cual se dirigía el rey. Sin más tardar, el rey sacó su espada, y desafió al duque, y después de algunas cuchilladas al aire el duque cayó muerto al suelo. No había nadie en la calle; según parecía no había ningún testigo que pudiese haber oído el golpe sordo que dió el cadáver al caer. Entonces el rey, acordándose del decreto que había hecho poco antes, soltó una carcajada, una carcajada feroz, siniestra, diabólica. Pero en el momento en que bajaba la calle, dejando en el suelo el cuerpo inerte del duque, una luz trémula apareció en la puerta de una de aquellas chozas miserables, y asomó una cara de mujer vieja, una cara de bruja. Y en el muro de aquel convento abandonado se oyó el graznido de un cuervo.

A la mañana siguiente toda Sevilla hablaba de la muerte del duque. Y como nadie sabía quién había cometido el crimen, el rey mandó buscar al corregidor de la ciudad.

—¿Y sabe la justicia de Sevilla quién mató al duque? —le preguntó el rey.

—Todavía no, señor—fue la respuesta.

—Entonces, que se le busque. Y si no le descubre dentro de ocho días, el que lo pagará con su propia vida será el corregidor, él mismo.

Salió triste el corregidor de la presencia del rey. Le era preciso descubrir al asesino. Lo había dicho el rey, y lo que decía el rey se cumplía siempre.

Así el corregidor fué a ver el sitio donde habían descubierto el cadáver del duque. Buscó en las chozas carcomidas en frente del convento abandonado, y halló a una vieja, que vivía sola en una de ellas, la única persona que vivía en esta calle.

Sí, ella había oído el choque de las cuchilladas y el golpe sordo que dio el cadáver al caer al suelo. ¿Y luego, qué? Pues alguien había soltado una carcajada. ¿Pero quién? ¿Conocía ella al que reía así? Sí, ella le conocía muy bien, porque le conocían bien todos los sevillanos. El que había soltado aquella carcajada diabólica era el mismo rey, nadie más que él reía así.

Entonces el corregidor se dirigió al Alcázar y fue recibido en audiencia por don Pedro.

—Ah, señor corregidor. ¿Ha descubierto la justicia quién mató al duque?

—Sí, señor don Pedro. El que mató al duque no es sino el mismo rey, don Pedro de Castilla.

El rey guardó silencio un momento. Entonces soltó
una nueva carcajada, y preguntó cómo lo había descubierto.

Y para que no se rompiese el decreto por razón de lo
que el mismo rey había hecho, hicieron cortar la cabeza
de una estatua del rey, que luego colocaron en el muro de
aquel convento abandonado. Así quedaron satisfechos
el rey y también la justicia de Sevilla.

COMMERCIAL SPANISH, 19

Insurance

The following letter and estimate enclosed with it give
an example of some of the terms used in marine insurance.

19 (*b*)

Compañía Hispanoamericana
de Seguros y Reaseguros,
Montera, 47,
Madrid
.11 de julio de 19—

D. Fernando Ferraz,
Claudio Coello, 63,
Madrid

Muy Sr. nuestro,

Seguro transporte aceite de palma

Adjunto a la presente nos permitimos enviarle
cotización para el seguro del transporte de aceite de
palma en bidones desde el puerto de Amberes al de Barcelona.

Queda entendido que las averías se abonarán en la
misma clase de moneda que se estipule el pago de la prima.

Agradeciéndole su conformidad o reparo a nuestra
cotización, aprovechamos la ocasión para saludarle muy
atentamente,

Compañía Hispanoamericano de Seguros y Reaseguros,
Rafael Martínez

19 (c)
Cotización para el seguro del transporte de aceite de palma en bidones

Embarques bajo cubierta:

Además de las condiciones generales impresas de nuestra póliza (pérdida total, gastos de salvamento, avería gruesa, incendio, naufragio, varada o abordaje), se responderá de todo riesgo accidental de mar debidamente justificado por la protesta del Capitán; robo parcial y derrames por rotura de los envases; falta de entrega y/o extravío de bultos completos; caída de bultos al mar en las operaciones de carga y/o descarga. Todo ello de conformidad con lo dispuesto por las cláusulas especiales emitidas por el Sindicato Vertical del Seguro y mediante la prima de 0,70%.

Embarques sobre cubierta:

1a modalidad: Los mismos riesgos que para los embarques bajo cubierta, incluidos el echazón y arrastre por las olas, mediante la prima del 1,15%.

2a modalidad: Únicamente a las condiciones generales impresas de nuestra póliza, incluidos echazón y arrastre por las olas y la caída de bultos al mar en las operaciones de carga y/o descarga, mediante la prima de 0,60%.

SPANISH LITERATURE, 19
Garcilaso de la Vega

Italian influence is evident in Spanish poetry in various ways after about 1530, and the courtly gentleman Garcilaso de la Vega (1503–36), with his friend Juan Boscán, was very largely responsible for introducing into Spanish literature the polished, stately forms and modes of poetic thought and expression then current in Renaissance Italy. Garcilaso was a soldier, a personal friend of the Emperor, Charles V, and he spent much time in the emperor's company, both at the Court in Toledo and on travels up and down the Emperor's wide dominions in Europe. Out of favour with the Emperor for a time, he spent a period in captivity (so many of Spain's best poets and writers have suffered imprisonment for one reason or another), and he was killed on a Spanish military expedition against the south of France in 1536.

His most famous poems are his "*Églogas*", pastoral compositions in classical vein, reminiscent of Virgil, full of the feelings of unrequited love. His sonnets (he and Boscán introduced the sonnet form into Spanish) are among the finest in the language.

The following sonnet is on an old theme, but it is beautifully written :

19 (*d*)

En tanto que de rosa y azucena
   se muestra la color en vuestro gesto,
   y que vuestro mirar ardiente, honesto,
   enciende el corazón y lo refrena ;
Y en tanto que el cabello, que en la vena
   del oro se escogió, con vuelo presto,
   por el hermoso cuello blanco, enhiesto,
   el viento mueve, esparce y desordena ;
Coged de vuestra alegre primavera
   el dulce fruto, antes que el tiempo airado
   cubra de nieve la hermosa cumbre.
Marchitará la rosa el viento helado,
   todo lo mudará la edad ligera,
   por no hacer mudanza en su costumbre.

LESSON XX

SOME DIFFICULT WORDS

ASK : Remember that *preguntar* implies asking a *question*, while *pedir* is used when the implication is " to ask FOR ".

My friend asked me where his brother was. *Mi amigo me preguntó dónde estaba su hermano.*

I am going to ask in that shop whether they sell ink. *Voy a preguntar en aquella tienda si venden tinta.*

I am going to ask for ink in that shop.   *Voy a pedir tinta en aquella tienda.*

Also, use *pedir* for " to ask " in the sense of *asking someone to do something* :

My father asked me to come and see you.   *Mi padre me pidió que fuese a verle.*

(Note also in this sentence the use of the verb *ir*, not *venir*, for " to come ". The point is that my father's words were " GO and see him ", not " COME . . .")

Preguntar por . . . is used only in the sense of asking *or a person* :

A man has just arrived who is asking for Sr Sánchez. *Un hombre acaba de llegar que pregunta por el Sr Sánchez.*

INTRODUCE (meaning " present ") :

He introduced us to his brother.   *Nos presentó a su hermano* (*introducir* implies " insert ").

It will be difficult to insert those papers into such a small envelope.   *Habrá dificultad en introducir esos papeles en un sobre tan pequeño.*

MONEY :

They have given me a lot of silver money (coins). *Me han dado muchas monedas* (*cuñas*) *de plata.*

I find the English money system difficult to understand (coinage).   *Encuentro que el sistema de la moneda inglesa es difícil de entender.*

This will cost a lot of money (quantity of money). *Esto costará mucho dinero.*

OFFICE :

room, *despacho, oficina.*

occupation, employment, *oficio* (which also means " church service ").

Post Office, *Casa de Correos, Estafeta.*

PLACE :

  spot, *sitio, lugar*
  seat, *asiento*
  market, etc., *plaza, plaza del mercado*
  job, occupation, *puesto, empleo, colocación*

PLAY (verb) : For playing musical instruments use *tocar*.

  She is learning to play the piano. *Aprende a tocar el piano.*

Otherwise use *jugar*.

  Let's play tennis this afternoon. *Juguemos al tenis esta tarde.*

PUT : Normally *poner*, but note that *meter* is used in the one sense of " putting something *inside* . . ."

  Don't forget to put water in the flower vase. *No olvide de meter agua en el florero.*

Compounds of *meter*, and the *-mitir* verbs are worth noting specially :

cometer, commit	*admitir*, admit
prometer, promise	*dimitir*, relinquish
someter, submit	*emitir*, emit
	omitir, omit
	permitir, permit
	remitir, send back
	trasmitir, transmit

RELATION :

  a person, member of a family, *pariente, parienta*
  narrative; matter that is in relation to, *relación*

SENSIBLE :

  with good sense, *sensato*
  capable of sensation, *sensible*

SENTENCE :

  in a court of law, *sentencia*
  grammatical, *la frase*

SUCCEED (with success) : *lograr*.

He succeeded in arriving on time. *Logró (en) llegar a tiempo.*

SUCCEED (in succession) : *suceder*.

The queen succeeded her father. *La reina sucedió a su padre.*

TAKE : Usually *tomar*.

Will you take a cup of tea? *¿ Quiere Vd tomar una taza de té ?*

BUT if the meaning is "carry away" or "lead", use *llevar* :

I will take these newspapers and a writing pad. *Llevaré estos periódicos y un block de cartas.*

Take my trunk to the station, please. *Haga el favor de llevar mi baúl a la estación.*

Daddy, will you take me to the beach? *Papá, ¿ quieres llevarme a la playa ?*

And note also :

Is this seat taken? *¿ Está ocupado este asiento ?*

"To take *off* (a garment)" is *quitar*.

Take off your raincoat, it isn't raining any more now. *Quite Vd su impermeable, ya no llueve.*

"To take *in*" (meaning "deceive") is *engañar*.

20 (a) Conversation

(*En el autobús entre la oficina de la línea "Iberia", en Sevilla, y el aerodromo.*)

ISABEL : ¡ Qué triste estoy de que hoy sea el último día de nuestra temporada en España ! ¡ Muchísimo me he divertido, Martín !

MARTÍN : Sí, pero has de recordar que probablemente podremos volver a pasar otras vacaciones aquí, dentro de un par de años, tal vez.

ISABEL : Espero que sí. Nos quedan tantas cosas por ver, en muchísimas partes, sobretodo aquí en el sur. ¡ Y pensar que no hemos podido ir esta vez a Granada !

MARTÍN : Tampoco hemos visto el este, Barcelona y la
Costa Brava y los Baleares, por ejemplo.

ISABEL : Verdad.   Sin embargo tendremos mucho gusto
en estar otra vez en casa.   Esto de tener que hacer y
deshacer las maletas casi todos los días es aburrido.   Mira,
¿qué hora tienes?   Parece que mi reloj se ha parado.

MARTÍN : Son las ocho y media.   El avión para Madrid
saldrá del aerodromo de San Pabio a las nueve, y llegaremos a Barajas, el aeropuerto de Madrid, a las once menos
cuarto.   Allí tendremos que esperar durante algún
tiempo, pues el avión para Londres en el cual tenemos los
asientos reservados no saldrá hasta las tres de la tarde.
Pero poco importa, podremos dejar las maletas en el
aerodromo e ir al centro de Madrid en el autobús, pudiendo
volver a eso de las dos.

ISABEL : ¿Cuándo comeremos?   En Madrid no se suele
comer antes de las dos, y entonces estaremos otra vez en
marcha.

MARTÍN : No te preocupes.   Se puede tomar cualquier
cosa ligera en uno de los cafés, y entonces una vez que
el avión haya salido se nos servirá un almuerzo excelente.
¡ Buena suerte hemos tenido con Antonio, que nos quiso
arreglar nuestros billetes !   El viajar en avión es tanto
más rápido que por otro modo alguno, y de veras me
asustaba un poco la idea del viaje de vuelta en el tren :
doce o trece horas de Sevilla a Madrid, veintidós de
allí a París, y luego otras doce a Londres, ¡ digamos
dos días y dos noches en el tren !

ISABEL : Tienes razón.   Además me gusta mucho el
viajar en avión.   Y dicen que las vistas que hay sobre
España desde un aeroplano son estupendos.   María
me hablaba de los colores tan vivos que se ven en las
montañas, y sobre las llanuras de Castilla.

MARTÍN : Aquí llegamos al aerodromo.   (*Bajan del
autobús.*)   El mozo bajará las maletas, sin duda, y las
veremos pasar, si quieres, al avión en este carruaje.
Probablemente tendré que enseñar los billetes en alguna
ventanilla.   Sí, aquí está.

(*Se acerca a la ventanilla, donde hay una pequeña
cola de viajeros.*)

MARTÍN: Como todavía no salimos directamente para el extranjero no tendré que hacer ninguna declaración acerca del dinero que llevamos. Ésta la haremos después en Madrid.

UNA VOZ: ¡ Atención ! Los señores viajeros para Madrid sírvanse pasar al andén número nueve.

ISABEL: ¡ Mira, Martín ! ¡ No tardes ! Dice aquella voz que los viajeros para Madrid deben salir de aquí para subir en el avión.

MARTÍN: No te aflijas, chica, no lo perderemos.

(Habiendo mostrado sus billetes y sus pasaportes, MARTÍN coge su cartera y sale del edificio con ISABEL y con el pequeño grupo de viajeros acompañado por el oficial del aerodromo que los conduce al avión. Aquí dejamos a MARTÍN e ISABEL, esperando que pasen un día agradable en su viaje aéreo entre Sevilla y Madrid, y luego entre Madrid y Londres.)

COMMERCIAL SPANISH, 20
Abbreviations

The following are some of the commoner abbreviations used in commercial Spanish :

a/c	= *a cuenta*	= to account
art. arto. }	= *artículo*	= article
brl	= *barril*	= barrel
cta. cte.	= *cuenta corriente*	= current account
ch/	= *cheque*	= cheque
doc., dna.	= *docena*	= dozen
d/v	= *días vista*	= days sight
E.U. EE. UU. }	= *Estados Unidos*	= United States
F.C., f.c.	= *ferrocarril*	= railway
fha.	= *fecha*	= date
Hno.	= *hermano*	= brother
m/	= *mi*	= my
m/f	= *mi favor*	= my favour
n/	= *nuestro*	= our

o/	= *orden* = order
pdo.	= *pasado* = past, " ult."
Q.B.S.M.	= *que besa su mano* ⎫ formulas sometimes in-
Q.E.S.M.	= *que estrecha su mano* ⎬ cluded before signature at foot of letter
s/	= *su* = your (his, etc.)
s/n	= *sin número* = not numbered
v/gr	= *verbigracia* = for example, " viz."

SPANISH LITERATURE, 20

Medieval Spanish Literature; the Romances

The oldest form of literature in Spanish was a type of song, composed probably by medieval minstrels who roved from place to place singing or reciting for a living. Their popular origin is indisputable; many of the longer narrative poems, commemorating the deeds of some famous hero in war, were so famous as to be incorporated, sometimes nearly verbatim, into the monkish medieval chronicles. The earliest and probably the best of these is the *Cantar de Mío Cid*, composed about 1140. Some of the shorter ones, which have survived in large quantity, seem to have been composed for community singing or to be sung while dancing; sometimes they capture a single incident and describe it in a lyrical way. In the form that has come down to us most of these " romances " or " ballads " belong to the fifteenth century.

The short " Romance " which follows here must have been composed by a prisoner, or by one who knew some- thing of a prisoner's thoughts :

20 (b)

Por el mes de mayo
cuando hace la calor
cuando canta la calandria
y responde el ruiseñor,
cuando los enamorados
van a servir al amor,
sino yo triste, cuitado,

que vivo en esta prisión,
que ni sé cuando es de día
ni cuando las noches son,
sino por una avecilla
que me cantaba al albor :
matómela un ballestero;
¡ déle Dios mal galardón !

PART 2
KEY TO EXERCISES AND TRANSLATIONS
KEY

1 (a) Exercise

1. El señor que acaba de llegar es ruso, pero vive ahora en los Estados Unidos de América.

2. Déme otro par de calcetines grises, por favor, Señora Martínez.

3. Se paró delante de cierta casa vieja al fin de la calle.

4. Su inquilino es un portugués muy grosero; es marinero, se emborracha a menudo y no tiene dinero.

5. El rey Jorge Sexto murió el seis de febrero de mil novecientos cincuenta y dos. Cien años antes reinaba la Reina Victoria.

6. Los médicos dicen que es malo el beber agua helada cuando tiene uno mucho calor.

7. ¡No he oído hablar nunca de tal cosa! ¡No me diga nada más acerca de ella!

8. El francés es bastante fácil de aprender si vive Vd un año o más en Francia, en Bélgica o en Suiza.

9. Aquí hay dos périodicos, uno lleva la fecha de ayer y el otro la de hace una semana. El primero es alemán y el segundo holandés.

10. La fe, la esperanza y la caridad son las tres virtudes cristianas. Tengamos siempre un poco más de caridad.

1 (b) Conversation

(*After dinner in the home of* MARTIN *and* ISABEL, *in London. Their Spanish friends* ANTONIO *and* MARIA *have been dining with them.*)

ANTONIO : So you are thinking of spending your holidays this year in Spain. Which part are you going to visit ?

MARTIN : First we are going by air to Paris, to avoid the

discomfort of crossing the Channel.   We would rather not
run the risk of Isabel being seasick.

ISABEL: Yes, indeed !   Anything to avoid that !

ANTONIO: Well, then, why don't you go to Madrid direct?
There are good services, both English and Spanish, that have
direct flights from London, and they take only two to three
hours to do this journey.

ISABEL : Well, out of the five weeks' holiday we have this
year we want to spend some days in the north of Spain,
at San Sebastian and Pamplona, and so we thought it
would be better to cross France from Paris by rail, and then
we should be exactly where we want to be.

ANTONIO : Yes, of course.   French trains are very fast, and
pretty comfortable too, especially if you have your seats
reserved in advance.

MARTIN : Yes, as we shall be beginning our journey in the
middle of July, this will be absolutely necessary, because
with the French holidays on the 14th trains will be very full.

ISABEL : But Maria, didn't you say that you were going to
Spain this summer too ?

MARIA : Yes.   You know Antonio always has to take his
holidays in August, so we are going to Córdoba to spend a
couple of weeks with my sister-in-law, who has a country
house near there.   Do you think there is a chance of our
meeting there ?   Martin, who is an architect, ought to go
down to Andalusia to see at least the Mosque in Córdoba,
and perhaps Seville and Granada.

MARTIN : Yes, I want to go there; it is a great many years
since I was in Andalusia.   I was only there once, when I
was a student, before the Civil War.

ANTONIO : Well, then, if you go through Cordóba while we
are there, you must come and see us.   My sister likes
having a lot of friends in the house, and she can easily
put you up.

ISABEL : Thank you, Antonio.   Obviously a good deal
depends on how much the journey and our stay in the North
and in Madrid are going to cost us, we want to be in Madrid
for a few days at least.   But I think we shall be able to
come and see you.   I very much want to visit Andalusia,
where I have never yet been.

MARIA : I am very glad.   About the first or second week in
August we shall expect you in Córdoba, then.   And so that
you can let us know when you are going to arrive, here is
my sister-in-law's address.   (*She gives it to her on a card.*)

1 (c)

1. (a) Señor Don Ramón Ramírez Valdés (or Sr. D. Ramón Ramírez y Valdés).
   (b) Señor Ramírez.
   (c) Don Ramón.

2. (a) Isabel (de) Avellaneda y Narváez.
   (b) Isabel (de) Avellaneda y Ramírez.
   (c) Doña Isabel.

3. Manuel Morales y Cía, S.A.,
   San Ignacio, 17, 3, dcha,
   Barcelona.

1 (d)

Fernando was an apprentice in the shoe-factory belonging to the now deceased Ichtaber, whom they called the " Flat-nosed man of Tolosa ", and I don't know if you will know, but Ichtaber was an elderly shoemaker and very well off. Fernando was courting a very pretty girl; but Ichtaber, the flat-nosed, when he saw her, began to make love to her, and asked her whether she would like to marry him. As he was rich, she accepted. The old man and the girl used to meet in the shoe-factory, and Ichtaber, in order to be alone with her, cunningly used to send Fernando, on one pretext or another, to the room behind the factory. He pretended not to mind, but he took his revenge.

" Yes," he said to her, " Ichtaber isn't a bad fellow, and he is well off, it is true; but as he is a shoemaker and flat-nosed and has spent all his life among leather, he smells very nasty."

" That's not true ! " she said.

" Well, you just notice. You'll see."

Fernando went to the factory, picked up a big bellows and filled it with that kind of tanning bark that is left over after hides have been tanned, and which smells filthy, then he made a hole in the partition between the factory and the room behind, and waited for his opportunity. The girl came in the afternoon, and Ichtaber said to his apprentice :

" Look, Fernando, go into the room behind for a moment and mend those lasts that there are in the box."

Fernando went out; he took up the bellows. He looked through the hole. Ichtaber was kissing the girl's hand; then Fernando aimed at her with the bellows, and sent through the hole in the partition a current of evil-smelling air. When Fernando looked next, Ichtaber, the flat-nosed, had his hand to his diminutive nostrils, and so had the girl.

Then Fernando went on blowing with the bellows intermittently, until he was tired.

Two days later the girl went again to the factory, and the same thing happened. After that she did not go any more, because, she said, Ichtaber, the flat-nosed, smelt disgustingly.

Ichtaber made love to another girl, but Fernando played the same trick with the bellows, and the shoemaker said to his friends:

" Upon my soul! It used to be different in my time. Girls were clean and healthy. Now, all of them smell worse than dogs."

2 (a) Exercise

Acabo de tener una conversación por teléfono con mi mujer, y me ha dicho que le compre una maleta nueva esta mañana antes de que almuerce. Necesita una para llevar a Mallorca el mes que viene. Probablemente tendré que comprarle una de cuero. También tendré que encargar un traje nuevo para mí, muchas veces tengo demasiado calor si llevo vestidos ingleses cuando hace mucho calor, y tengo ganas de comprar un traje ligero como los que tienen la mayoría de los españoles para llevar en el verano. No tengo miedo de que haga frío, cuando hemos estado en Palma otros años por la primavera he hallado siempre que estoy bastante abrigado contra el tiempo si llevo un impermeable y una bufanda.

2 (b) Conversation

(*In the train. A second-class compartment in the express from Paris; near Biarritz.*)

ISABEL (*waking up*): What time do you make it, Martin?
MARTIN (*who has been awake for some time*): Seven o'clock. Have you slept well?

ISABEL : Yes, fairly well, although I wasn't very comfortable. When do we get to the frontier?

MARTIN : At half-past. You have all the time you need to wash your face, and that is very necessary. I advise you to go at once, because there may be a queue.

ISABEL : Really, you are very rude. But of course, husbands are privileged to say such things, and . . .

MARTIN : Yes, indeed. At Irún we can have coffee, and then you will feel better. Look, how lovely it is! There in front are the Pyrenees, like a great wall.

ISABEL : Yes, and on the other side there is the sea. And that in the distance, is it the Spanish coast?

MARTIN : It is the Cantabrian coast near San Sebastian.

(ISABEL *goes off down the corridor with her sponge-bag.* MARTIN *smokes a cigarette and watches the scenery.*)

A GENTLEMAN (*who got in at Bayonne*) : You are going to Spain, aren't you? Is it your first visit?

MARTIN : It is my wife's first visit, yes, but I have been to Spain several times, some years ago, when I was a bachelor.

THE GENTLEMAN : And where are you going? To San Sebastian, or Madrid, or farther south?

MARTIN : Well, I want to show my wife some of the places I used to know, and so we are going to spend two or three days at San Sebastian. Then we shall go on to Pamplona or Burgos, and then more or less straight to Madrid. Afterwards we may go down through Andalusia, but in five weeks we must be back in London, because that will be the end of my holidays.

THE GENTLEMAN : That will be a really good trip. I hope you enjoy yourselves.

MARTIN : Thank you.

(ISABEL *comes back.*)

ISABEL : What station is this?

MARTIN : It must be Hendaye. Here the French police may ask for passports. Then the train goes across the international bridge over the Bidassoa, and then we get to Irún at once. How fortunate it was that I consulted that agency in London, which arranged our passports and all the tickets and seat-reservations! This journey is rather long, but it has been very comfortable.

(*At the station at Irún. The train has just arrived.* MARTIN *has got the luggage down from the rack.*)

PORTER : Do you need a porter?

MARTIN : Yes. Take these two suitcases and this bag. Do we go with you to the customs ?

PORTER : You will find me there, I will wait for you. You have to go through that door to show your passports, and to fill in some forms that they will give you.

(*At the Customs house, after the inspection of passports.*)

CUSTOMS OFFICER : Are these your cases ? Have you any other luggage ?

MARTIN : Only these two, and this bag. I don't think we have anything to declare, all we have is for our personal use on holiday, during the next few weeks. (*He opens the cases.*)

CUSTOMS OFFICER : Very well. (*He marks the luggage with chalk.*)

MARTIN : Now we can go and find the train for San Sebastián, and as there is plenty of time, we will try to get that cup of coffee I have been wanting !

2 (c)

Muy Srs. míos,

En contestación a su atenta carta fecha 16 del corriente, tengo el gusto de comunicarles que nuestro representante Mr Henry Smith efectuará la visita que nos piden, por el día 28, acompañado de las últimas novedades en géneros de punto.

Esperando queden complacidos con ello, se despiden de Vds, suyo atento ss.ss., q.e.s.m.

George Johnson & Co,

H. W. B.

2 (d)

Dear Sirs,

In accordance with the information in your letter of the 20 inst., we have had the pleasure of receiving a visit from your representative Sr D. José Pérez, and we have offered him any assistance we may be able to give him during his stay here.

We regret that present circumstances do not permit us to order goods from you, but we hope that there may be a better opportunity at some future date.

Yours very truly,

Enrique Alvarez, Ltd.

Notes : 1. *Aviso* means "intimation" or "communication," not "advice", which is *consejo.* 2. *Para lo que pueda ofre- cérsele* means literally "for anything that he may need." 3. *Sentir,* meaning "to be sorry" or "regret", requires the Subjunctive in the next clause. 4. *No nos anime a* implies "does not encourage us to ".

2 (*e*)

Arsenio is quite sure that the ring on the door bell is going to produce some alteration in the normal course of events, and that this alteration will be fatal to his master's amorous supper party. On tiptoe he goes to the door, and noiselessly opens the peephole. Then, overcome with shock and fright, he goes over to Juan Gabriel while the bell is ringing for the second time.

" It's your Uncle Dámaso ! "

" What ! "

" It's your uncle, in person."

Juan Gabriel drops into a chair and almost bursts into tears. His normal customs are always interrupted for days whenever his Uncle Dámaso comes to see him.

" Are you sure ? "

" I saw the hat and basket."

So there is no doubt whatever. The hat and basket are Uncle Dámaso's unmistakable characteristics. For at least forty years he has never taken off his hat, even to sleep, and when he goes on a journey he always takes with him a few dozen new-laid eggs from his own hens. He is quite certain that all the hens in the world, except his own, have their eggs go wrong inside them and then lay them too late. He has never eaten anyone else's hens' eggs, because they always taste of straw, onions, wire, or dirty children. The bell rings for the third time, and Juan Gabriel, before giving the fatal order for the door to be opened, dares to indulge in a few slender hopes.

" Maybe he is only coming for an hour or so."

2 (*f*)

If you were to ask a Frenchman (before the war) what his idea of an Englishman was he would probably answer :

They are hypocrites with practical sense. It is a curious thing that national character is usually summed up by the voice of universal opinion as a pair of features, one a quality, the other a defect. Thus, to the pair hypocrisy–practical sense, which represents the Englishman, correspond clearness–licentiousness for the Frenchman, thoroughness–clumsiness for the German, dignity–cruelty for the Spaniard, vulgarity–vitality for the American. It is as if, in this big village of the world, each individual nation had been sketched down by its neighbours to its fundamental features—more or less accurately understood—and in this operation a good and a bad quality had remained, witnesses to the double origin of the human soul.

3 (a) Exercise

1. El teniente Barno es un hombre muy enfermo. Se le ha enviado a orillas del mar para un período de convalescencia.

2. No toque aquella bandeja. La pintura está aún húmeda.

3. El césped está cubierto de nieve esta mañana. ¡ Qué bonito !

4. Los obreros que empezaron la obra la semana pasada están cubriendo el tejado de tejas.

5. Yo era carpintero, pero ahora soy vendedor de tabacos.

6. Espere aquí un momento. Sólo son las cuatro menos cuarto.

7. ¿Quién es? ¿Quién está ahí?—Soy yo.

8. Necesito nuevos botones para mi manga, éstos están rotos. Muy bien, ésos sirven.

9. Mi yerno es muy joven todavía. Cuando muera su padre, será rico.

10. La viuda Twankey estaba muy enfadada con su hijo.

Notes : 1. " He is very sick " would be *Está muy enfermo*, but the noun " man " in the predicate requires that the verb is *ser*. 4. The literal *está siendo cubierto* is clumsy and unSpanish. In a sentence containing a passive verb, it is usually best in translating to reverse the subject and object, and make the verb active, as in the translation of this sentence given above. 8. *Está bien* would do as well as *muy bien*. 9. The subjunctive after *cuando* when futurity is indicated will be dealt with later in the book under the general heading of the Subjunctive.

3 (b) Conversation

(*Entrance hall of a hotel in San Sebastian.* MARTIN *and* ISABEL *come in from the street, followed by the hotel porter with their cases.*)

ISABEL : Here we are at last. Good Heavens ! What have I done with my hat ? I must have left it in the taxi !

PORTER : It hasn't gone yet, madam. The driver is talking to someone in the street. Shall I ask him to look for your hat ?

ISABEL : Yes, please ! I mustn't lose it. (*The* PORTER *goes off.*) I took it off because it was so hot when we came out of the station.

MARTIN : It doesn't matter much, really, because you won't need it here. As far as I can see, not many Spanish women wear hats in the street. But it will be better if the porter does get it back, because you will want it when we get back to England. How careless you were !

ISABEL : You can say that, this time, and I will let it pass. But I warn you, one of these days it will be you who forgets something, and it may easily be something important.

(*The* PORTER *returns with the hat.*)

ISABEL : Thank you very much indeed ! (*Aside to* MARTIN) Look, Martin, give the porter a tip. You have got all the Spanish money we have.

MARTIN : Of course; I will give him one up in our room, where he will be taking our luggage. (*To the* RECEPTION CLERK) Good morning. My name is Johnson, and I have reserved a room here for three nights. A room with two beds and a bathroom.

THE CLERK : Yes, sir. You wrote to us, didn't you ? It will be number thirty-one, on the second floor, facing the sea. Will you please sign this form and the Visitors' book ? Porter, here is the key of number thirty-one. Take up this gentleman's luggage.

ISABEL : What ? What do I have to write here ? They want me to write my Christian name and surnames, my home address, the number of my passport, and other things, and I don't know what it all means !

MARTIN : Don't worry, it is very easy. I will do it this time, and all you will have to do is sign it at the bottom of the form. (*He writes.*) There, it is done now. Now don't let's be any longer going upstairs. We will change our clothes and tidy up a bit, and then go out and breathe this San Sebastian air, which they say is so pure.

---

3 (c)

Dear Sir,

We beg to inform you that we are the exclusive agents for the export of certain American manufacturers, and we wish to draw your especial attention to our rebuilt typewriters. You will of course understand that these typewriters have been used, but completely taken down, inspected, and cleaned with the greatest care in our factory. We guarantee our typewriters completely.

We enclose in this letter our list of prices.

We supply these typewriters with keyboards for Spanish, French, Portuguese, Italian, or any other language, without any addition to the price.

We are willing to grant you the exclusive agency for our goods in your town and its neighbourhood, if you will favour us with an initial order for five typewriters.

Should you be interested in purchasing any further types of writing materials, we shall be happy to send you, on your request, price lists and samples.

Hoping that you will favour us with an early and favourable reply,

We are,

Yours very truly,

X.Y.Z. & Co.

3 (d)

(JOSEFINA *wants to go to the Theatre, while her husband* RAMÓN *wants to stay at home.* RAMÓN *comes into the drawing-room of their house in Madrid and sees his wife in full evening-dress.*)

RAMÓN : My dear girl !
JOSEFINA : Well, do I look nice ?
RAMÓN : Not . . .

JOSEFINA : What do you mean, don't I ?

RAMÓN : Oh, yes, you look very nice, but that isn't what I mean.

JOSEFINA : Well, what are you looking so surprised about ?

RAMÓN : I'm surprised to see you in this dress.

JOSEFINA : Do you expect me to go about the house without one ?

RAMÓN : This isn't much more than half a one, anyhow ! The neck-line seems very . . .

JOSEFINA : Ah, you think it's too low ? No, it's just rather smart. But if you like I'll put a flower here, in the middle.

RAMÓN : Don't let's discuss the neck-line now. What have you put on evening-dress for if we are staying at home ?

JOSEFINA : Staying at home ?

RAMÓN (*angrily*) : But we settled everything about this at dinner.

JOSEFINA : Don't be angry Moncito,[1] don't be angry !

RAMÓN : Huh ! This is going to be expensive !

JOSEFINA : What ?

RAMÓN : You are calling me Moncito !

JOSEFINA : Well, what about it ?

RAMÓN : When you call me Moncito instead of Ramón ! It makes me really frightened ! Poor Moncito ! *I* know. (*Walks about.*)

JOSEFINA : Oh, Ramoncito, you do get annoyed so easily ! And I can't have a quarrel this evening, the coffee has upset my nerves.

RAMÓN : It's going to upset mine, too.

JOSEFINA : But you didn't have any !

RAMÓN : No, I mean the coffee you had.

JOSEFINA : Ah ! Indeed ! What a delicate way of showing your sympathy.

RAMÓN : Well, why not ?

JOSEFINA : Well, now, let's understand each other. And we'll begin by understanding that we're never to do anything but just what *you* like, dear, just what *you* like. (*Ramón looks at her.*) I understand that you (and I haven't the slightest idea why) wanted to go to some other theatre tonight, instead of going to the Princess's. But I did *not* understand that we weren't going out at all. (*He looks at her again.*) No, I didn't, and don't look at me like that !

RAMÓN : Oh, all right. I suppose I don't understand what I'm saying myself or what you said either,[2] because after all the reasons I gave you, you said we would do what I wanted and not go out, and that you were very pleased because I've got to get up early tomorrow.

JOSEFINA : Indeed ! And I said all this, did I ? How careless I must be ! And after saying all this I went and dressed for the theatre ! How careless ! And you know I've done just what we always do on Wednesdays !

RAMÓN : No, it isn't just what we always do on Wednesdays, because on Wednesdays you always dress *before* dinner.

JOSEFINA : Or after, it depends . . .

(*But in the end they do go to the theatre.*)

Notes : 1. *Moncito* is a diminutive of Ramón, much as " Charlie " is of Charles. 2. Ramón's remark about " talking Greek and hearing in Chinese " needs a freer translation in English to be readily understood.

3 (*e*)

When you kissed me, your lips planted a rose-tree in my lips, and its roots grew and filled my whole heart.

It was autumn. The vast sky's sunlight drew up in columns of splendour all that is golden in the world.

Dry summer has come; all is over now—two buds of sorrow, sprung from the rose-tree, have opened, dully, in my eyes.

4 (*a*) Exercise

1. En el estanco no quedaban cigarros ingleses ni norteamericanos.

2. Algún día le encontraré pero no me dé Vd más queso.

3. A la mañana siguiente me despertó el canto de un tordo en el naranjo oloroso delante de la ventana de mi alcoba.

4. Cordelia era la hija menor del viejo Rey Lear.

5. Su suegra es una persona muy superior; bien pudiera ser la Madre Superiora de un convento.

6. Los jóvenes andaluces no dejaron nada más que una taza y un platillo sucios.

7. Ella fue a él y le dio una bofetada en la cara. Él es demasiado inteligente para hacer eso otra vez.

8. Tres pañuelos de algodón, dos camisas de seda, y un cinturón de cuero.

9. Una tarde encantadora él y ella fueron a contemplar la dorada puesta del sol a través del mar.

10. " Ésta es la regla más vieja de todas en el libro " dijo la Reina.

11. El violinista me dijo que nunca había encontrado a nadie que supiese reparar su violín.

12. Nadie pudo hacer nada que aliviase su dolor.

13. Ningunas novelas, por muy bien que estén escritas, me gustan más que las que he leído de Cervantes.

14. Esto no tiene nada que ver con aquello. ¡ Quítelo Vd !

15. El equipaje era tan pesado que el mozo no pudo menos que dejarlo caer.

16. No debéis comer helados, ni chocolates tampoco, hasta que hayáis tomado el té.

17. Sin hablar a ninguna de las señoras, el cura entró lentamente en la iglesia.

18. En aquel sitio a la orilla del mar había cuatro millas de arena, y en la playa no vimos a nadie.

19. Ya no me siento cansado, así seguiré trabajando. Diga a Jorge que no venga a buscarme todavía.

20. ¿ Ha estado él en Barcelona alguna vez?   ¿ No? Entonces es inútil preguntarle algo acerca de ella.

Notes : 1. *Estanco,* literally a store where goods subject to excise duty are sold, is the word universally used in Spain for a tobacconist's shop.   Postage stamps are almost invariably sold there too.   3. *Canción* is a song usually involving words and music.   Here " canto " is the appropriate word; a famous sixteenth-century poet, Fray Luis de León, wrote of *las aves con su canto suave no aprendido.* 4. *Menor* and *mayor,* placed *after* their nouns, imply " younger " and " older ", respectively, instead of " smaller " and " larger ", their meanings if they go before.   5. *Superiora* occurs only in this context.   No other comparative in -*or* ever has any feminine form ending in -*ora.* 8. It frequently occurs that when an English noun is used as an adjective, the corresponding Spanish requires *de* plus the noun to give the necessary meaning.   There are thus three examples in this sentence. 11 and 12. A relative adjectival clause referring to a negative antecedent requires the verb in the Subjunctive.

4 (b) Conversation

(*The first morning in San Sebastian.*)

ISABEL (*coming out of the hotel*): Where shall we go first?
The only thing I must do is to buy a toothbrush; I have
lost mine somewhere on the journey.

MARTIN: There is a chemist's close by. We can buy you
one on our way back from our walk. Let's go now and
see this famous bay, that they call the Concha. At this
time of day it is sure to be full of people, and as I think
the tide is high there are certain to be some people bathing.

ISABEL: Here we are. How lovely it is! And what vivid
colours! I see now why they call it the Concha, it is shaped
like a shell. What are those hills called? With the little
island between them they almost close the entrance to the
bay.

MARTIN: The one on the right is Monte Urgull, and the one
on the left is Monte Igueldo. They are both public parks,
and there are very fine views from them, over the sea and
country all around. We can walk to one of them this
afternoon when it begins to get cooler. What terrific
sun!

ISABEL: Look, what I should like to do more than anything
is to have a bathe, the water is really most inviting. Shall
we have time to bathe before lunch?

MARTIN: Yes, because in Spain nobody lunches early. We
can stay here in the sun until two o'clock. Let's go to the
hotel and get our bathing-suits, and then go to that establish-
ment over there, we can leave our clothes there while we are
bathing.

(*In the hotel dining-room, at half-past two.*)

ISABEL: My first meal in Spain this year! What are we
going to have to eat?

MARTIN: We shall soon see. In this hotel, which isn't one
of the most important ones, there may be no choice.
(*The* WAITER *appears.*)

WAITER: Are you taking soup?

MARTIN: Yes, please; and will you get us some bread?
There isn't any on this table.

WAITER: I will bring you some at once, sir. How would you
like the eggs done, fried or an omelette?

ISABEL : I should like them fried, but you are very fond of Spanish omelettes, aren't you, Martin ?

MARTIN : Yes, but today I'll have mine fried too. (*To the* WAITER) Two fried eggs each, please. What is to follow ?

WAITER : Today there is Valencian Paella, or roast veal with potatoes and other vegetables.

MARTIN : Bring us veal, we'll try the Paella another day. And for wine, a bottle of Rioja, if you have any.

WAITER : Yes, sir. I will bring it in a few minutes. (*He goes.*)

MARTIN : This seems all right. After our bathe we've got good appetites. If the veal is as good as it smelt on the plate that that other waiter has just taken to that table over there, we shall be having a good meal. What would you like for dessert ?

ISABEL : I don't know yet. Perhaps some fruit. Maria told me that plums are always good in San Sebastian in July.

MARTIN : Here comes the waiter with the eggs. Now let's eat !

---

4 (c)

Señor :

He leído en el " A.B.C." de hoy que necesita Vd una persona que sepa francés para trabajar de secretario particular, y por lo tanto me permito dirigirme a Vd para ofrecerle mis servicios.

Soy natural de Sevilla, donde hace cinco años que terminé mis estudios en la Escuela de Comercio. Desde entonces he estado desempeñando el puesto de ayudante de Tenedor de Libros en la sucursal de la casa de Záuregui, en Madrid. Mis jefes con gusto darán las referencias necesarias acerca de mi persona. Domino perfectamente las lenguas inglesa y francesa, y tengo bastante práctica en trabajos de traducción. Soy buen taquígrafo, y puedo agregar que tengo buena presencia y que soy trabajador. Tengo 26 años y soy soltero.

Puedo, pues, desempeñar el puesto que se ofrece.

Esperando me otorgue una entrevista personal, me es grato ofrecerme de Vd,

atto y s.s.

Julio Oliver Quintana

4 (d)

Dear Sir,

     We are in receipt of your letter of yesterday's date, and in view of the fact that we are interested in your proposal to join our firm, we beg to request that you will attend for personal interview at the above address on Thursday next, 14 inst., at 7 p.m.

     Looking forward to the pleasure of meeting you,

We are,

Yours faithfully,

" Alianza Española "

4 (e)

We were approaching Seville ! My heart was beating fast. For me, Seville had always been the symbol of light, the city of love and laughter. How much more so at this moment, when I was going there in love ! Orange groves were already to be seen, and among the emerald-coloured leaves there hung full-juiced oranges that were bursting with ripeness, like globes of rubies, as an Arab poet has said. At the next stations, Brenes, Tocina, and Empalme, I noticed some little animation, which could not have been caused by the travellers, who were far from numerous. Black-eyed girls with red carnations in their hair were standing on the platforms, smiling at those of us who were looking out of the windows. At every level-crossing the cottages had pots of flowers at the windows, and even the poorly-dressed old women who kept the crossings, furling their flags as they let the train go through, wore in their grey hair a carnation or a gilliflower.

4 (f)

Five or six days went by without don Pedro needing to ride his new horse. Then one day he ordered his servant to clean and harness the horse because he intended to go to Mieres. The servant appeared a few moments later and said :

" Do you know, sir, that León (this was the nag's name) has white stains on him that won't come off ? "

" Give him a good cleaning, then, you fool. He must have rubbed himself against the wall."

Although the servant did all he could, he was unable to get rid of the stains. Then the priest said angrily :

" I am going to prove to you, Manuel, that you have forgotten what elbow-grease is. You'll soon see how quickly these stains can be got rid of."

And taking off his cassock and rolling up his shirt-sleeves, he took the brush and scraper, and himself began to clean the horse. But his hopes proved vain. Not only did the stains not disappear, but they grew steadily larger.

" Here, bring me some hot water and soap," he said, finally, vexed and perspiring.

Then the truth was revealed ! The water immediately turned red, and the white stains on the horse spread until they covered almost his whole body.

To cut a long story short, they scrubbed him so hard that half an hour later the brown horse had disappeared, and a white one stood in his place.

Manual stepped back a few yards, and with consternation in his face exclaimed :

" Upon my soul, if it isn't Pichón ! "

5 (a) Exercise

Hace frío esta mañana, pero aun si hiciera más calor, yo tendría frío todavía. Siento el frío hasta en mis huesos. Hace quince años que vivo aquí, y no creo que nunca haya hecho jamás tanto frío como ahora, excepto una vez hace tres o cuatro años cuando heló seis semanas seguidas. Después de una helada hay siempre mucho lodo, por muy fuerte que brille el sol, y esto es siempre muy desagradable. Durante aquella helada, hacía una media hora que trataba yo de derretir el agua en la cañería de mi cuarto de baño cuando el mayor de los caños explotó, y resultó un revoltijo terrible.

¿Cuánto tiempo lleva Vd en esta ciudad ? ¿Solamente dos años ? Entonces no podría haber recordado esto. Debe haber pasado antes que Vd viniera. Déme una taza de té, deseo beberla cuando esté caliente.

Notes: 1. " No matter how powerful." This has the same meaning as " however powerful," and the idiom in such cases is found in the formula " *por* plus adjective plus *que* plus a *subjunctive* verb." 2. " How long have you been living in this town ? "—The translation given above is a useful alternative to the equally correct *¿ Cuánto tiempo hace que vive Vd en esta ciudad ?*

5 (b) Conversation

(*A café in the principal square in Pamplona.* MARTIN *sits down on the terrace.*)

MARTIN (*to himself*) : How hot it is this morning ! (*To a* GENTLEMAN *who is sitting at the next table*)   Good morning ! I had not seen you.   How do you do ?

THE GENTLEMAN : Very well, thank you, how are you ? It is two days since I have seen you.

MARTIN : Yes, yesterday, as the weather was so splendid we went on an excursion to Roncesvalles. Today my wife is very tired, and she hasn't got up yet. (*To the* WAITER, *who is approaching*) Black coffee, please. (*To the* GENTLEMAN)   Are you here on holiday ?

THE GENTLEMAN : Not exactly, because I am a representative of a business house in Madrid, and I have some business to do here. But as I have an uncle and aunt here in Pamplona, whenever I come here I feel at home, and on holiday. How do you like the hotel ?

MARTIN : We think it is very good. A friend of mine recommended it to me in England, and we do really like it. It is very quiet and well situated, with magnificent views of the hills from the balcony of our room.

THE GENTLEMAN : Had you just arrived when we met the other evening ?

MARTIN : Yes, and what an extraordinary journey we had had !

THE GENTLEMAN : Why was it extraordinary ?

MARTIN : Well, we came up from San Sebastian on that narrow-gauge line. Once outside the neighbourhood of San Sebastian the train goes through a lot of tunnels that are positively frightening, and between them there are superb views of the mountains of Navarre. It takes less time to get here than one might think, but how dirty we were when we did finally reach the station at Pamplona !

THE GENTLEMAN : You would have done better to go the other way, through Alsasua, more comfortable trains run on that line.   But still, it is all good experience.

MARTIN (*seeing* ISABEL, *who has come out of the front door of the hotel into the square*) : Here is my wife. (*The gentlemen stand up, and the necessary introductions are made.*) What would you like to drink ? The waiter will be back in a minute.

ISABEL : Orangeade, a long, cool one. The heat this morning is stifling.

MARTIN : Wait till this afternoon. It will be much worse then.

ISABEL : Maybe. But this morning I want to go to some place in Pamplona where it is fairly cool. Can you advise us ?

THE GENTLEMAN : The only thing I can suggest is that you should go to the Cathedral, it is very interesting and very famous.

MARTIN : Let's go there at once. (*To the* WAITER *who comes with the orangeade*) How much do I owe you ? I want to settle while I have a minute to spare, we are going as soon as my wife has finished her orangeade. (*He gives a bank-note to the* WAITER, *who gives him his change.*)

ISABEL : There ! That's it. I'm sure I have drunk it much too fast, but at least I'm not thirsty any more. Let's go now to the Cathedral, it will be much cooler there. If I don't go there I shall melt ! (MARTIN *and* ISABEL *say good-bye to the* GENTLEMAN *and go.*)

---

5 (c)

Santa Bernarda, 87,
Madrid
14 de mayo de 19—

José Pérez y Cía,
Encina, 7,
Madrid

Muy Sres nuestros,

Nos permitimos dirigir a Vds la presente para suplicarles se sirvan darnos algunos informes en cuanto a la persona cuyo nombre y señas figuran en el papelito que adjuntamos.

Dicha persona nos ha indicado la apreciable firma de Vds como referencia, y les quedaríamos muy agradecidos por cualesquier informes tuvieran a bien suministrarnos. Excusados nos parece asegurarles que haremos el uso más discreto de todo informe que Vds tengan la amabilidad de comunicarnos.

Sin otro particular por ahora, nos ofrecemos de Vds, muy attos y afmos ss.ss.

q.l.e.l.m.

Martínez Rosas y Cía.

5 (d)

Ramón Campos de Olivera y Cía,
Garaje Moderno,
Canfranc
18 July, 19—

Sres G. y J. Ramírez,
Adelfas, 38,
Sevilla

Dear Sirs,

I beg to acknowledge receipt of your letter of the 10th inst., for which I thank you. I have much pleasure in replying to your offer, and I regret that I have been absent for a few days and unable to reply earlier.

I have no objection to advertising your garage by distributing cards, which I should receive from you, to any cars crossing the frontier at this point en route for Seville. This is frequently the case with French people resident in Morocco, who return home from France via Canfranc. I shall naturally direct my chief attention to them.

As payment for these services I suggest the following :

150 pesetas monthly from October to March,
250   ,,   ,,   ,, April to September,

since in the latter period there is a greater volume of traffic.

Your cards should be stamped with the word CANFRANC which would enable you to gauge the extent of business that you receive through my recommendation.

I should add that this arrangement will be without

obligation on either side, and subject to cancellation by either party without notice.

Yours faithfully,

R. Campos de Olivera

---

5 (e)

Doña Perfecta felt as though a flame of fire rose from her heart to her lips. She felt suffocated, and only her black eyes, blacker than night itself, answered her daughter.

" Mother! I hate everything that is not Pepe! " exclaimed Rosario. " Hear me confess to you, I want to confess to everyone, and to you first."

" You will kill me! You are killing me! "

" I want to confess, so that you will pardon me. This weight is bearing down on me, and crushing life out of me! "

" It is the weight of a sin! Add to it the curse of God, and then try to move under the burden, unhappy girl! Only I can take it away from you! "

" No! Not you! You cannot take it away! " cried Rosario in despair. " But listen to me, I want to confess it all. . . . Afterwards cast me out of this house, cast me out of my home."

" I cast you out? "

" I shall go, all the same."

" Never! I will show you what you have forgotten, I will show you a daughter's duties."

" Then I shall escape from here. He will take me with him."

" Did he say this, is this his suggestion and arrangement? " asked Doña Perfecta, hurling the words at her daughter like lashes from a whip.

" Yes, it is his suggestion. We are going to be married. It must be like this, Mother. . . . I will indeed love you, I know I must love you. God will damn me if I do not."

She folded her arms and, kneeling down, kissed her mother's feet.

" Rosario, Rosario! " exclaimed Doña Perfecta in a terrible voice. " Stand up! "

There was a brief pause.

" Has this man written to you? "

" Yes."

" Have you seen him again since that night? "

" Yes."

" Have you written to him, too? "

" Yes, I have written to him, too. Oh! Why are you looking at me like this? You cannot be my mother! "

" I wish to God I were not! Go and rejoice in the harm you are doing to me! You are killing me, killing me! " shouted Doña Perfecta, in the greatest agitation. " You say that this man . . ."

" He is my husband. I shall be his, protected by the law. . . . Why are you looking at me like that? You are making me afraid! No woman could look like that! . . . Mother! Do not let me be damned! "

" What you have done has damned you already. Now, obey me and I will forgive you. . . . Answer me: when did you last have letters from this man? "

" Today."

" Infamous treason! " exclaimed the mother. " Did you arrange to meet? "

" Yes."

" When? "

" Tonight."

" Where? "

" Here—here. I confess it all, everything. I know that it is a crime. . . . I am a sinner, but you, Mother, you must rescue me from Hell. Say that you will, say one word to me! "

" That man here, in my house! " cried Doña Perfecta, striding to the middle of the room.

Rosario followed her, still on her knees. At the same moment three bangs resounded through the house, crashing as though three cannons had been fired. It was Maria Remedios, pounding with her whole heart on the knocker. The house shook as if in awful terror. Mother and daughter remained still like statues, listening.

A servant went down to open the door, and a moment later Maria Remedios, more like a basilisk wrapped in a cloak than a woman, entered Doña Perfecta's room. Her face seemed ablaze with anxiety.

"He is there, he is there," she said as she came in. "He has gone into the orchard through the little private door!"

---

6 (a) Exercise

1. No me lo diga Vd ahora, ¡ cállese !
2. Abriendo la ventana, vi que brillaba el sol.
3. No lo compraron para dármelo a mí, sino para mi padre.
4. ¿Dónde te has escondido? Quiero dar un paseo contigo enseguida.
5. El cura no puede dárnoslos hoy, porque su hermano todavía no se los ha devuelto a él.

Notes: 2. Not *en abriendo*. *En* rarely precedes the Present Participle in Spanish, and if it does the meaning is then that of a Perfect Participle: "after having . . . (opened)". 3. *Sino* is required instead of *pero*, because the word "but" introduces words which *contradict a previous negative*. If "but" introduces a clause which contains a verb, however, either *pero* or *sino que* must be used, not *sino* alone, e.g.,

> *No es que no lo entienda, sino que no lo quiere entender.*
> It isn't that he doesn't understand it, but he doesn't want to.

5. Note the use of *devolver* "for to return a thing borrowed," i.e., "to give back."

6 (b) Conversation

(MARTIN *and* ISABEL *are crossing the principal square in Burgos. It is half-past nine on a fine July morning.*)

ISABEL : I like this town immensely, Martin. Its atmosphere is most interesting. Why didn't you tell me about it before we came here ?

MARTIN : I don't know. I've always liked it a great deal too. The fact is, there are such a lot of beautiful towns in Spain that one can't talk about all of them at once. Let's go now and see a little museum that is close by here. It contains things to do with the Cid.

ISABEL : Shan't we go first to the Cathedral? I saw its towers this morning from our bedroom window in the hotel, and it looks magnificent.

MARTIN : We'll go there later. But first, you ought to know something about the Cid, who was one of the most important figures in medieval Spain. He lived in the time of our William the Conqueror, and when he was exiled by the King of Castile he went to Valencia with a sort of private army, fighting the Moors. He drove them out, and reigned as a prince in Valencia until his death.

ISABEL : You talk like a schoolmaster. But what is that great piece of wall over there with that gate in the middle ?

MARTIN : We go up that way to the museum I told you about, it is over the old entrance to the city. As you know, Burgos in the Middle Ages was the capital of Castile, and one of the most important towns in the whole of Spain.

(*They reach the entrance to the museum.*)

MARTIN : Two tickets for the museum, please.

THE KEEPER : Yes, sir. But I am sorry that at this time in the morning I can't change that twenty-five-peseta note. Haven't you any less ?

MARTIN : Let's see. Yes, I have got enough change. (*The KEEPER gives him the tickets.*) Are we the first here this morning ?

THE KEEPER : No, sir. Two visitors have just gone in.

MARTIN : Let's go up, Isabel.

(*In the museum.*)

ISABEL : Look who's here ! Antonio and Maria ! What luck ! We didn't know you were in Burgos.

MARIA : Fancy meeting you here, Isabel ! I'm very glad to see you. We came yesterday, and as we were rather tired after our very long ride through France we are spending the day here resting.

ANTONIO : It's the car that needs a rest more than we do. They are repairing it now in the hotel garage. Well, how are you ? What sort of a journey have you had ?

MARTIN : We're all right, thanks. We went up from San Sebastian to Pamplona, because I'm very fond of Navarre and its mountains, and we came here yesterday. Tomorrow we are going on towards Madrid.

ANTONIO : That's lucky, so are we ! I have just reserved a

room in a hotel at the Escorial for tomorrow night. Will
you come with us? There will be enough room in the car
if we rearrange the luggage a bit, and you will be able to
avoid the trouble of the train journey, and all that.

ISABEL : Thanks very much, Antonio. We are very glad to
accept. I always think travelling by car is much better
than by train, because in a car you go through the middle
of the towns and villages, which are much more interesting
than the stations.

MARTIN : Thank you, Antonio. I'll telephone to the Escorial
to reserve a room, too. Let's go now and have something
cool to drink in a café.

ISABEL : We haven't seen much of this museum!

MARTIN : I'll tell you all about it afterwards. Come on down
these stairs.

---

6 (c)

(*A* FOREIGNER *and a Spanish* FRIEND *go into a Madrid bank.*)

FOREIGNER : This is where I can change my travellers' cheques,
isn't it?

FRIEND : Yes. Go to that counter with the label " Ex-
changes ", and the clerk will tell you what to do. In some
banks there is a counter with the words " Foreign Exchange ", but as this is not a big branch there isn't one here.

FOREIGNER (*to the* CLERK) : I have here some travellers'
cheques from my bank in England, and I want to change
thirty pounds into pesetas.

CLERK : Yes, sir. Have you your passport with you?

FOREIGNER : Yes, here it is.

CLERK : Good, then sign the cheques, please.

FOREIGNER : Do I have to endorse them too?

CLERK : No, that is not necessary.

> (*After making some calculations on a form the* CLERK
> *returns to him his passport and the remaining cheques
> that he is not cashing that day, and he gives him a
> metal token stamped with the number* 71.)

FOREIGNER (*to his* FRIEND) : What do I do with this?

FRIEND : You have to wait now until the cashier, that man
behind the counter over there where you see the label
" Cash ", calls the number seventy-one. It is the cashier's
business to settle in this way all transactions in which the
bank pays cash.

FOREIGNER : Will he be a long time?

FRIEND : No, I don't think so, because your transaction is a very simple one.

CASHIER : Number sixty-nine !

FOREIGNER : It isn't my turn yet.

FRIEND : No, but it soon will be.

CASHIER (*a minute later*) : Number seventy-one !

FOREIGNER (*giving his metal token to the cashier*) : That's me.

CASHIER : Shall I give you your money in two 1,000-peseta notes and the rest in smaller notes ?

FOREIGNER : Yes, that will do nicely.

    (*He receives his money and they go out into the street.*)

6 (*d*)

Antoñona, taking advantage of the hour in which the servants dined and Don Pedro slept, had penetrated thus far without being observed, and had opened the door of the room and closed it behind her so gently that Don Luis, even if he had been less absorbed in meditation than he was, would not have noticed it.

She had come resolved to hold a very serious conference with Don Luis, but she did not quite know what she was going to say to him. Nevertheless, she had asked heaven or hell, whichever of the two it may have been, to loosen her tongue and bestow on her the gift of speech; not such grotesque and vulgar speech as she generally used, but correct, elegant, and adapted to the noble reflections and beautiful things she thought it necessary to say, in order to carry out her purpose.

When Don Luis saw Antoñona, he frowned, and showed by his manner how much this visit displeased him, at the same time saying roughly :

" What do you want here ? Go away ! "

" I have come to call you to account about my young mistress," returned Antoñona quietly, " and I shall not go away until you have answered me."

She then drew a chair towards the table and sat down in it, facing Don Luis with coolness and effrontery.

Don Luis, seeing there was no help for it, restrained his anger, armed himself with patience, and, in a less harsh tone than before, exclaimed :

" Say what you have to say ! "

7 (a) Exercise

1. ¿Dónde están mis huesos? dijo el perro. ¡Démelos en seguida!

2. No me gusta esperar a que ellos entren para comer.

3. Tráigame seis sellos de cincuenta céntimos, y cuatro de dos pesetas, cuando vaya al correo.

4. Todavía no conocemos al Señor Sánchez, preséntenos, por favor.

5. Aguardándole horas seguidas en el jardín, Elena cogió grandes ramilletes de madreselvas y geranios.

6. No lo pongas aquí, quítalo, dijo la madre a la niña revoltosa.

7. ¿Ha escrito para pedirles que nos lo manden?

8. "Lo siento," sollozó la muchacha, "Lo dejé caer pero no quise romperlo."

9. Me gusta aquella mesa, que tiene la alfombra roja debajo de ella.

10. Vd ha de entrar después que yo, pero antes que él.

11. ¿Quién es aquel hombre con la nariz grande y roja?

12. ¿Cuáles son los cisnes que pertenecen a la reina? Son aquéllos que nadan en el estanque, pero no se pueden ver desde aquí.

13. El autobús que él conduce se fabricó en la factoría que visitamos la semana pasada.

14. Aquélla es la puerta por la que se pasa a los retretes de señores.

15. ¿De quién es el manojo de plátanos que Jorge halló en el coche?

Notes: 3. *De a* . . . is sometimes used in this type of expression instead of *de*. E.g., *Un paquete de a cinco pesetas*—obviously *un paquete de cinco pesetas* might mean five pesetas wrapped up together. 8. *Sentir* meaning "to be sorry" occurs in either of two constructions. One says *Lo siento*, meaning "I am sorry", but if one means "I am sorry that . . ." (i.e., if there is a continuation of the sentence after the words "I am sorry") the Spanish is *Siento que* . . . and the following clause contains a Subjunctive; or *Siento* . . . followed by a dependent Infinitive. One does *not* say *lo siento que* . . . 10. *Después que* and *antes que* are needed here, not *después de* and *antes de*, as the expressions are elliptical, and imply " after I *go in*, before you *go in*." 15. *Plátano* is much more commonly used in Spanish than *banana*.

---

7 (*b*) Conversation

At El Escorial

(*The four friends are sitting in a hotel garden, under some trees. From it there is a very fine and extensive view.*)

MARTIN : Now that we have seen the palace and visited the town, and had a splendid lunch, what are we going to do this afternoon ?

ANTONIO : Good heavens ! How energetic you are ! After all that, all I want to do is to have a siesta.

ISABEL : Yes, of course. Even if it is very hot this afternoon, it's very pleasant in this garden. I would rather stay here, where there is a splendid view of the palace and the mountains ; I don't want to go in and sleep in my room.

ANTONIO : Well, you must excuse me. I do need an hour or two's sleep. Shall we go to our room, Maria ?

MARIA : No, you are more tired than I am, and that's quite natural, because you have been driving the car for hours and hours together ever since we left London a week ago. You go to sleep, and I'll stay here with Isabel and Martin.

ANTONIO : Very well, good-bye. (*He goes.*)

MARIA : Which part of the palace did you like best this morning, Isabel ? The church, Philip II's rooms, or the tombs ?

ISABEL : I really don't know what to say. The church is very much like others I have seen in Spain, except that there are a few very interesting things in it, those famous statues of Charles V and his family, for instance. Philip II's rooms were much less gloomy than I expected, someone told me in England that I shouldn't like them at all, because they were all dark and severe. On the contrary, they impressed me a great deal, because they are not too big, like many rooms in royal palaces, and they are furnished with tables and chairs and other things so well arranged that one can easily imagine how the king and his family lived there and slept in those very beds.

MARIA : Yes, quite. But did you like the tombs, and the royal mausoleum, down underneath ?

ISABEL : Yes, that was exciting. That round chapel, with the coffins of all the kings of Spain since the sixteenth century, all so imposing in marble, I shall never forget it. But a place like that can't be exactly gay. The monument I liked best was the tomb of Don Juan de Austria, who is lying there so beautifully carved in marble that he seems to be asleep. He was the one that the guide said had fought against the Turks, wasn't he, Martin?

MARTIN : Yes, the Spanish fleet under his command destroyed the Turkish Navy, which was then threatening Christian Europe, at Lepanto, off the coast of Greece, in 1571.

ISABEL : What a head you have for dates! I just forget them at once.

MARTIN : What time do you expect to be leaving tomorrow, Maria?

MARIA : I don't know, but it will probably be about ten o'clock. Antonio wants to spend a few days at a place he knows in the Sierra de Guadarrama before we go on to Madrid. You can't see it from here, it is farther round to the left, but it is very beautiful. I went with him there once, a good many years ago; you go up the road from Cercedilla to the top of the pass of Navacerrada, and there right on the pass is the hotel, six thousand feet up. We shall get there in time for lunch, I hope. What about you? Are you leaving early for Madrid?

MARTIN : Yes, we shall catch a train, it doesn't matter which. Now they have electrified this piece of the railway line the journey from here to Madrid is very pleasant. I should like to get to Madrid fairly early, because we have to find a *pensión* that will suit us. I have telephoned already to one I know, but their telephone wasn't working; anyhow, I couldn't get through to them.

ISABEL : But at this time of year we are sure to have no difficulty in finding a room in some *pensión*, because there are lots of people away on holiday.

MARTIN : Of course. And now, if you don't need me here any more, I am going for a walk. I want to see that thing I've heard so much about, " Philip II's chair ".

MARIA : You want to do that at this time of day? The man was quite right when he said that only mad dogs and Englishmen go out in the midday sun.

(*But Martin does go off for his walk.*)

7 (c)

Dear Sir,

It is anticipated that a 5% increase in customs duties on imported pottery and china goods will be imposed as from the 25th of next month. We therefore intend to replenish our stocks before this increase takes place.

Having consulted our stock books, I have made out an order (which I enclose) for goods to the value of £400, which on receipt of the said goods will be credited to your account with us.

I must repeat that it is essential for these goods to reach this country before the 25th of next month, as otherwise they would be subject to the increased import duties, and this order would then be useless.

Yours faithfully,
(Henry Smith)

7 (d) (A reply)

Juan Rodríguez,
San Gabriel, 97,
Madrid
20 de abril de 19—

Al Sr D. Henry Smith,
284, Newgate St.,
London, E.C.3

Muy Sr mío,

En contestación a su atenta carta fecha 15 del corriente, he de comunicarle, que con fecha de hoy, los productos detallados en su extracto de pedido no. 3257 han sido enviados por medio de la agencia de transportes " la Europea " de la cual le adjunto su recibo de mercancías.

Sin otro particular, y de nuevo en espera de sus gratas órdenes, se despide de Vd,

s.s. q.e.s.m.

(Juan Rodríguez)

7 (e)

" Ave María Purísima ! Half-past twelve and a calm night ! "

The night-watchman whose duty it was to call this round the streets of the town was in process of so doing, when the miller's wife and the Corregidor, riding on the miller's donkeys, Señor Juan López on his mule, and the two constables with them on foot, reached the door of the Corregidor's house. The door was shut. It seemed as though everything had finished for the day, as far as concerned the Government, as well as the people it governed.

" This is bad," thought Garduña. And he knocked on the knocker two or three times.

There was a long pause, but no one opened the door or answered the knocking. Señá Frasquita had turned very pale. The Corregidor had bitten all his finger-nails in his emotion. Nobody said a word.

Pum ! Pum ! Pum ! The two constables and Señor Juan López knocked again on the door of the Corregimiento. Nothing happened. No one answered. The door remained closed ; not a fly stirred.

The only sound was the trickling of water in the fountain in the courtyard inside the house. Minutes went by, seeming like eternity. Finally, about one o'clock, a small window on the second floor opened, and a woman's voice said :

" Who is it ? "

" That's the children's nurse," murmured Garduña.

" It's me ! " replied Don Eugenio de Zúñiga. " Open the door ! "

There was a moment's pause.

" And who are you ? " replied the nurse.

" Can't you hear me ? I am the master of the house, the Corregidor ! "

There was another pause.

" Go away, and good night to you ! " replied the good woman. " My master came in an hour ago, and went straight to bed. You go to bed too, and sleep off the wine you must be so full of ! "

And the window shut with a bang.

8 (*a*) Exercise

Present Indicative.	Past Historic.	Present Subjunctive.
1. muestra	mostró	muestre
mostramos	mostramos	mostremos
consiente	consintió	consiente
consentimos	consentimos	consintamos
duerme	durmió	duerma
dormimos	dormimos	durmamos
2. pienso	pensé	piense
piensan	pensaron	piensen
prefiero	preferí	prefiera
prefieren	prefirieron	prefieran
corrijo	corregí	corrija
corrigen	corrigieron	corrijan
3. comienzas	comenzaste	comiences
comenzáis	comenzasteis	comencéis
vistes	vestiste	vistas
vestís	vestisteis	vistáis
sirves	serviste	sirvas
servís\	servisteis	sirváis
4. sugiere	sugirió	sugiera
sugieren	sugirieron	sugieran
pide	pidió	pida
piden	pidieron	pidan
atraviesa	atravesó	atraviese
atraviesan	atravesaron	atraviesen

5. Muriendo, contando, gimiendo.
6. Duerme, vuelve.
7. Sintiese, sintiésemos; encontrase, encontrásemos; impidiese, impidiésemos.

8 (*b*) Exercise

1. Empiece a poner la red ahora, antes que comience a llover, para que así tal vez podamos jugar al tenis esta tarde.
2. Ella pidió un diccionario mejor, y él sugirió que siguiera la costumbre usual y que comprara un ejemplar de este grande.

3. El mísero profesor corrigió los temas de los alumnos la misma tarde, y se los devolvió al día siguiente.

4. " Lo siento, prefiero ir por otro camino," dijo el Arzobispo.

5. " Siento muchísimo que prefieras eso, porque no hay otro camino," respondió su hermana.

6. Ríete, y el mundo reirá contigo; llora, y llorarás solo.

7. La reina atraviesa la carretera, mirando a la izquierda para ver si viene algún coche, y luego huele el azahar en el naranjo cerca del estanque.

8. En Madrid riegan las calles varias veces al día para impedir que haya demasiado polvo; a menos que llueva, por supuesto.

9. " Ciérrate los ojos y duérmete en seguida, niño travieso," repitió la niñera.

10. Tan pronto como el tren salió de Granada, los niños empezaron a reñir violentamente entre sí, para ver cuál de ellos se sentaría junto a su madre.

Note : The verbs *empezar, comenzar, seguir,* and *corregir,* used in this exercise, have in addition to their radical changes, orthographic changes that are explained in the next lesson.

Oler has the special peculiarity that when its *o* changes to *ue,* the initial *h* must be added; it is a rule of Spanish orthography that no word may begin with the diphthong *ue* or *ie.*

8 (c)

The sun was rising behind Peñalara as we left the Escorial, and as it was the end of July, the heat was greater than we could comfortably enjoy. A cool breeze sprang up from the north soon after we reached the open country, however, and we arrived at the foot of the mountain railway, at Cercedilla, about ten o'clock without feeling too hot and tired. The railway runs up the left of the valley, while the road winds its way up on the right, amongst the pine-groves and crags that lie along the lower slopes of this steep mountain-side. Half-way up, the road passes through the little collection of houses known as El Ventorrillo, at an exposed point from which a magnificent view can be had over the whole of the lower part of the valley, and at any hour of the day the sun plays on the Siete Picos, to the right, La Maliciosa to the left, and on the open plains of Castile, with their indistinct vermilion-coloured horizon away in the distance to the west. We reached the hotel at the head of the valley in time for a late lunch.

8 (d) Exercise

(a) We are despatching it to you by registered post.

(b) I have learned by today's post that our clients wish to receive them within the next month.

(c) Kindly reply by return.

(d) The " P.O. Box " is the box in which the Post Office nearest to the address of a business man or private individual deposits all the latter's correspondence, so that his representatives can collect it at any hour. He can thus receive his post earlier than by the usual delivery, because when the mail arrives at the Post Office correspondence addressed to the Post Boxes is distributed immediately, whilst if it is to be delivered home, there must always be a slight delay, because the postman, on leaving the Post Office, has to cover a long round.

8 (e)

Again the sombre swallows will return
To hang their nests beneath your balcony eaves,
And on swift wings athwart your window-panes
Again will wheel and cry.

But those that did not fly away till late,
That stayed to watch your beauty and my joy,
That lingered there and came to know our names,
No, they will not return.

Again upon your garden walls will climb
The honeysuckle, thick, fragrant, and sweet,
And in the afternoon, more lovely still,
Their flowers will open wide.

But those, that glistened with the dew, whose drops
We watched, all trembling on the blooms, to fall
Like tears from out the scorching heat of day,
    No, those will not return.

Again the burning words of love will fall
Upon your listening ear, and shall perhaps
Awaken from its sound, unheeding sleep,
    Your deeply dreaming heart.

But as I knelt, still, silent, and devout,
As men before his altar worship God,
Make no mistake, as I have worshipped you,
    None else will ever love.

9 (a) Exercise

1. rezo, reza; pago, paga; saco, saca; venzo, vence; esparzo, esparce; corrijo, corrige.
2. (Past Historic) recé, rezó; pagué, pagó; saqué, sacó; vencí, venció; esparcí, esparció; corregí, corrigió.

(Present Subjunctive) rece, rece; pague, pague; saque, saque; venza; venza; esparza, esparza; corrija, corrija.

9 (b) Exercise

1. Págueme lo que me debe tan pronto como pueda.
2. Saqué de mi bolsillo todo mi dinero, y luego ella sacó de su bolso todo el suyo.
3. Recoja aquellas naranjas antes que los niños las esparzan por todo el suelo.
4. Distingamos claramente entre esto y aquello.
5. Nuestro viejo jardinero construyó un hermoso muro, largo de cincuenta metros, al fondo del vergel.
6. Yo conozco a Martín y él me conoce a mí, pero no voy a esperar hasta que aparezca aquí.
7. Busque en la enciclopedia y averigüe todas las fechas de las cuales no está seguro.
8. Le pegué porque él me pegó a mí primero.
9. " Cuando lleguemos a Barcelona, le compraré un crisantemo blanco," dijo el panadero.
10. Esperamos acabar nuestro trabajo mucho antes que anochezca.

9 (c) Conversation

(*Madrid.   Vestibule of a building in the Calle de Goya.   MARTIN and ISABEL have just got out of the taxi that has brought them from the station.*)

MARTIN : Here we are at last. (*To the* CONCIERGE, *who is looking out of his room*)   Good morning.   Will you please tell me which floor we go to for the *pensión*, is it the third or the fourth ?

CONCIERGE : The fourth, sir.   But unluckily the lift isn't working today, you will have to walk up.

MARTIN : What !   Isn't it working ?   The last time I was here it was almost always out of order.   Never mind, I will carry the suitcases.   (*To* ISABEL)   Can you manage that bag of yours and my little case ?

ISABEL : Of course.   Let's go up.

(*At the* pensión *door.*)

MARTIN (*to the servant who opens the door*): Good morning. May I speak to the señorita (i.e., proprietress) ?

SERVANT : Yes, sir.   What name shall I say ?

MARTIN : Johnson.   Perhaps the señorita will remember me. I stayed here for a while six years ago, and I have come this time with my wife.   We want to know if there is a room vacant, to stay here for a couple of weeks.

SERVANT : I will go and see, sir.   I will tell the señorita. Come in and take a seat here, please.   (*The servant goes in,* MARTIN *and* ISABEL *enter the* pensión.)

(*Some hours afterwards, when they have fixed up their stay at the* pensión, MARTIN *and* ISABEL *are in their room, which is a large one with a balcony overlooking the street.*)

ISABEL : How glad I am to be here at the end of this part of the journey !   I like seeing new places, but I don't like so much travelling about.   Here we can unpack our cases and feel at home.   Do you think that servant will be able to get some clothes washed for us ?   Some of my things need washing most urgently.

MARTIN : Yes, of course.   Laundry work in Spain is done magnificently and very fast.   It is because with this sun everything they wash dries at once, and besides, Spanish washerwomen are excellent at ironing.   I have some shirts and a pair of pyjamas to be washed, too.   Let's arrange our things a bit now, and then we can go for a walk, because it is half-past six, and it's getting cooler.

ISABEL : At what time do they serve dinner in this *pensión* ?
MARTIN : If I remember rightly, not before ten. People in Madrid always dine very late.
ISABEL : Then we shall have lots of time for our walk. Come on !

9 (d)

Dear Sirs,

I desire to subscribe to your review entitled " Rango " for a period of three months. I request you therefore to inform me of the price of the subscription for this period, and of the best way of remitting the payment to you.

Yours very truly,

Peter Brown

9 (e)

Casa Editorial " Rango ",
Alcalá, 215,
Madrid
10 de octubre de 19—

Mr. Peter Brown,
304, Smith Street,
London, S.W.1

Muy Señor nuestro,

En contestación a su atenta carta fecha 3.10.56 sentimos comunicarle que la subscripción mínima de esta revista es por un período de seis meses. El precio de dicha subscripción es de sesenta pesetas y el pago habrá de hacerse por adelantado, pudiendo efectuarse en la forma que más le convenga.

Sin otro particular y en espera de sus gratas órdenes se despiden de Vd, suyos afmos.

q.e.s.m.

Casa Editorial " Rango "

9 (f)

A sudden clash of swords was heard, then a cry, a dying cry, a cry that rent the heart, striking with terror all who heard it, freezing them to the very marrow of their bones; a cry of one who was bidding his last farewell to this world.

The noise ceased, a muffled man passed by and pulled his hat down carefully over his eyes. Gliding alongside the wall of a church, he crossed over and was lost in the darkness.

He passed down a narrow, high-walled street, the Street of the Coffin, that was clothed in gloom as though eternally shrouded in a cloak of darkest crape; at night the only light in it was the lamp burning beside an image of Christ. As the muffled man passed near the Cross, the lamp shone for one bright moment on the drawn sword which he still held in his hand.

10 (a) Exercise

1. No pudiendo abrir la lata, la puso otra vez en el estante del armario.

2. " Ven acá y dime la verdad, Juanito," dijo su abuela.

3. Si yo condujese aquel coche demasiado aprisa, lo más probable es que me saldría de él.

4. Trataré de ver a la duquesa ahora, antes de que vaya a Australia.

5. ¿Quisiera Vd que supiera Jorge lo que estamos haciendo?

6. " Oye, sal en seguida, y espera en el jardín hasta que yo esté listo," dijo el muchacho a su hermana.

7. No podemos entrar en aquel tranvía, porque no cabemos.

8. Anduvo despacio, y finalmente llegó a la plaza del mercado.

9. Me dijo ella que yo no trajera dinero, pero yo tenía la cartera en el bolsillo.

10. Cuando hayas terminado tu trabajo, puedes salir, pero hasta entonces, no.

10 (b) Conversation

(*An hour after the previous episode,* MARTIN *and* ISABEL, *after walking up and down the Paseo de la Castellana and the Paseo de Recoletos, sit down in the plaza de la Cibeles, in front of the General Post Office.*)

ISABEL : From here we shall see everything. There is so much to see : lots of people and cars, imposing buildings, and a certain amount of shade to sit in. What shall we drink ?

MARTIN : I feel like having something to eat. As I told you, we shall not get dinner in the *pensión* until ten. I shall ask the waiter for two packets of potato crisps and I shall have beer to drink. What do you want ?

ISABEL : A little glass of that sweet wine we tried yesterday at the Escorial will do for me. It was Málaga, wasn't it ?

(MARTIN *orders what they want when the* WAITER *comes, and the* WAITER *brings it.*)

(*Half an hour later.*)

MARTIN : Look, Isabel, I'm in rather a difficulty. Have you got any money with you ?

ISABEL : No. Since you always pay for everything, and I didn't want to go shopping this afternoon, I left at the *pensión* the little I have got. What ! Have you left yours behind too ? Whatever are we going to do ? We've no money to pay the waiter ! And you, always so correct, how have you managed to do anything so silly ?

MARTIN : Yes, I was a fool, I admit. I've just remembered that I left my money in my wallet, locked in my little case. It isn't much, I shall have to change some travellers' cheques tomorrow at a bank. But the important thing now is, how are we to get away from here without any money ?

ISABEL : Well, if we go away without paying, and the waiter sees us, he will make a tremendous fuss, and the police will take us to prison. That will be a fine beginning for our holiday in Madrid !

MARTIN : Now, my girl, don't exaggerate. What we can do is this. As I don't know anyone here to borrow money from, I will go back to the *pensión* now and collect my wallet, and you will stay here till I come back.

ISABEL : Me stay here ! But I'm frightened ! I've never been alone in a foreign city at this time of day ! What should I do if some man spoke to me ?

MARTIN : Nobody will say anything to you. Besides, if you want to, you can make yourself understood well enough in Spanish to explain our difficulty to anybody. But listen. What you can say if anyone comes is this : " My husband is coming." That's all. Just the same to the waiter if he asks if you want anything else to drink, as to anybody else, and nobody will trouble you at all. I'm going. But what a bore! I haven't even a peseta to pay a tram-fare. I must walk. Good-bye. Don't forget: " My husband is coming."

(Three-quarters of an hour later, MARTIN returns in triumph in a taxi, with his wallet. MARTIN pays the waiter, and he and ISABEL return in the direction of the pensión. *And* ISABEL *has not had to explain anything to anybody, nor even to say, this time, the magic words " My husband is coming ".)*

10 (c)

(From her hotel in Madrid, MARIA wishes to put a telephone call through to a friend in London.)

ANTONIO : Since I can't find the telephone directory and I don't know the number you have to dial to make this call, I think the best thing would be to call up Enquiries; the number is 03.

MARIA : I think so, too. May I use the telephone?

ANTONIO : Of course.

MARIA : Thank you.
      (MARIA takes up the receiver and dials 03.)

OPERATOR : Spanish National Telephone Company. Enquiries. Can I help you?

MARIA : I want to put a call through to London.

OPERATOR : Oh, yes. Dial number 09, for Trunks.

MARIA : Thank you.
      (MARIA puts down the receiver, and immediately takes it up again and dials 09.)

OPERATOR : Spanish National Telephone Company. Trunks. Can I help you?

MARIA : I want to put a call through to London.

OPERATOR : What number, please?

MARIA : DWC 1989.

OPERATOR : London, England, DWC 1989.

MARIA : Yes, that's right.

OPERATOR : What is your number please?

MARIA : 37 75 51.

OPERATOR : Good. Replace the receiver, we will call you later.

MARIA : Can you please tell me how long it will be?

OPERATOR : Half an hour.

MARIA : Thank you.
      (MARIA puts down the receiver.)

MARIA : And now we just have to wait.

ANTONIO : How long will it be?

MARIA : She said half an hour, but one can never be certain about that, you know.

ANTONIO : It depends on how busy the line is. Sometimes . . .
   (*Telephone bell rings.*)

MARIA : Through already ! How quickly . . . !
   (*She takes up the receiver.*)

MARIA : Hello !

VOICE : 36 85 64.

MARIA : I'm sorry, it's the wrong number.

VOICE : Sorry.
   (MARIA *puts down the receiver.*)

MARIA : What a bore ! This waiting gets on my nerves.
   (*Telephone bell rings.*)

MARIA (*taking up the receiver*) : Hello !

OPERATOR : 37 75 51.

MARIA : Yes, Hello !

OPERATOR : Don't put the receiver down, please.
   (*Several voices are heard through the receiver. Then a clear, definite voice :*)

THE CLEAR VOICE : London, Hello !

MARIA : At last ! Hello ! . . .

10 (*d*)

MARSILLA : My name is Diego Marsilla. I was born
   In Teruel, which, founded but yesterday,
   Is now a mighty city, whose proud walls
   Amid the horrors of atrocious strife
   Were fashioned, and cemented with the blood
   Of her brave citizens. I think when God
   Decreed my birth, His purpose was to form
   A man and woman, patterns of pure love;
   So, to maintain in perfect equipoise
   Their mutual affection, first He shared
   The twin halves of a single radiant soul
   Between them both, and then said : " Live and
       love."
   And at the sound of that creative voice
   My Isabel and I came into being :
   Both saw the light the selfsame day and hour.

Already from our earliest years were we
Devoted lovers. The very day we met.
Before we met indeed, we loved each other.
For love began to inflame our souls when God
Moulded them from mere nothing, and they felt
The quickening touch of the Creator's hand.
And so the miracle of our young love,
Of love made flesh before we both were born,
Destined my Isabel and me to love,
And so to love on with all our heart, as first
With all our soul.

11 (a) Exercise

1. ¿Cuánto pagó Vd por aquel coche?
2. Creo que hizo aquello sólo para engañarme.
3. Esta casa fue construida por un buen arquitecto.
4. Mañana por la tarde partiré para Sevilla.
5. Permanecí dos horas en el cine.
6. Voy a Buenos Aires por seis u ocho meses.
7. Por haber ahorrado tanto dinero, ya se había hecho muy rico.
8. Quiero que vaya Vd al correo por mí; estoy muy ocupado y no puedo salir.
9. Compró este libro para mí, pero será inútil.
10. Le busqué en el jardín, porque teníamos que salir para la estación a las cinco.

(*Notes:* 6. *u* is required instead of *o* to translate " or " because it precedes another word beginning with " o ". The best modern Spanish writers try to avoid the use of this *u*, but in a few cases, as in the one above, its appearance is inevitable. 9. If the meaning were " for my sake "—i.e., " to prevent anyone else from buying it ", the Spanish would be *por mí*.)

11 (b) Conversation

(MARTIN *and* ISABEL, *coming out of the* pensión, *at ten o'clock one morning, meet* ANTONIO *and* MARIA.)

ISABEL : How marvellous ! We didn't know you were in Madrid.

MARIA : We only arrived last night, and as Antonio has some things to do in this very street, I came with him to call on you. But are you going out ?

ISABEL : We were going to see if we could find some presents to take back to our families in England. Would you like to come too ? You would be doing us a great favour, because of course you know the shops much better than we do. Look Martin ! (MARTIN, *who has been talking to* ANTONIO, *turns round.*) Maria is going shopping with us; she says that you, Antonio, have some things to do round about here, and that she can come with us.

MARTIN : What a splendid idea ! Then you ladies obviously won't want me with you. You will enjoy yourselves much better without me. And as I get rather bored having to wander from shop to shop not knowing what we are looking for, I will leave you, and we'll meet at lunch-time. By the way, would you like to lunch with us here in our *pensión* ? They put on a very good meal, and besides, the dining-room is much cooler and quieter than a restaurant.

ANTONIO : We shall be very pleased, shan't we, Maria ? So we shall meet here again about two o'clock ?

MARTIN : Let's say in the café opposite at half-past one, for a drink. I will go up to the *pensión* to let the manageress know.

ISABEL : Where will you be going then, Martin ?

MARTIN : Never mind. I have lots of things to do. One of them is to go to the bank to change some cheques. We shall certainly be wanting money if you are going shopping. Good-bye ! Have a good time !

>   (*They separate, and the ladies go on down the street. At the corner they catch a bus which takes them to a stop near the Gran Vía, where they get out. Soon afterwards they go into one of the nearby big shops.*)

MARIA : I'm sure you'll find all you want for presents in this shop. They keep all sorts of things of every quality.

ISABEL : Yes, it is very much like some of the very fine shops I have seen in Paris. And like some of the London ones, of course, too.

MARIA : What do you want to buy, Isabel ? Are you looking for anything in particular ?

ISABEL : Yes. Some Spanish lace handkerchiefs for my mother, a silver bracelet for my little sister, some dolls dressed like Spanish dancers like those I have seen in some of the shop-windows, for two little friends I have, and other things—oh, yes, over there are a lot of postcards with views of Madrid. I must buy at least a dozen to send to my friends in England.

MARIA : Here are some very pretty lace handkerchiefs.

ISABEL (*to the* SHOPGIRL) : Excuse me, are these the prices, marked on the label?

THE ASSISTANT : Yes, madam, all the prices are marked.

ISABEL : Very good, I will take these five. Can you change this hundred-peseta note?

THE ASSISTANT : Yes, madam.

(*She wraps up the handkerchiefs and hands them to* ISABEL. *The two ladies go on through the shop, looking for the other things that* ISABEL *wants to buy.*)

11 (c)

Dear Sir,

With reference to yours of the 27th ult., we beg to inform you that the goods to which you refer were despatched to you by goods train on April 10th, as is evidenced by our rail consignment note no. 3257.

Since these goods have not reached you we think it desirable to make the appropriate claim, and on hearing of your approval we shall proceed with this step,

Yours faithfully,

José Domínguez

11 (d)

(From *El Sí de las Niñas, of Moratín*)

DIEGO : Yes, she isn't wealthy, but I don't want money, I have enough. I have sought out a woman who is modest, reserved, and virtuous.

SIMÓN : That is what is most important, and besides, who is there for you to leave your money to, anyway?

DIEGO : That's just it. And you know how important it is for a wife to be skilful and hardworking, and to know how to look after the house, and be economical, and manage everything properly. . . . I'm tired of always struggling with housekeepers, each one worse than the one before, wasteful, meddlesome, gossiping, hysterical, old, ugly as sin. No, from now on there's to be a new way of life. I shall have someone by me who will be faithful and loving, and we shall live together in peace like the angels. And let people talk and put rumours round. . . .

SIMÓN : But if both parties are satisfied, what right have people to talk ?

DIEGO : No . . . but I know what they will be saying. . . . They will say that it is an unequal match, that the ages aren't suitable, or . . .

SIMÓN : Well, there doesn't seem to be much difference. Seven or eight years, at the most.

DIEGO : What ? What do you mean, seven or eight years ? She is only a few months over sixteen !

SIMÓN : Well, what of that ?

DIEGO : And as for me . . ., although, thanks be, I am still hale and hearty, for all that I shan't see fifty-nine again.

SIMÓN : But that isn't anything to do with it. . . .

DIEGO : Well, what are you trying to say ?

SIMÓN : I mean. . . . Well, either you haven't explained very well what you mean, or I don't understand you. Let's get this clear. Who is this doña Paquita going to marry ?

DIEGO : So that's it ? She's going to marry *me*.

SIMÓN : You ?

DIEGO : Yes, me.

SIMÓN : Heavens. . . . That's a fine mix-up.

DIEGO : What do you mean ?

SIMÓN : And I thought I had guessed right !

DIEGO : Well, what had you thought ? Who did you think I was arranging for her to marry ?

SIMÓN : Don Carlos, your nephew. He's a fine lad, plenty of talent and well-educated, a splendid soldier, and a thoroughly likeable fellow. I thought you were arranging that *he* was to be the bridegroom.

DIEGO : Well, I wasn't.

---

12 (*a*) Exercise

1. Luis invitó a Juana a acompañarle al cine.
2. La madre de ella rehusó permitirlo.
3. Consiguieron salir de la casa de Juana mientras que su madre estaba arriba.
4. Decidieron sentarse en la última fila de las butacas.
5. Juana quería fumar los pitillos de Luis.
6. Tardaron mucho en volver a casa.

7. Juana había olvidado de tomar consigo su llavín.
8. No se atrevió a sonar el timbre.
9. Luis le ayudó a entrar por la ventana del comedor.
10. Ella se asustó al ver a su padre que les aguardaba.

12 (b) Conversation

(*The Paseo del Prado.* MARTIN *and* ISABEL, *on their way to spend an hour or two in the Museum, are walking towards the entrance.*)

ISABEL : This is where we are going to spend the morning, isn't it ? I do very much want to see these pictures I have read so much about.

MARTIN : Yes. I am always immensely glad to come into this museum, too. It contains one of the best collections of fine paintings in the whole world, especially of paintings of the Spanish school.

ISABEL : Are you going to show me all there is to see ?

MARTIN : No, that would be impossible in a single morning. The best thing will be to go to the rooms with the pictures by the most important painters, el Greco, Velázquez, and Goya, and study them first. If we try to see much more on our first visit we shall only have a very confused idea of what we have seen. (*To the* DOOR-KEEPER) How much is it ? (*He pays the amount asked for and they go inside.*)

MARTIN : Let's go first through these rooms on the left where there are a good many Italian pictures, which are very fine and interesting, and we shall soon get to the Velázquez rooms.

ISABEL : But how marvellous they are ! I could spend days and days here without getting tired of looking at so many lovely paintings.

MARTIN : We will come back on Sunday.
       (*They go through four or five rooms on the left-hand side of the Museum.*)

MARTIN : Oh, yes. Here's the picture that I always think wonderful. They always hang it in this small room where it is all by itself.

ISABEL : I know it's called " Las Meninas ", but I don't remember what you have told me about it. Who is that figure on the left, he seems to be painting a portrait ?

MARTIN : It is a self-portrait of Velázquez. The story is that one morning in the summer of 1655, Velázquez was in his studio in the old palace in Madrid, painting the portraits of the King and Queen, Philip IV and his wife, Mariana. When there was a moment's pause their daughter the Infanta Margarita María came in to see them, followed by two Maids of Honour—they are the " Meninas "—two dwarfs and three other people belonging to the Court.   After this visit Velázquez had the idea of painting, not what he himself saw at that time, but what the King saw.   So he did, and he even painted, in the background of the picture, a mirror in which you can see the reflections of the King and Queen. It is said too that when the King saw this picture for the first time—Velázquez had painted it in secret—he looked at it in silence for some time, and then, taking a brush, he added, on the breast of the figure of Velázquez, the red cross of the Order of Santiago, thus indicating without a word how he was rewarding him for having painted such a magnificent picture.

ISABEL : How magnificent it is, really ! I like those delicate colours, they are almost transparent, and the light that falls so naturally from the right. Doesn't it seem as though we are there, in that room ?   It seems so real to me that I almost feel as though I could smell the smell of this studio.

MARTIN :   Well, historians say that the palace smelt very nasty !

ISABEL : How prosaic you are !   Is that where we are going tomorrow ?   You said you were going to take me to see the Royal Palace.

MARTIN : No.   The one that is there now is a very fine one, and replaced the old one in the eighteenth century.   But it is on the same site, to the west of Madrid, looking down over the valley of the Manzanares.

ISABEL : Let's go into the next room now.   Are all these paintings by Velázquez ?

MARTIN : Yes, and there are some very famous ones here, too.   There are " Las Lanzas " and " Las Hilanderas ", for instance.

(*And we leave them to spend the rest of the morning in the Museum, studying the pictures.*)

12 (c)

Dear Sir,

As the settlement of your account for goods delivered to you from us, as per invoice no. 3105, was due some time ago, and as we have not received any news from you concerning this matter, we request you to credit the amount to our current account in the Bilbao branch of the Banco de Vizcaya, in order that settlement may be complete.

Yours faithfully,

González y Cía.

12 (d)

As they went along they discovered some thirty or forty windmills that are on that plain; and as soon as the knight had espied them, " Fortune," cried he, " directs our affairs better than we ourselves could have wished : look yonder, friend Sancho, there are at least thirty outrageous giants, whom I intend to encounter; and having deprived them of life, we will begin to enrich ourselves with their spoils : for they are lawful prize; and the extirpation of that cursed brood will be an acceptable service to Heaven."

" What giants? " said Sancho Panza.

" Those whom thou seest yonder," answered don Quixote, " with their long-extended arms; some of that detested race have arms of so immense a size, that sometimes they reach two leagues in length."

" Pray, look better, sir," said Sancho; " those things yonder are no giants, but windmills, and the arms you fancy, are their sails, which, being whirled about by the wind, make the millstone turn."

" It is clear," cried don Quixote, " that thou are but little acquainted with adventures. I tell thee they are giants; and therefore, if thou art afraid, go aside and say thy prayers, for I am resolved to engage in a dreadful, unequal combat against them all."

This said, he clapped spurs to his horse Rocinante, without giving ear to his squire Sancho, who bawled out to him, and assured him that they were windmills, and no giants. But he was so fully possessed with a strong belief of the contrary, that he did not so much as hear his squire's outcry, nor was he sensible of what they were, although he was already very near them; far from that.

" Stand, cowards," cried he as loud as he could; " stand your ground, ignoble creatures, and fly not basely from a single knight, who dares encounter you all."

At the same time the wind rising, the mill-sails began to move, which, when don Quixote spied :

" Base miscreants,'' cried he, " though you wave more arms than the giant Briareus, you shall pay for your arrogance.''

He most devoutly recommended himself to his lady Dulcinea, imploring her assistance in this perilous adventure; and so, covering himself with his shield and couching his lance, he rushed with Rocinante's utmost speed upon the first windmill he could come at, and running his lance upon the sail, the wind whirled about with such swiftness, that the rapidity of the motion presently broke the lance into shivers, and hurled away both knight and horse along with it, till down he fell, rolling a good way off in the field. Sancho Panza ran as fast as his ass could drive to help his master, whom he found lying, not able to stir, such a blow had he and Rocinante received.

" Mercy on me ! '' cried Sancho, " did I not give your worship fair warning ? Did I not tell you they were windmills, and that nobody could think otherwise, unless he had also windmills in his head ? ''

" Peace, friend Sancho,'' replied don Quixote : " there is nothing so subject to the inconstancy of fortune as war; for I believe, and it is therefore true, that that necromancer Frestón, who carried away my study and books, has transformed these giants into windmills, to deprive me of the honour of the victory ; such is his inveterate malice against me; but in the end, all his pernicious wiles and stratagems shall prove ineffectual against the prevailing edge of my sword.''

13 (a) Exercise

1. Me alegro de que haya recordado que no me gusta azúcar en mi té.

2. El autor siente mucho que no haya enviado su manuscrito al redactor a tiempo para publicarse.

3. Cierre con llave la puerta del invernadero, deje salir el gato, y suba a la cama sin hacer ruido.

4. Tal vez sea verdad, tal vez no. Sin embargo es lo más importante que sepamos exactamente lo que ocurrió.

5. El viejo irlandés se incorporó en la cama y les dijo que le trajesen sopa.

6. Su madre le prohibió que saliese con aquella chica.

7. Ella sabía que su madre de él no quería que fumase.

8. Él dijo que la acompañaría a la casa después de la función.

9. Vd no puede negar que lo entienda perfectamente.

10. ¿ Cree Vd que pueda llegar aquí antes de las dos ?

13 (*b*)

The Legend of the Christ of the Vega (i)

In the middle of the sixteenth century, in the lovely and very ancient city of Toledo, there lived a gallant young nobleman named don Fernando de Medina del Ríoseco. He was very rich, and lived in a splendid palace that he had inherited from his ancestors and which was full of precious tapestries, splendid furniture, and magnificent arms. But in spite of all this wealth, the palace was gloomy. No gentle voices of women or children were to be heard in its great halls and corridors and staircases : deep silence reigned there, only rarely broken by the slow step of some serving-man dressed in black, who might walk quietly through those sombre rooms.

Not far from this palace, in a little cottage at the foot of the rock upon which the Alcázar stands, there lived two women, María del Valle, a poor widow, and her daughter Catalina, a very beautiful girl of eighteen. Life was not easy for them, they had to work very hard for their living. Twice a day, very early in the morning and at nightfall, Catalina went down for water to the River Tagus with her donkey, and later on, when she had filled the water-pots that the donkey was carrying, she would return again up the hill.

One morning at dawn, when the first rays of the sun were already gilding the topmost towers of the Alcázar and the Cathedral, the young nobleman, Fernando de Medina del Ríoseco, mounted on a fine sorrel-coloured horse, rode down the same path that Catalina usually took, and at the same moment she with her donkey was beginning to

return up the hill with her pots full of water.   Just as they
were about to meet, Fernando's horse stumbled on the root
of a cork-tree that was growing there at the side of the path,
and threw Fernando at the foot of the tree.   Catalina came
up, fearful lest she should find that this gallant young man
was dead, for she saw that his face was streaming with blood
and that he was not moving.   It was clear that he needed
help, and as there was no one but herself on that path,
she took off the handkerchief that she wore tied round
her neck and dipped it in the water that the donkey was
carrying.   Then she gently bathed the young man's face,
removing the blood gradually, and when she saw that he was
no longer bleeding, she tied the handkerchief round Fernando's head so as to keep the wound clean.   At this moment
Fernando opened his eyes, and saw Catalina, looking like
an angel, kneeling beside him, with the rays of the sun,
now fully risen, reflected in her eyes and her golden hair.
They looked at each other, and they fell in love at once.
Half an hour later, when Fernando felt that he was completely well again, they went together back up that path
to the city.   On the next morning Fernando and Catalina
met again in the same place, and again on many other days.
The longer they spent together, the more they loved each
other.   And they thought that they were happy.

One evening, however, a cloud came, darkening the rosy
sky beneath which these two lovers had been so happy.
While they were walking beside the Tagus, under the
poplar-trees that grow along the river-bank, Fernando gave
Catalina the bad news that on the following morning he
would have to leave for the war in Flanders with his regiment, and that he would probably have to be absent for
two or three years.

" But I love you, Catalina ; I love you with all my heart,
and when I come back, we will be married."

" I love you, too, as you know I do," replied Catalina,
" but will you truly swear that you will marry me when
you return ? "

" Yes, of course I swear it," said Fernando.

" But we must have a witness, and there are none here.
Who is to be the witness of our promise ? "

At this moment they saw that they were not far from a little chapel that there is in the middle of the beautiful Vega of Toledo, the one that is now called the chapel of the Christ of the Vega. They went in, and Catalina said to Fernando :

" There is our Lord Jesus Christ, crucified on that wooden cross. He shall be our witness. Let us swear before Him that we shall be married when you return."

And in that dark, quiet chapel, amid the scent of incense and burnt-out candles, they swore their oath.

And on the following morning Fernando set out along the road to Madrid, to join his regiment.

(*To be concluded.*)

13 (*c*)

Dear Sir,

I shall be grateful if in accordance with usual procedure you will duly authorize the installation of an extension line to my telephone no. 4763 to the following premises :

Ildefonso de las Morenas Gaztambide, Sta Marta, 14, Salamanca.

Yours faithfully,

Ildefonso de las Morenas Gaztambide

13 (*d*)

Dear Sir,

We are in receipt of your letter of the 18th inst., in which you request us to install an extension line from your telephone no. 4763 to the address indicated above, and we regret to inform you that through technical difficulties we find it impossible to install this line for you at present.

We are, however, filing your request in order to proceed with it when circumstances eventually permit.

Yours truly,

Joaquin Llopis

(Regional director)

13 (e)

At the same instant two men came into the court, the one dressed like a country fellow, the other looked like a tailor, with a pair of shears in his hand.

" If it please you, my lord," cried the tailor, " I and this farmer here are come before your worship. This honest man came to my shop yesterday ; for, saving your presence, I am a tailor, and Heaven be praised, free of my company : so, my lord, he showed me a piece of cloth : ' Sir ', said he, ' is there enough of this to make me a cap ? ' Whereupon I measured the stuff, and answered him, ' Yes, if it like your worship.' Now as I imagined, do you see, he could not but imagine (and perhaps he imagined right enough) that I had a mind to cabbage some of his cloth ; judging hard by us tailors. ' Prithee,' said he, ' look there be not enough for two caps.' Now I smelt him out, and told him there was. Whereupon the old knave (if it like your worship), going on to the same tune, bid me look again and see whether it would not make three ; and at last if it would not make five. I was resolved to humour my customer, and said it might. So we struck a bargain ; just now the man is come for his caps, which I gave him, but when I asked him for my money, he will have me give him his cloth back again, or pay him for it."

" Is this true, honest man ? " asked Sancho.

" Yes, sir," replied the farmer, " but pray let him show the five caps he has made me."

" With all my heart," cried the tailor, and with that, pulling his hand from under his cloak, he held up five tiny caps, hanging upon his four fingers and thumb.

" There," said he, " you see the five caps that this good fellow asks for, and I swear by God that I have not wronged him of the least snip of his cloth, and let any workman be judge."

The sight of the caps, and the oddness of the cause set the whole court laughing. Sancho considered for a while, and then said :

" It seems to me that there is no need of long deliberation on this suit, for it may be decided at once by using plain common sense. Therefore the judgement of this court is that the tailor shall lose his making, and the farmer his cloth, and that the caps be given to the poor prisoners in jail."

---

14 (*a*) Exercise

1. No se me puede acusar de crímenes que no haya cometido.

2. Indíqueme dónde puedo encontrar un hotel en que pueda pasar la noche.

3. En mi vida no la olvidaré. Ni tú tampoco.

4. " Tan pronto como llegue el correo, hágamelo saber, por favor," dijo el huésped.

5. Luego que hubo llegado, le llevamos sus cartas.

6. El escritorio está colocado de modo que recibirá Vd la luz de la izquierda.

7. Dondequiera que vaya Vd, no encontrará mejores bicicletas en el mercado.

8. Tropezando entre las rocas desnudas, y perdiendo nuestro camino muchas veces, seguimos hasta que llegamos a la cumbre.

9. Se pondrá una multa severa a los viajeros que se apeen antes que se pare el tren en una estación.

10. Aunque es mi mejor amigo tendré que pegarle si vuelve a hacer eso.

11. Por las tardes, mientras que duerme la abuelita, hago calceta o zurzo calcetines.

12. Cierre la puerta del cuarto de baño para que el vapor no llene la casa.

13. Sí, iré a su fiesta, a condición de que no me hagan cantar.

14. Aunque la muchacha parecía completamente una persona mayor, sólo tenía quince años.

15. El Primer Ministro debiera haber consultado el Parlamento antes de hacer tal cosa.

14 (*b*)
The Legend of the Christ of the Vega (ii)

Two years later, on a beautiful autumn evening when the setting sun was just beginning to touch the surface of the river with gold, and when the dusty roads across the Vega were turning yellower than ever, a girl, who was now twenty years old, climbed up the tower of the Visagra Gate, the point on the town walls from which there is the best view of the road from Madrid. She did this every afternoon, but on this day she was more eager than ever, because news had come of the arrival in Madrid of a regiment of soldiers who had fought in Flanders. And as the sun set on this evening, Catalina saw that along the road from Madrid a little cloud was approaching, and as it came closer it was clear that it was a cloud of dust, made by a man galloping along on horseback.

Yes, there was no doubt of it, it was he, Fernando. Catalina came down at once from the tower to that little square that is there by the gate. When the rider came up to her, Catalina cried :

" Fernando, my Fernando, here I am ! "

But scarcely reining his horse, Fernando did not deign to glance at this woman. She seemed poor, and she was hindering him as he rode along.

" Away, vile creature ! " he said, and without recognizing her, or rather without wishing to recognize her, he crossed the square and went on up the street towards his palace, leaving Catalina transfixed with grief there at the foot of the tower.

However, Catalina was a girl of spirit, and she was not willing to leave matters as they were. Two or three days later she complained to the Corregidor of the city, and her complaint was heard before all the members of the high court of justice.

" But are you saying, Catalina del Valle," said the Corregidor, " that don Fernando de Medina del Ríoseco, before he went to Flanders, swore that he would marry you on his return ? And that now that he has returned he refuses to fulfil his promise ? Is there any witness of this oath ? "

" Yes, I do say this. And I have a witness, too."

" Well, who is he ? Why have you not brought him to this tribunal ? "

" It is Our Lord, the Holy Christ of the Vega," replied Catalina.

" Then we must see if He swears that what you have said is true," said the Corregidor.

And so the whole tribunal was transferred to that chapel in the midst of the Vega, which smelled of incense and of burnt-out candles. Don Fernando was with them, too, for the Corregidor had sent to find him; but he came in proud and haughty, whilst the others were all humble, not daring to think what might be going to happen on this very unaccustomed occasion.

They all waited for the Corregidor to speak, and in a gentle, calm voice he repeated the story that Catalina had told him, before the cross where the holy image of Christ was hanging. At length he added :

" Dost Thou say that there was indeed such a promise ? "

So that the oath could be taken, a notary held the book of the Gospels up to the image. And at that moment there was heard in the chapel a rustling sound, as it were of invisible wings, and then a gentle voice, saying :

" Yes, I swear it."

And at the same moment the right arm of the image fell down upon the book of the Gospels, and was left hanging from the shoulder, as it has remained from that day until now. All those present in the chapel knelt down and crossed themselves. Even Fernando, who was now beside Catalina, knelt, and said to her in a low voice :

" Will you pardon me, Catalina? I have done wrong, a great wrong, but now, will you marry me ? "

" Yes, of course I will marry you; I promised I would," she replied.

As the sun was setting on that lovely autumn afternoon, when the members of the tribunal had gone away, the two lovers walked for a long time beside the Tagus under the poplar-trees. And on the following morning they were married, in the little chapel of Our Lord, there in the midst of the Vega.

---

14 (c)

Dear Sirs,

We have today received from you goods corresponding to your invoice no. 3253, and we regret to inform you that they have arrived in a much damaged condition: about 10% of the lamps have arrived broken, and a further 5% will not light.

We know that we are not in a position to claim compensation for this damage, since the goods were not insured in transit, but since the damage caused is largely due to very inferior packing, we must insist that if this should occur on any future occasion we shall have to place our future orders elsewhere.

Yours truly,

Baltasar Flores y Cía.

14 (*d*)

Muy Señores nuestros,

En contestación a su atenta carta fecha del 28 del último mes de febrero, nos complace comunicarles que los daños recibidos en las mercancías correspondientes a nuestro envío no. 3253 serán renumerados en la forma más conveniente a sus propósitos.

Entendemos que en gran parte fueron causados por el mal estado del embalaje, lo cual se debió sin duda a un cambio provisional de personal en tal departamento. Afortunadamente dicho personal ha sido ya restituido por otro más competente.

Les rogamos encarecidamente nos perdonen por las molestias ocasionadas; garantizándoles un esmerado servicio en lo futuro.

De nuevo en espera de sus gratas órdenes, nos despedimos de Vds, afmos y s.s.

John Harrison, Lambert & Co.

14 (*e*)

That night they reached Antequera, and after a few long days' riding they arrived at the place where the company of soldiers had just been formed. They set off on the road to Cartagena, putting up that night and the next four nights in villages through which they happened to pass. There Tomás noticed the great authority of the company's quartermasters, the easy-going ways of some of the captains, the careful work of the billeting officers, the industry and complicated accounts of the paymasters, the complaints of the villagers, the people who paid money to buy exemption from the duty of billeting soldiers in their houses, the insolence of the raw recruits, the quarrels that arose with innkeepers, the soldiers who asked to take more baggage than they needed, and finally, the almost absolute necessity of doing everything he was told and which seemed wrong. Tomás had dressed gaily, throwing aside his sober student's dress, and put on easy, bright-coloured clothes. He got rid of all his books except two : a Book of Hours and an unannotated copy of Garcilaso's poems. These he carried in his two saddle-bags.

They reached Cartagena sooner than they would have liked, for a soldier's life in lodgings is free and easy, and every day new, pleasant things turn up. There they embarked in four Neapolitan galleys, and there Tomás also noticed how extraordinary life is on board a galley, where most of the time bugs bite, galley-slaves steal, sailors irritate, mice ravage and the rolling of the sea disturbs the passengers' stomachs. Big squalls and storms made him afraid, especially two that beset them in the Gulf of Lions : the one drove them on to Corsica, and the other back to Toulon, in France. At length, tired-eyed with lack of sleep and soaked to the skin, they reached the fine and very lovely city of Genoa. There they disembarked in sheltered water at Mandrache, and after a visit to a church, the captain and all his companions settled down at an inn, where they forgot all the past storms in the enjoyment of the present.

15 (a) Exercise

Si viviese en el campo compraría los más de mis víveres en la tienda de la aldea, pero una o dos veces al mes haría mandar un surtido de géneros en lata desde uno de los almacenes de la ciudad más próxima. Entonces si unos amigos fuesen a verme tendría en la casa bastante para comer, aun si llegasen más amigos de los que esperaba. El año pasado cuando mi mujer y yo alquilamos una casita pequeña en la costa del este para los meses del verano, le dejábamos una llave a una vieja que vivía cerca, para que si le enviábamos desde Londres una postal diciéndole la hora de nuestra llegada, pudiera entrar a encender fuegos si sintiese que la casita estaba húmeda. Luego si llegásemos a la medianoche, no tendríamos mucho que hacer antes de acostarnos.

Aquella casita nos gustó tanto que el año que viene puede ser que la compre, si no encuentro otra que me venga mejor. Descubrimos una muy encantadora que se hallaba a unas diez millas del mar, pero no tenía cuarto de baño, y además el agente era un tipo tan desagradable que no quise tener nada que ver con él.

Si Vds pasan en automóvil por aquellas aldeas el año que viene y si al mismo tiempo nosotros estamos allí, deberán ir a hacernos una visita. Todo lo que tendrán que hacer es preguntarle al dueño de la tienda del pueblo si sabe si hemos llegado y él les dará nuestras señas como si nos hubiese conocido toda la vida.

15 (b) Conversation

(*In a café in the principal square in Toledo*, 10 a.m. ANTONIO *and* MARIA *are on their way from Madrid to Córdoba, and their two English friends have come with them as far as Toledo. The latter will be returning to Madrid by train the same evening.*)

ANTONIO : Martin, you know Toledo better than I do, and as we only have a few hours here, I think you had better organize us so that in the available time we can see as much as possible.

MARTIN : Yes, when I was a student in Madrid a good many years ago I used to come here often, and as most of Toledo is one big historical monument, I don't think it can have changed much since my last visit. So if you will look at this plan of the town, I will tell you what we can do. First we will go to the Cathedral, down one of these streets to the left. Of course there is enough there to occupy us not only all day, but for days on end; but as today we must see at least half a dozen churches we shall not be able to spend in the Cathedral more than half an hour.

MARIA : Of course. But are all the streets as narrow as this one, or is there a broad, new one, somewhere ?

MARTIN : No, there is no really wide street anywhere in Toledo, they are all very old and narrow.

ISABEL : Where shall we go after we have seen the Cathedral?

MARTIN : We will turn down to the right to see a very important painting by El Greco, the famous painter of the sixteenth century, we shall find it in the church of St. Thomas. It is called " The burial of the Count of Orgaz ", and I am sure you must have seen many photographs of it. I will explain it to you later on. Then we will go on down the hill towards the house of the same painter, El Greco, where he himself used to live. It is a museum now, but it is completely restored and furnished, and it is very interesting not only because of its style of architecture but on account of its situation, too. From the garden there are magnificent views across the river. Then near by we shall find two very interesting little churches, the Tránsito and Santa María la Blanca. Both of them were formerly synagogues, in the Middle Ages.

ANTONIO : I can follow the route you mean fairly well on the plan of the town. Isn't that where that famous factory is, where they make cutlery and other things with local Toledo decorations?

MARTIN : Yes. It is just beside Santa María la Blanca, and I should be glad to spend a few minutes there, because I want to buy a pair of scissors for Isabel. I lost a good pair of hers a little while ago. If you want to, you can study there, close to, the method they use to engrave the metal with designs and Moorish decorations in gold.

ISABEL : Thanks, Martin. I wasn't expecting that. I should like to buy a present for you, too. What do we do then?

MARTIN : The church of San Juan de los Reyes is close by, at the extreme end of the hill. From there there is a view of the whole Vega, with the River Tagus and the bridge of San Martín that crosses it. We could find a place there to have our meal, since we have brought these good packed lunches with us from Madrid.

MARIA : We shall certainly be ready to eat by that time.

MARTIN : After lunch, if you are still energetic and if it isn't too hot, we can go and see the little chapel at the foot of the hill, called the Cristo de la Vega; you know the legend about it already. The walls and the old gates of the city are very interesting from that side. Then to finish, we can come in through the Visagra gate and go on up the hill to the Puerta del Sol, which is really a medieval gate, not a public square like the Puerta del Sol in Madrid. Behind it there is another very fine little church called the Cristo

de la Luz, which in the time of the Moors was a mosque.
I don't know if we shall have time left then to go up to the
Alcázar, to see the damage done during the Civil War,
when it was besieged by the Reds for seventy-seven days.
There are lots of stories told about this episode.

ISABEL : And then, my dear Martin, I shall be extremely
tired and I shall not want to do anything but sit in a café
until it is time for our train.   But come on, if we don't want
to waste time now, we must go to the Cathedral, mustn't
we ?

15 (c)

Dear Sir,
     We learn this morning from your mechanic that
you are in urgent need of your car, and we note the instructions that he delivered to us concerning repairs to the
brakes.

With reference to the paintwork, our painter has pro-
cured a catalogue showing suitable paints from the O.U.E.
Company of Madrid (Sta Lucia, 38, telephone 03854),
and we think that the nearest shade to that of your car is
" Steel Grey ", which in this copy of the catalogue is
numbered *nine*. We shall be glad of your immediate
instructions on this point, and request you to inform us at
once if the number of the shade is different in your copy
of the catalogue.

Yours very truly,
(For " Garaje Excelsior ")
Lucas Fernández

15 (d)

The Divine Sheperd

Shepherd, who with thine amorous, sylvan song,
Hast broken the slumber which encompassed me,
That madest thy crook from the accursed tree
On which thy powerful arms were stretched so long,
     Lead me to mercy's ever-flowing fountains,
For Thou my Shepherd, Guard and Guide shalt be.
I will obey thy voice, and wait to see
Thy feet all beautiful upon the mountains.
     Hear, Shepherd !—Thou who for thy flock art dying,

Oh, wash away these scarlet sins, for Thou
Rejoicest at the contrite sinner's vow.
Oh, wait, to Thee my weary soul is crying;
Wait for me. Yet why ask it, when I see
With feet nailed to the cross, Thou'rt waiting still for me?

(This translation is one of several from older Spanish poetry
made by the American, Henry Wadsworth Longfellow.)

16 (a) Exercise

Estaba claro que esta casa era más vieja de lo que al
principio creímos. Más de una de las viejas puertas de
roble estaban carcomidas y verdes de edad, y las ratas
habían hecho más daño del que pudimos ver en la foto-
grafía que el antiguo dueño nos había enviado. En los
jardines había un viejo lago mayor que aquél en que
nadábamos cuando vivíamos en aquel hotel a unas veinte
millas más cerca de Londres. El dueño actual quiere
venderla pero pide mucho más de lo que vale. Desde
luego tiene ciertas ventajas. En esta granja hay más
vacas de las que había en la que visitamos la semana pasada.
Si alquilásemos esta granja podríamos mandar más leche
que antes a la lechería de Maidstone. No tenemos que
decidirnos en seguida, el agente nos deja más de tres semanas
para tomar nuestra decisión.

16 (b) Conversation

(*Two or three days after arriving at Córdoba,* ISABEL *and* MARTIN
are returning to ANTONIO'S *family's country cottage, after
spending the morning looking round the town.* ANTONIO
is driving them back, with MARIA.)

ANTONIO : What do you think of Córdoba, Isabel ? Which
of the things you have seen here have you liked best ?
ISABEL : Really, Antonio, I don't know. There are so
many interesting things that I can't decide. Of course
the Mezquita is the most surprising thing of all. I had no
idea of its enormous size. Inside, with all those columns
and the particular Moorish type of arches, it was like a
thick forest.
MARTIN : Yes, and in spite of that choir in the very different

sixteenth-century style, it seemed to me that the two types of architecture blend very well together.

MARIA : Can you tell me, Martin, as an architect, why the choir was built there in that style ?

MARTIN : They say that the Emperor Charles V, wanting to turn the Moorish Mosque into a Cathedral worthy of the Christian God, and not wanting to use that beautiful Moorish Mihrab as a chapel for the High altar, had the central part of the Mosque pulled down to build the present choir.

MARIA : But he did not really have very much pulled down, because I heard someone say that there are, still, more than five hundred columns there.

ISABEL : I liked the outside part, too, the Court of the Orange-trees, where everything seemed to be sunlight and peace.

ANTONIO : Yes, you have been lucky with the weather, though of course, here in Córdoba at the end of July it is always very sunny, and extremely hot, too. I like hot weather, and I shall not be very keen to return to England when we leave here next week.

ISABEL : Yes, indeed. And tomorrow we, too, have to begin our journey back. It's sad !

MARTIN : Yes, but it has been grand to see this part of Anda-lusia again. Not only the Mezquita and the town, which are, of course, immensely interesting, but country life too. Your sister's country cottage is a very pretty place, Antonio.

ANTONIO : Yes, she is very fond of living in the country, and country life is much healthier for her children than living all the year round in Córdoba. The boys are very interested in my brother-in-law's farm, alongside. Has my sister told you that the eldest boy is going to be an Agricultural Engineer ? He is to begin his course at the University of Madrid in October.

MARIA : Yes, he is a very intelligent boy, and I'm glad he has chosen that as a career. According to his father, there is great need of agricultural specialists in Spain.

ISABEL : Well, you have driven the car so fast, Antonio, that we are here at the cottage already. What a magnificent view of the Sierra there is from here !

(*The four get out of the car at the door of the cottage, and go into the pleasant, shady drawing-room, where* ANTONIO'S *sister is awaiting her guests' return.*)

16 (c)

Dear Sir,

In view of your activities as exporter in the cork trade, we beg to offer you our services in the event of your desiring our collaboration here in Almería.

For your information, we should let you know that we are agents of several shipping companies, both Spanish and foreign; that we are fully solvent; and that we have under our control shipping services for all parts of the world.

In addition, we are actively concerned in the business of chartering vessels, and we can assure you with full confidence that we are in a position to offer you vessels for loading in any Spanish port for any port of destination abroad.

We trust that you will seriously consider our proposition, and that we may in the near future count you among our best clients.

Yours faithfully,
(For " Combustibles, S.A.")
Juan José Alcover

16 (d)

CRESPO (*kneeling*): Behold, upon my knees I ask it—upon my knees, and weeping such tears as only a father's anguish melts from his frozen locks! And what is my demand? But that you should restore what you have robbed: so fatal for us to lose, so easy for you to restore; which I could myself now wrest from you by the hand of the law, but which I rather implore of you as a mercy on my knees!

CAPTAIN: You have done at last? Tiresome old man! Be thankful that I do not add your death, and that of your son, to what you call your dishonour. Only for the sake of your daughter's beauty I will spare you both—let that be enough. If you want to avenge yourself by arms, I have little to fear. If you want to put me before your civil court, you have no jurisdiction over me.

CRESPO: Will not my tears——?

CAPTAIN: Who cares for the tears of a woman, a child, or an old man?

CRESPO: No pity?

CAPTAIN: I spare your life, is that not enough?

CRESPO : Upon my knees, asking back my own at your hands
  that robbed me ?
CAPTAIN : Nonsense !
CRESPO : For my honour, now, as Mayor in Zalamea ?
CAPTAIN : You have no authority over me, the War Council
  will send for me.
CRESPO : You are resolved ?
CAPTAIN : I am; wearisome, tiresome old man !
CRESPO : Is there no way——— ?
CAPTAIN : Yes. Your best way is to say no more about it.
CRESPO : No other ?
CAPTAIN : No !
CRESPO (*rising, and taking the wand of Justice*): Then, by God,
  you shall pay for it ! Ho, there !
      (*Enter villagers.*)
VILLAGER : Sir !
CAPTAIN (*aside*): What are these villagers about ?
VILLAGER : What is your command, sir ?
CRESPO : Take this Captain to prison.
CAPTAIN : This is too much ! With a man like me, in the
  King's service, you can't do this !
CRESPO : We will try. You will not leave this place, unless
  you are a prisoner, or dead.

---

17 (*a*) Exercise

1. No tarde, o puede que partamos sin Vd.
2. ¿Puedo comerme una manzana, por favor ?
3. Es posible que llegue el tren antes de lo previsto.
4. No puedo dejar de pensar que Vd se podía haber
partido la pierna en aquel accidente.
5. Trabaja con ahinco para ganar mucho dinero.
6. ¡ Que viva mil años !
7. Su madre dijo que podían permanecer en la fiesta
hasta las siete.
8. Él no debería salir esta mañana, tiene un constipado
muy fuerte.
9. El viajero no sabía que hubiera debido levantar el
sombrero.
10. Hubieran debido darme una toalla limpia, ésta es
una porquería.

Notes : 4. *Partir* is better than *romper* for " to break " in the sense of breaking an arm or leg. 8. *Debiera* is, of course, a common alternative to *debería*. 10. *Una porquería* implies something disgustingly filthy. " Very dirty " is, of course, *muy sucia*.

17 (*b*) Exercise

Ricardo, un obrero que vivía en una calle humilde de Granada, recibió una noche muy tarde la visita de dos sacerdotes misteriosos, que le preguntaron si quería trabajar para ellos. Ricardo consintió, porque era pobre, y los sacerdotes le prometían buen pago. Le sorprendió, sin embargo, el hecho de que el trabajo tenía que hacerse de noche, y que los sacerdotes le cubriesen los ojos con un pañuelo durante el paseo para que no viese a donde iba. Cuando los sacerdotes le quitaban la venda de los ojos, Ricardo vio que estaba en medio de un pequeño patio, donde le dieron lo que necesitaba para la construcción de una pared que cerrara un hueco detrás de la escalera de la casa. Trabajó con ahinco toda la noche, pero antes que terminase uno de los sacerdotes vino a él y le dijo : " No cierre la abertura todavía. Tenemos siete cadáveres que enterrar detrás de aquella pared."

" Usted tiene que ayudarme a meter estos cadáveres en el hueco ", continuó el sacerdote. Lleno de miedo, Ricardo siguió al cura a otra parte de la casa, donde hallaron siete cajas grandes y muy pesadas. Todas estaban bien tapadas, pero Ricardo pudo ver por las grietas en las tapas que no contenían cadáveres sino cuñas de oro. Las colocaron en el hueco, el cura le ayudó entonces a terminar el muro, después de lo cual Ricardo fue bien pagado por su trabajo, y con los ojos vendados otra vez fue conducido de vuelta a su casa.

Pasaron muchos años sin que Ricardo oyese decir nada del cura ni del tesoro escondido. Sin embargo un día el propietario de algunas viejas casas vino a él y le dijo " Quiero que me repare una casa que según dicen los vecinos está frecuentada por los fantasmas de dos viejos curas que vivían allí." Ricardo fue con él a verla, y luego que llegaron reconoció el patio y el muro que él mismo había construido detrás de la escalera. " Ahora bien," dijo al

propietario, " yo repararé esta casa, y como me gusta se
la alquilaré y viviré en ella. Yo no tengo miedo a los
duendes." El propietario consintió, y en poco tiempo los
vecinos se sorprendieron muchísimo al notar la mucha
prosperidad de Ricardo y su familia, que vivieron felices
muchos años en aquella vieja casa.

17 (c)

Dear Sir,

We have ready in our warehouse the compressed air
apparatus RATMA which you recently ordered through our
representative D. Andrés Alcover, but before despatching
it we should inform you that this apparatus, just received
from our workshops, is now somewhat higher in price than
that shown in our catalogue. The present price is 1235
pesetas, with 10% discount, instead of 1150 pesetas, the
former price.

On account of this, we have not yet despatched the compressed air apparatus to you, and we request you to let us
know whether you still wish to take delivery. On receipt
of an affirmative reply, we will despatch the apparatus to
you without delay.

Yours faithfully,
Autoaccesorios Ramón Serrano y Cía, S.A.

17 (d)

Upon a darksome night,
Kindling with love in flame of yearning keen
—O moment of delight !—
I went, by all unseen,
New-hush'd to rest the house where I had been.

Safe sped I through that night,
By the secret stair, disguisèd and unseen,
—O moment of delight !—
Wrapt in that night serene,
New-hush'd to rest the house where I had been.

O happy night and blest !
Secretly speeding, screened from mortal gaze,

Unseeing, on I prest,
Lit by no earthly rays,
Nay, only by heart's inmost fire ablaze.

'Twas that light guided me,
More surely than the noonday's brightest glare,
To the place where none would be
Save one that waited there—
Well knew I whom or ere I forth did fare.

O night that led'st me thus !
O night more winsome than the rising sun !
O night that madest us,
Lover and lov'd, as one,
Lover transformed in lov'd, love's journey done.

Upon my flowering breast,
His only, as no man but he might prove,
There, slumbering, did he rest,
'Neath my caressing love,
Fann'd by the cedars swaying high above.

When from the turret's height,
Scattering his locks, the breezes play'd around,
With touch serene and light
He dealt me love's sweet wound,
And with the joyful pain thereof I swoon'd.

Forgetful, rapt, I lay,
My face reclining on my lov'd one fain.
All things for me that day
Ceas'd, as I slumber'd there,
Amid the lilies drowning all my care.

(This translation is one made by the late Professor E.
Allison Peers, and occurs in his translation of the *Complete
Works of Saint John of the Cross*, published by Messrs Burns
Oates & Washbourne, to whom I am indebted for their
permission to quote it here.)

18 (a) Exercise

1. Hablaría con más cortesía, si yo fuese Vd.
2. Vd no debiera tratar de hacer demasiadas cosas a la vez

3. Sabía que pronto tendría que comprar un diccionario nuevo.

4. Todas las tardes a las seis y media iba a la tienda a comprar un periódico.

5. ¿ Quiere Vd indicarme cómo llegar a la Casa de Correos, por favor ?

6. El chófer del taxi no quiso aceptar una propina de la vieja señora.

7. Ella dijo que volvería tarde.

8. Yo no podría leer eso, aunque tuviese mis gafas.

9. Mis amigos me invitaron a pasar un mes en Barcelona, pero no pude ir.

10. Yo no quisiera creer que Vd hubiera podido hacer tal cosa.

18 (b) Conversation

(*The last evening of* MARTIN *and* ISABEL'S *stay at* ANTONIO'S *sister's country cottage. After dinner.*)

MARTIN : It looks as though we shall have only one day to see all that there is to be seen in Seville, because we leave here tomorrow morning. We shall reach Seville about half-past nine, and so we shall have almost exactly twenty-four hours to spend there. What do you advise us to try to see in that time ?

ANTONIO : Well, let's see. You will be going first to your hotel, which is in the Plaza de San Fernando, and fairly near the Cathedral. That is one of the finest monuments of Spanish Gothic style. You will need at least an hour and a half or two hours to see it, and the Patio de los Naranjos and the Giralda. If you want to go up to the top of the Giralda, and I advise you to, because there is a magnificent view from there, you will need half an hour more.

ISABEL : From the photographs I have seen of it, it must be very high indeed, but as we shall have a very similar view from the aeroplane, on the following day, we could leave out that climb.

ANTONIO : Of course. Then you can go next to the Picture Gallery. There are many very fine paintings there that you certainly must see. The museum is about 500 yards from your hotel, not far from the station.

MARTIN : By then it will be lunch-time, or at least time for a bit of a rest.

ANTONIO : Yes. And with the heat that you are certain to find I don't know whether you will feel energetic enough to spend the afternoon walking about. But you mustn't miss seeing the Alcázar and its gardens, and you can sit about there in the shade if you find the heat too strong. The Alcázar, as perhaps you know, is the old palace of the Moorish kings, and although it has been modernized a good deal, it is well worth seeing. A little later, when it won't be quite so hot, you can walk on through the gardens of Maria Luisa, as far as the side of the Guadalquivir, where you will see the Torre del Oro, which is Moorish, too, and which used to be part of the walls of the town.

ISABEL : Shall we have time to look round the shops ? They say that the Seville shops are wonderful.

MARIA : Yes, especially the ones in the Calle de las Sierpes, where they don't allow any cars, so as to leave the street clear for pedestrians.

ANTONIO : In a single day you won't be able to see much more than these places of special interest. Of course you need much more time to see a city as fine as Seville. You won't have time, either, in just one day, to go to a bull-fight.

ISABEL : We went to one in Madrid. It wasn't bad, but I don't care for them much. Martin likes them, though.

MARTIN : Yes, I do like the liveliness of it all, and the bright colours, and the skill and cleverness of the bull-fighters, but as it is the only day we shall be spending in Seville we shall not go to a fight, but go about on foot looking at the buildings and gardens that Antonio has told us about. But aren't you going to recommend us to look at the Barrio de Santa Cruz ? I remember from my last visit how delightful those winding streets were, each house with its own special courtyard and many of them with a fountain.

ANTONIO : Yes, of course you must go there if you can in the short time you will have.

ISABEL : Good. Well, thank you very much, Antonio, for having explained to us so well what we can do. And now it's getting late, and since I have to pack my cases, I think that Martin and I had better go up to our room, because tomorrow we must be up very early to catch the train. So good night !

     (MARTIN *and* ISABEL *go up to their room.*)

18 (c)

Carriage of passengers' luggage by Spanish railways is subject to the following conditions :

Ordinary trains : (These include express trains, fast trains, mail expresses, mail trains, slow mail trains, through trains or trains carrying through coaches, whether propelled by steam or electrically driven engines.)

In these trains the passenger has the right to free registration of 30 kilograms of luggage (15 kilos in the case of children travelling at half fare).   Registration can only be effected up to 15 minutes before the departure of the train on which the passenger is to travel, but may take place several days in advance at the Parcels Office at the station on payment of Left Luggage charges.

In addition to registered luggage, passengers may carry hand baggage, provided that it is not so bulky as to inconvenience other travellers.   Explosive substances, firearms, and evil-smelling or dangerous objects are not permitted to be carried in this way.

Luggage should be collected within three hours of the arrival of the train, and will travel in the same train as the passenger.   On the expiration of the three-hours' period, Left Luggage costs will be charged.   Excess luggage will be paid for by fractions of 10 kilograms, according to the corresponding tariff.

18 (d)

We departed out of Salamanca, and came on our way as far as the bridge, at the entrance whereof standeth a beast of stone, fashioned much like a bull.   As soon as we came near it, the blind man willed me to approach, saying :

" Lázaro, put thine ear to this bull, and thou shalt hear a terrible noise within."

As soon as he had said the word, I was ready like a fool to bow down my head, to do as he had commanded, thinking that his words had been most true ; but the traitorous blind man suspecting how near it my head was, thrusteth forth his arm upon a sudden, with such force, that my sore head took such a blow against the devilish bull, that for the space of three days my head felt the pains of his horns.

Wherefore he was right glad, and said : " Consider now what thou art, thou foolish fellow ; thou must understand that the blind man's boy ought to know one trick more than the devil himself."

It seemed then immediately that I awakened out of simplicity, wherein I had of long time slept (like a child), and I said to myself :

" My blind master hath good reason, it is full time for me to open mine eyes, indeed, and to provide and seek mine own advantage, considering that I am alone without any help."

19 (a)

A Medieval Legend from Seville

Pedro the Cruel, King of Spain about the middle of the fourteenth century, had many palaces and other residences in various parts of his dominions, but the one he liked best was the Alcázar in Seville. Situated in a very peaceful part of the great Andalusian city, and in the midst of some very beautiful gardens, it is still today to be seen with much of the glory of its medieval splendour, which illustrates so well the mixture of the Spanish and Arabic civilizations.

Its halls, ornate with coloured glazed tiles, and with intricate relief-work painted in bright colours, are the same halls where don Pedro took his ease with his Court, to which many notoriously corrupt men and women belonged.

So evil was the Court, and so frequent were the duels and murders which were daily discovered, that don Pedro was obliged to make a decree, which ordered that anyone who fought in a duel should have his head cut off in the spot where the duel had taken place.

One night shortly afterwards, the King, who liked to take nocturnal walks, often with some amorous intention, was walking through the Barrio de Santa Cruz, through those winding streets and little squares which even today constitute one of the most typical parts of Seville. The night was dark, and don Pedro was walking along muffled in his cloak. But suddenly, as he was going down a lonely street between a deserted convent on one side and some tumble-down cottages on the other, the King noticed that someone was following him. It was his rival, a duke, who was no doubt on his way to the house of the same woman to whom the King was going. Without delay the King drew his sword, and challenged the duke, and after a few passes and thrusts the duke fell dead. There was no one in the street, there seemed to be no witness who could have heard the dull thud that the corpse made as it fell. Then the King, remembering the decree that he had made such a short while before, uttered a loud laugh— fierce, sinister, and diabolical. But just at the moment when he went away down the street, leaving the lifeless body of the duke there on the ground, a flickering light appeared at the door of one of those wretched cottages, and an old woman's face, a hag's face, looked out. And from the wall of the deserted convent there was heard the croaking of a crow.

The next morning all Seville was talking of the duke's death. And since nobody knew who had committed the crime, the King ordered the corregidor of the city to be sent for.

" And does the Law in Seville know who killed the duke? " the King asked him.

" Not yet, sire," was the reply.

" Then let him be found. And if he is not discovered within eight days, the corregidor himself shall pay for the crime with his own life."

The corregidor went sadly out of the King's presence. He now must find the assassin. The King had said so and what the King said always had to be done.

So the corregidor went to see the place where the duke's body had been discovered. He sought in the decrepit cottages opposite to the deserted convent, and he found an old woman, who lived alone in one of them, the only person who lived in this street.

Yes, she had heard the clash of swords and the dull thud that the body had made as it fell. What else? Some-one laughed, loudly But who was it? Did she know the man who laughed like that? Yes, she knew him very well, because everybody in Seville knew him. The man who had uttered that diabolical laugh was the King himself, no one but he laughed like that.

Then the corregidor went to the Alcazar and was received in audience by the King.

" Ah, Señor Corregidor. Has the Law discovered who killed the duke? "

" Yes, sire. The man who killed the duke is none other than the King himself, don Pedro de Castilla."

The King was silent for a moment. Then he uttered another loud laugh, and asked how it had been discovered.

And so that the decree should not be broken through what the King himself had done, the head was cut off a statue of the King, and it was then placed on the wall of that deserted convent. Thus the King and the Law in Seville were satisfied.

19 (b)

Dear Sir,
Insurance re-Palm Oil in Transit

We enclose herewith our quotation for insurance in transit of Palm Oil in cans from Antwerp to Barcelona.

It is understood that claims for damage will be met in the currency stipulated on payment of the premium.

Trusting that this quotation will meet your requirements,
Yours faithfully,
Compañía Hispanoamericano de Seguros y Reaseguros,
Rafael Martínez

19 (c)
Quotation for Insurance of Palm Oil in Cans
Goods Shipped below Deck

In addition to the general published conditions of our policy (complete loss, salvage expenses, serious damage or loss through fire, shipwreck, grounding or piracy) all accidental risks will be covered if duly authenticated by the Captain's declaration; theft of part of the contents and leakage through damage to the cans, loss through goods undelivered and/or disappearance in transit of complete cases; loss through cases falling into the sea during loading and/or unloading operations.   All the above subject to the special clauses published by the Sindicato Vertical de Seguros, and at the premium of 0·70%.

Goods Shipped on Deck

1st estimate : Risks covered as for the transport of goods shipped below deck, but to include loss through goods being washed overboard, at the premium of 1·15%.

2nd estimate : Coverage only as per the general published conditions of our policy, including loss through goods being washed overboard, and through goods falling into the sea during loading and/or unloading operations, at the premium of 0·60%.

19 (*d*)

While yet the bloom of rose and lily's glow
Their colours blend in your fair countenance,
And still your frank but ever ardent glance
Inflames my heart and yet restrains it so;
And while like gold deep-delved your tresses flow,
The fairness of your light-poised neck to blanch,
Meantime the wind beguiles their lightsome dance,
Disorders all, disturbs their modest show;
Gather the rosebuds of your happy hour
Of golden spring, for jealous wrathful Time
Will blanket soon with snow the mountain's prime.
Cold winds will sadden all the rose with rime,
His lightfoot years will steal away your dower.
So are his ways; steadfast they will abide.

I am indebted to my friend and former pupil, Dr. J. E. Varey, of Westfield College, London University, for permission to print his translation of Garcilaso's Sonnet.   (L. D. C.)

20 (*a*) Conversation

(*In the bus between the Iberia line's office in Seville and the aerodrome.*)

ISABEL : What a pity today is the last day of our stay in Spain ! I've had a very good time here, Martin.

MARTIN : Yes, but you must remember that we shall probably be able to come back and spend other holidays here, in a couple of years, perhaps.

ISABEL : I hope so.   There are such a lot of things we haven't seen, in all sorts of places, especially here in the south. Just think !   We haven't even been able to see Granada this time.

MARTIN : We haven't seen the east, either, Barcelona and the Costa Brava and the Balearics, for instance.

ISABEL : Yes.   But it will be good to be home again.   It is boring to have to pack and unpack the suitcases almost every day.   Look, what time is it ?   My watch seems to have stopped.

MARTIN : It is half-past eight.   The plane for Madrid leaves the San Pablo aerodrome at nine, and we get to Barajas, the Madrid airport, at a quarter to eleven.   We shall have to wait some time there, because the plane for London with our reserved seats doesn't leave till three.   But it doesn't matter much, we can leave the luggage at the airport and go into the centre of Madrid by bus, and come back there about two.

ISABEL : When shall we have lunch ?   Lunch isn't usually served in Madrid before two, and by then we shall be on our way again.

MARTIN : Don't worry.   We can have something light in one of the cafés, and as soon as the plane has taken off they will serve us an excellent meal.   It was lucky for us that Antonio managed to arrange our tickets for us.   Travelling by air is so much faster than by any other way, and I was really rather appalled at the idea of the return journey by train : twelve or thirteen hours from Seville to Madrid, twenty-two from there to Paris, and then twelve more on to London.   Altogether about two days and nights in the train !

ISABEL : You are right.   Besides, I very much like travelling by 'plane.   They say that there are the most wonderful views over Spain too from the air.   Maria was telling me about the strong, lively colours to be seen in the mountains and over the plains of Castile.

MARTIN : Here we are at the aerodrome.   (*They get out of the bus.*)   The porter will unload the luggage, of course, and if you like we can watch it go by, on this trolley.   I shall probably have to show the tickets at some counter.   Yes, here it is.

(*He goes up to the ticket-office, where there is a small queue of passengers.*)

MARTIN : As we aren't yet going abroad directly, I shall not have to make any declaration about the money we have with us. We shall be doing that later on, in Madrid.

A voice is heard : Attention, please ! Travellers for Madrid please go to platform number nine.

ISABEL : Look, Martin ! Don't be long ! That voice says that travellers for Madrid must go out of here and get into the plane !

MARTIN : Don't worry, we shall not miss it.

(*After showing his tickets and their passports, MARTIN picks up his briefcase and leaves the building with ISABEL and the little group of passengers, accompanied by the aerodrome official, who leads them to the plane. And here we leave MARTIN and ISABEL, hoping that they spend a pleasant day travelling by air from Seville to Madrid, and then on to London.*)

20 (*b*)

It was the budding month of May when the warm sun fills the sky,
When the skylark sings its clear note and the nightingales reply,
When, on their faithful service bent all lovers hasten by—
Save one—the broken-hearted—who must in dungeon lie.
I know not when the day begins, or twilight draweth nigh,
But for a little singing-bird, that sang, at dawn, on high.
An archer slew that little bird. God ! May that archer die !

SHORT BIBLIOGRAPHY OF RECOMMENDED BOOKS
General

Spain, a Companion to Spanish Studies; ed. Professor E. A. Peers (Methuen).
Spain, by Salvador de Madariaga (Cape, 1942 edition).
Spain, by Sacheverell Sitwell (Batsford).
The Civilization of Spain, by Professor J. B. Trend (Home University Series).
Brief History of Spanish Civilization, by Altamira (Constable).
The Face of Spain, by Gerald Brenan (Turnstile Press).
The Spanish Temper, by V. S. Pritchett (Chatto & Windus).
A History of Spain and Portugal, by W. C. Atkinson (Pelicans).

Imperial Spain, by T. H. Elliott (Pelicans).

The Spanish Labyrinth, by G. Brenan (Cambridge University Press, paperback).

The Spaniards and their History, by R. Menéndez Pidal and W. Starkie (Hollis and Carter).

The Heritage of Spain, by Adams (Harrap).

Conversations and Idioms

Brush up your Spanish, by Baeza (Dent).

Brighter Spanish, by Baeza (Dent).

Spanish Phrase Book, by W. W. Timms and M. Pulgar (Teach Yourself Books).

Commercial

El Comercio, Teoría, Práctica, Correspondencia, by McHale (Heath).

Correspondencia Comercial, by R. Bori (Montesó, Barcelona).

Literature

The Literature of the Spanish People, by Gerald Brenan (Cambridge University Press).

Historia de la Literatura Española, by Romera Navarro (Heath).

A Literary History of Spain (E. Benn); several volumes, e.g., *The Middle Ages* by A. D. Deyermond, *The Golden Age, Prose and Poetry* by R. O. Jones.

Escritores y poetas de España, by K. Vossler (Austral).

The Picaresque Novel, ed. Northup (Harrap).

The Mystics of Spain, by E. A. Peers (Allen & Unwin).

St John of the Cross, and other essays, by E. A. Peers (Faber).

Cervantes, by Professor Entwistle (Oxford University Press).

Don Quijote, Don Juan, y la Celestina, by R. de Maeztu (Austral).

Theory of Drama in the Golden Age, by Chaytor (Manchester University Press).

Libros y Autores Modernos, by C. Barja (Campbell's Bookstore, Los Angeles).

The Romantics of Spain, by E. Piñeyro, trans. Peers (Oxford University Press).

Novelistas Españoles modernos, by Balseiro (Macmillan).

The Genius of Spain, by S. de Madariaga (Oxford University Press).

Contemporary Spanish Literature, by Aubrey Bell (Oxford University Press).

Lorca, by Roy Campbell (Bowes and Bowes).

FRANCIA

San Sebastián

NCIAS
GADAS
toria
NAVARRA   Pamplona
groño

Huesca

Soria
Zaragoza   Andorra
ARAGÓN   Lérida   CATALUÑA   Gerona

Ebro   Barcelona

Tarragona

Teruel
Cuenca   Castellón
de la Plana

ISLAS BALEARES   Palma de
Mallorca

VALENCIA   Valencia

Júcar
Albacete

MURCIA   Alicante
Segura   MAR
MEDITERRÁNEO
Murcia

ería

ESPAÑA

INTERNATIONAL BOUNDARIES
REGIONAL BOUNDARIES
PROVINCIAL BOUNDARIES
MAIN ROADS
RIVERS

50   0   50   100 Miles
50   0   50   100   150 Kilometres

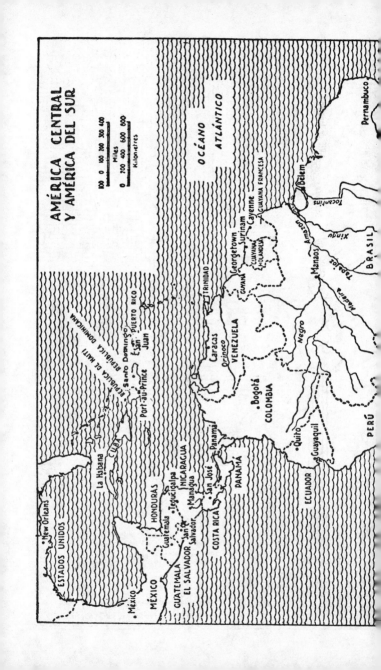

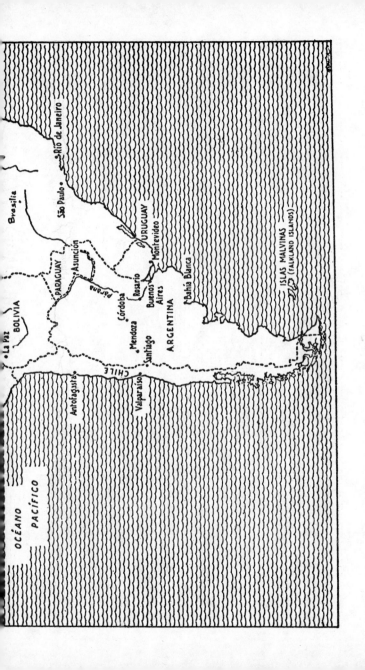

SPANISH

JUAN KATTÁN-IBARRA

A stimulating and clearly structured introductory course designed to help you achieve basic fluency in both spoken and written Spanish.

This book assumes no previous knowledge of Spanish, and takes you to the point at which you can read and write simple texts and join in everyday conversation. The twenty-four carefully-graded units focus on communication in a wide range of practical situations and provide all the Spanish you need to feel confident about travelling, shopping, ordering a meal, and coping generally with everyday life in Spain. A special feature of the book is the inclusion of the alternative language forms and customs of Spanish-speaking Latin America.

Each unit contains lively dialogues, introducing useful vocabulary and essential grammar which is clearly and simply explained and then practised in a variety of exercises. Information sections and authentic illustrative material complement the dialogues and offer a valuable insight into the Spanish way of life. A key to the exercises, verb tables, a grammar index and a comprehensive Spanish–English vocabulary are also provided.

TEACH YOURSELF BOOKS